What Price Israel

ISRAEL *shall not live on one soil but in the souls of men chastened and transfigured, in laws and institutions of righteousness, in human relations ennobled and disciplined by a sense of responsibility. And men shall then look into each other's eyes and see the reflection of their own unfulfilled longings, and the hearts of men shall go out to each other in understanding, for they will know that all suffer hurt and heartache and dream the same dreams of freedom, security and peace. And together they shall build the Kingdom of God.*

MORRIS LAZARON

What
Price
Israel

by

Alfred M. Lilienthal

HENRY REGNERY COMPANY

Chicago · 1953

FOREWORD

In 1948, a new white flag with a single blue six-pointed star was hoisted to a mast on the east coast of the Mediterranean Sea. Thus was born the national state of Israel, with its own government, army, foreign policy, language, national anthem and oath of allegiance. The resulting confusion has seriously affected the position of the free world in the Middle East, has dangerously complicated the lives of Jews everywhere, and now endangers Judaism, the oldest monotheistic faith in the world.

The ancient cry "next year in Jerusalem," resounding down the centuries, made Judaism indestructible. It held forth a perpetual goal not to be achieved through human intervention. Judaism's power to survive depended on its being unrelated to any particular geographic tract. States could come and go; but a set of beliefs, isolated from temporal happenchance, could forever endure. A "Kingdom of God" was never at the mercy of physical force.

Judaism has been a universal religious faith to which loyal citizens of any country could adhere. By contrast, Zionism is a nationalist movement organized to reconstitute Jews as a nation with a separate and sovereign homeland. The establishment of the State of Israel has consequently freed the Jews "to do what they could not do before," to use the words of Arthur Koestler in *Promise and Fulfillment* "to discard the knapsack and go their own way with the nation whose life and cul-

v

ture they share, without reservations or split loyalties";
or else they could choose the only alternative—emigrate to the sovereign State of Israel.

But this one and only set of alternatives has not been
accepted by American Jewry. For the mere declaration "I am not a Zionist" (while others in Israel and
in the United States were continuing to speak and to
act in the name of the "Jewish people") has not constituted a decision. The word "Jew" is now being
used simultaneously to denote a universal faith *and* a
particular nationality; and the corresponding allegiances
to religion and to state have become confused.

For centuries before he was granted political equality
in Western Europe and in the United States, the Jew
lived under the discipline both of the sovereign state
in which he was physically located and of the religio-
political community to which he belonged. In that
past, religious ties were intimately linked with political
status. And this past continues to cast its shadow, even
on fully emancipated Americans, particularly those
who have come from eastern Europe.

Suppose Israel had, as seemed quite possible for several
years, joined the Soviet bloc or fallen behind the iron
curtain. It would not be difficult to imagine the situation in which this would have placed Jewry in the
United States.

During the events which altered the relationship between the Kremlin and Israel the reaction in this country was to treat the Israeli crisis as if it were the crisis
of the Jewish people all over the world. But if the
political problems of Israel continue to be the political
responsibility of Jews in the United States, disaster
must follow. Innumerable situations will involve Israel
in policies and politics which nationals of no other coun-

try may dare underwrite. Next time, the enemy of Israel may not be the enemy of the United States.

In the United States, a number of people may indeed achieve something of a separate group identity merely by believing they do belong together; but American tolerance toward separatism ceases when group thought and group action run counter to the mores and interests of America. And the moment has come for the American Jew, I think, to free metaphysical practices, essential to worshiping God, from his nationalist activities related to a foreign state.

This book has been written, against the concerned counsel of many who are close and dear to me, because I feel I owe a duty to my country above any duty I owe to my family and friends. The question "What is a Jew?" is now tied to the more important question "How can we hold the Middle East?" My determination to complete this book was strengthened by the knowledge that no American Christian could, nor any Jew would, write it. Some of my material has been the subject of whispers, and I decided it was time that muted talk be brought to the surface and be debated.

I have received innumerable admonitions "not to say anything that might harm the Jewish people." But, indeed, my efforts are intended to benefit American Jewry. Criticism expressed in these pages and directed against guilty leadership could involve all Jews only by the process of generalizing—the favorite weapon of anti-Semites.

And yet, I do not underestimate for one moment the wrath that will descend upon me for having written this book. Every conceivable kind of pressure will be exerted, I am afraid, to prevent a fair consideration of the material set forth in its pages. But the gravity of the problems discussed, and their far-reaching consequences for the United States as well as for Judaism, merits a minimum of group emotionalism and a maximum of individual thought. Such an approach is what I request from my readers.

I am thinking of them, and of my subject, in the spirit of Western man. The significance and, indeed, the meaning of Western man is his free will. The American way of life, drawing upon the Judeo-Christian heritage, is nothing if it is not the person's right to choose freely and the person's duty to face the consequences of his choice. And what is totalitarianism if it is not a vice of determinism, of having an irrevocable choice made for the individual even before he is born? I have written this book because I, an American of Jewish faith, have not the slightest doubt that American Jewry, too, has a free choice—and must face the consequences of whatever it will choose.

During the Palestine controversy of 1947, world opinion was polarized into two contrary viewpoints—"the Zionist case" versus "the Arab case." The third position—that of the integrated American (Englishman, Frenchman, etc.) of the Jewish faith—seemed swallowed up by what appeared to be the overwhelming tide of "Jewish unity." But the response I received to a magazine article, "Israel's Flag Is Not Mine" (*Reader's Digest*, 1949), indicated that there must be untold thousands who live in this alleged no man's land. It is time for them to speak up and tell their self-appointed leadership: "So far and no further."

To these as yet inarticulate Americans of Jewish faith, this book is dedicated—to them and to the Americans of Christian good will who gladly grant their Jewish fellow citizen equal though not special rights.

Contents

What Price Israel

CHAPTER I

The Historic Duality

THE FATHER of the new state of Israel lies in an unknown grave. For without the anonymous poet who wrote the 137th Psalm, there would be no "Jewish State" today.

After the Northern Kingdom of Israel was swept away by the Assyrians in 721 B. C., and the Second Jewish Commonwealth was destroyed by the Romans in 70 A. D., the nation concept of Judaism was kept alive through the words of this psalmist:

> By the rivers of Babylon there we sat down; yet we wept when we remembered Zion. How shall we sing the Lord's song in a foreign land? If I forget thee, O Jerusalem, let my right hand forget her cunning; let my tongue cleave to the roof of my mouth, if I remember thee not; if I set not thee Jerusalem above my chiefest joy.

Here is the seed of nationalist-segregationalist Zionist thinking. Yet there was another tradition deeply imbedded in the minds of the followers of Yahweh, the

1

name by which the monotheistic God Jehovah was first known. In their Babylonian captivity, into which the Judeans were taken in 586 B. C. by Nebuchadnezzar, the prophet Jeremiah spoke to them in these words of advice:

> *Build ye houses and dwell in them and plant gardens and eat the fruit thereof; take wives and beget sons and daughters. . . . And seek the peace of the city whither I have caused ye to be carried away captives and pray unto the Lord for that city, for in the peace thereof shall ye have peace. (Jer. 29:5–7)*

This is the philosophy of integration around which the universal precepts of the Judaic faith were built. The Hebrew prophets, Amos, Jeremiah, Micah, Hosea, the two Isaiahs and Elijah (to which exalted number Jesus properly belongs) were not interested in the restoration of political power. They were concerned with the injustices of their day, the remedy for which, they believed, could be found only in a universal God of mercy, of justice and righteousness. This God demanded an undeviating code of moral values.

The second Isaiah, writing *circa* 536 B. C., endowed the burgeoning faith with a vision of the Messianic coming. His "next year in Jerusalem" was unrelated to any particular nation or sovereignty, and referred to a Kingdom of God which would bring forth a perfected society of perfected men. In the Old Testament, this prophet described the mission of the Judeans as their duty "to open the blind eyes" and "to serve for a light of the Gentiles . . . For my House shall be called a House of prayer for all people."

The history of the peoples who came after the Judeans and who became known, many generations later, as "Jews," is a continuous struggle between these conflicting ideologies—nation versus faith—chosen people versus universality—segregation versus integration.

When Cyrus the Persian crushed Nabonidus, the last Babylonian king, permission was granted to the captives (in 538 B. C.) to return home and rebuild the Temple. Some returned,[1] but the great majority preferred to remain in exile. Many had prospered and progressed in the stimulating atmosphere of Babylon. They had learned to pray elsewhere than in the Temple of Jerusalem and they began to develop what later became the modern Jewish synagogue, the mother of the Christian and the Mohammedan service. "Israel" came to designate the worship of Yahweh.

Greek and Syrian and Roman sway followed Persian suzerainty over Judea. Those who returned to Jerusalem had developed in exile the nationalist spirit and the chosen-people complex—the idea of preeminence and predestination. This concept was kept alive by their leaders who governed them as a nation within the Persian empire. The priest Ezra, and after him Nehemiah (the former cupbearer to Artaxerxes I who became Persian Governor and rebuilt the walls of Jerusalem), attempted to break up Judean intermarriages with semi-heathen peoples and Babylonian conquerors.[2] The Temple became the center of both national and religious Judean life.

But the almost continuous foreign rule exposed Judeans to alien mores and ways of life. The flourishing Greek civilization made a particular impression upon Judeans in Jerusalem. There were those who preferred the less regimented life of the Greeks, enjoyed Greek literature, Greek clothes, Attic architecture. These

3

Hellenists strove to bridge the gap separating those who believed in Yahweh from those pagans who celebrated Hellenic life.

Such Hellenists were opposed by the Pietists or Hasidim, who insisted on strict observance of the laws and customs set forth in the Torah (and later prescribed in the Mishnah and the Talmud). This legislation regulated hygiene, inheritance, property, agriculture, dress, diet and business exactly in the Judean fashion of ten centuries before.

The Hasid would call the Hellenist a traitor, and in return he would be called an old fogey. But between the articulate extremists of Hassidism and Hellenism was a majority who refused to take sides. Yet it was a passive majority who left it to their priests to decide for them. When the Hellenists wished to build a Greek gymnasium in which to practice Greek athletics, the priests refused permission on the grounds that the proposed activity was repellent to Judean puritanism. The cruelty of Antiochus Epiphanes, the Syrian ruler of Palestine, further weakened the case of the Hellenists.

The last years of Judea under Roman rule were characterized by the struggle between the aristocratic priestly sect of the Sadducees, who believed in the most literal interpretation of the written law, and the religious Pharisees, who added the oral law and the interpretative process. Jesus, said to have been a Pharisee, inveighed against the reactionaries who had captured his party and made it scarcely distinguishable from the Sadducee opposition.

The Nazarene opposed the subordination of spirit and substance to law and form: "The Sabbath was made for man—not man for the Sabbath." The human failing of exalting one's own creed and nationality, as illustrated in the parable of the Good Samaritan, offended Christ's sense of universality. But the admonition fell on ears as deaf as had been those unpenetrated by Amos' cry before: "Are ye not as children of the Ethiopians unto me, O children of Israel?"[3]

The Judeans rebuked Jesus as they had rebuked their other prophets. They were far more concerned with political deliverance from Roman control than with religious reform. They willingly embraced successive Messianic imposters—politicians in religious disguise. Unsuccessful revolutions against Rome, led by the ultra-nationalist patriots, the Zealots, only succeeded in reducing a crushed Judea to a Roman province.

In an uprising (132 A. D.) against the emperor Hadrian, Bar Kokba, supported by Rabbi Akiba, attempted to rally his countrymen around the flag of statehood. Three years later the revolt collapsed and the procurator Tinnius Rufus had Jerusalem plowed under. On the site of the ancient Temple a new edifice was erected in honor of Capitoline Jupiter.

During the Second Commonwealth, the Judeans were governed by the Kohen Gadol, the rabbi-priests who claimed to be in direct line of descent from the priest Zadok[4] of Samuel's day; or by the Hasmonean Kings (as the family of the Maccabees was known); or by the Council of the Sanhedrin. But all the time there was constant strife. One sect was always purging another to gain control.

Neither the two kingdoms nor the united nation displayed, in more than nine centuries, any particular genius for government. As Dr. Julian Morgenstern has pointed out, there were "only two brief simultaneous periods in the life of each kingdom, neither lasting more than fifty years, when there was any indication of national strength and glory."[5] The singular feature of true spiritual worth was the development of obstinate and unwavering monotheism.

When Ptolemy Lagi returned to Egypt, after the conquest of Judea in 320 B. C., many Judeans accompanied him. By 250 B. C., Alexandria contained the largest number of Judaists in the world (far outstripping Jerusalem). Many had fled to the land of the Nile, three hundred or more years before, upon the Babylonian invasion; and these Alexandrians of Palestinian origin never returned to Jerusalem. They were influenced by their Greek surroundings and in turn influenced it with their religion. The Bible was translated into Greek because that language had replaced Aramaic and Hebrew among the Judeans in Egypt.

Philo, himself a Jew, heaped praise upon the Proselytes. In his *Letter Against Flaccus* he discerned that the "Jews considered Jerusalem where the Holy Temple is situated as their *home*, but regard as their *country* the country in which they have been living since the times of their fathers, grandfathers, and great-grandfathers, and in which they themselves were born and brought up."[6]

As the sole monotheistic religion in a pagan world, Judaism had made converts in many lands. The universal aims of the second Isaiah had found expression in great missionary activities. Judean traders spread their faith eastward, as far as India and China, and others carried the religion to what is now Italy and France. Whole peoples of varying ethnic strains became proselyte Judaists, especially during the two centuries before the birth of Christ. Judeans migrated to the Arabian desert and converted semitic peoples in Yemen.

Pagans as distant as those of the Kerch Strait and the Crimea accepted Yahweh.[7]

In Roman days, there were already more people of the Judaic faith throughout the world than in the Holy Land.[8] Many Romans, including members of the nobility, embraced the simple teachings of Judaism, won by the appeal of what Jewish historians have called a "system of morals, anchored in the veneration of the One and Holy God"[9] and "the purity of Judean home life.[10] Most of the proselytes accepted the idea of monotheism and the moral law without the ceremonial precepts. A smaller number, called "proselytes of righteousness," respected the initiatory rites of Judaism and all its law and custom.

With the advent of Christianity, the parent faith ceased proselytizing. Monotheism was now carried to the pagan world by the disciples of Jesus (and later by Islam). The Apostle Paul, born Saul of Tarsus, removed the ceremonial law and freed those who were willing to accept Christianity from the minute formalization of the ancient worship of Yahweh.

Judaism now concentrated on keeping its own flock. In Babylonia, the friendly Persians welcomed the Judean emigrees from the rival Roman Empire, and here they joined their coreligionists who had remained "in exile." These former Judeans were ruled by a prince of their own (supposedly of the House of David) who was called Resh Galuta, "head of the exiles"; for their separate mode of life required some such self-government regulated in accordance with the Talmud, their own compilation (and rearrangement in Aramaic) of the written and oral laws. The spiritual leadership of Judaism was centered in that "state within a state" in Babylonia.

The marked trend toward adjustment to the habits of the people amongst whom the Judaists lived was cut short by the clash between Judaism and Christianity. The sacred Judaistic mission of carrying the monotheistic message to all people was now buried underneath the formal law and ceremony. The Jewish leadership insisted upon separateness, to keep out, first, the Hellenic influence, and then, the Christian competition. This dovetailed with the intents of the growing Christian Church. The Edict of Milan (313) granted toleration to the Christian Church; the Code of Theodosius II brought, in 492, Church and State closer together; and the Code of Justinian discriminated, in 555, against the older faith. These decrees, and others that followed, built a wall between Christians and non-Christians. They built a wall, too, around the "nation within a nation." They emphasized that members of the older monotheistic faith belonged to a particular and peculiar group which now received the distinctive label "Jews." Segregation, initiated by intolerance from without, and not discouraged by vested interests from within, had started.

In Western Europe, the Jews almost invariably were settled in certain quarters of the towns to protect them against an unfriendly world; but far from all of these Jewish quarters were surrounded by ghetto walls. In Spain, where some Sephardic[11] Jews had lived since about 300 A. D., they had, in 711, helped Islam to move into the country and win over the Peninsula. In the struggle between the conflicting powers of Mohammedanism and Christianity, Spanish Jewry held the balance of power. They thrived in business and held important public posts in the Moslem land. The poet, Judah Halevi, and the philosopher, Moses Maimonides, helped to bring their coreligionists closer to the people amongst whom they dwelt.

This Golden Era in Spain came to an end when a Mohammedan factional struggle brought to the throne Almohades, who hated Jews as much as Christians. The Judaists's choice was either conversion to Mohammedanism or expulsion. And many Judaists were willing to accept the prayer "God is one and Mohammed is his prophet" which sounded not unlike their own brand of monotheism.

Christian rulers finally pushed down from the north to dislodge the Mohammedan Moors from Spain, and they first protected the Judaist colony. But then the religious fanaticism of the day prevailed in Spain, too. The terrible cry of "Christ killers," or "deicides," was then being heard throughout Europe and soon reverberated in the land of Castile and Aragon. Some Spanish Jews were willing to give up their "Jewish way of life" though not their religious beliefs: they moved out from the Juderias, the special "Jewish Community," and pretended to have become Christians, though secretly they continued to worship their own God. Culturally and politically integrated, these "Marranos" nevertheless went underground (to use the modern parlance)—not for nationhood, but for faith. In point of fact, history ought to have coined a more flattering word for these faithful Judaists: in Spanish, "Marranos" means the "Accursed Ones"—a name applied in contempt by Jews of their day to those who betrayed the Jewish ritual but held fast to the ethical concepts of Judaism. The Inquisition banned from Spain all Mohammedans, Jews and heretics. The Marranos fled to other parts of Europe, to North Africa and even to South and Central America. But the Marranos who came to Bordeaux and

Marseilles still called themselves "nation Portugèse."
Rabbi Solomon-ibn-Adret spoke of Spain as his country. Maimonides went to Egypt—and still signed his
name "Moses, son of Maimon, the Spaniard." So deeply
rooted was the tradition of integration.

In the rest of Europe, the abandonment of Judaism
was the price Judaists had to pay for sharing the limited
cultural, social and political blessings of the feudal peas-
antry. The only rights possessed by unconverted Jews
were the group rights of the ghetto which was recognized by the State as a corporate medieval entity.[12] The
ghetto leaders made their contractual arrangements with
the Church-State for their closed corporation and ruled
"their own." There was joint ghetto responsibility for
obligations, and taxation often was on a unit basis. Jewish courts had all civil jurisdiction, Rabbinic law governed all business, synagogue life, dance, dress and morals. The Jew was immersed in the Talmudic details
within the ghetto and hardly thought of the Christian
outside world save to hope that it would permit him
to live unmolested.

Where ghetto walls were not erected, nationalist-
minded Jewish leaders strove for complete segregation.
A Jewish "deputation" approached the rulers of the
city of Speyer, in 1084, requesting that a ghetto be set
up.[13] No less a scholar, and nationalist, than Professor
Salo Baron points out, in his history of Jewry, that "Talmudic rabbis insisted upon separatism on practical as
well as ritualistic grounds," and that the general laws
regulating ghetto life in Portugal had been adopted
upon a nationwide Jewish request.[14]

There was one Judaist who tried the different approach of knocking down the ghetto walls. Moses Mendelssohn, whose contribution to the triumph of Human

Rights predates the French Revolution, led a fully integrated life amongst the Christians of Berlin, and at the same time maintained his faith. Mendelssohn believed that some of the barriers of prejudice could be hurdled if Jews spoke and wrote the language of the country in which they lived. German Jews were then using Hebrew or Yiddish (German dialect written in Hebrew characters). Mendelssohn opened a school for Jews in Berlin, where French and German were included in the studies. He himself translated the Pentateuch into German and implored the German Jews to take advantage of the 1782 Patent of Toleration, to send their children to public schools where they could learn a trade. In his book *Jerusalem*, Mendelssohn pleaded for more compliance of the ancient Jewish law with the customs of the country. But the Jewish adjustment he sought was refused by the Rabbinate. A rabbinical edict forbade members of their congregations to read or own a copy of Mendelssohn's Pentateuch translation.

The French Revolution ushered in the gradual emancipation of western Jewry. Revolutionary France's great intellectual spirits—Mirabeau, Abbé Grégoire and Saint-Étienne—fought to assure that "equality" and "fraternity" was extended to all religious groups of France. Their attitude was summed up in these words of Clermont-Tonnerre, delegate to the French National Assembly: "To the Jews as a nation we grant nothing; to the Jews as men we grant all." And the Jews of France were given complete equality. As Napoleon Bonaparte cut through Europe, he imposed Jewish equality everywhere. In 1807, he convened a Sanhedrin of Jewry from all parts of his Empire. When these representatives were asked whether or not they regarded France as their country, and Frenchmen as their brothers, they answered: "Aye, even unto death." They specifically promised the Emperor to recognize their fellow citizens of other faiths as their brethren. There has never been, since Napoleon, Jewish nationalism in France.

By 1874, full rights had been granted to Jews in England, Germany, Holland, Belgium, Denmark, Norway, Austria and Switzerland. The Jews of Western Europe had won the right to profess their religion and to be otherwise considered fully privileged nationals of the countries in which they resided.

But while this great transformation was taking place in the West, the ghetto walls of Eastern Europe had not been scaled. Prior to the Hitler mass slaughter, the followers of Judaism throughout the world totalled sixteen million, and almost one half of them lived in Eastern Europe. For centuries the Jews in Poland had been meticulously organized into "kehillahs," governed by their own all-powerful Joint Councils, the Va-ad Arba Aratos. With the three partitions of Poland, Russia inherited the world's largest body of Jews. The Czars confined them to living in Russia's western provinces within the "Pale of Settlement" and its strong internal organization. Poland and Russia remained virtually untouched by the emancipation.

When the teachings of Moses Mendelssohn began to impress some eastern scholars, their efforts to spread these ideas were stymied by rabbinical and lay leaders of eastern Jewry who feared cultural integration. In the middle of the 19th century, the German rabbi, Max Lilienthal, tried to set up modern Jewish schools in Russia where the Russian language and several secular subjects were to be taught. He was defeated by rabbinical suspicion combined with Czarist repression.

Rather, the eastern Jew turned to Jewish Nationalism for his emancipation: the political rights he wanted he was taught to see as group rights and they were to be won in Palestine. Zionism began to transform religious hopes and a yearning for individual freedom into a political program of nationalist utopia.

The first presentation of Zionism was given by Moses Hess in his book *Rome and Jerusalem* (1862). The next philosopher of Zionism was Leo Pinsker who, twenty years later, wrote in his *Auto-Emancipation* that the Jews formed, in the midst of the nations among whom they reside, a distinctive element which cannot be readily digested by any country. (Strangely, these were practically the same words for which the *Dearborn Independent* and Henry Ford, Sr. were to be sued more than sixty years later, by American Jews of Zionist leanings.) Pinsker's goal was a "land of our own," though not necessarily the Holy Land. Under his leadership, a first Jewish National Conference[15] met in 1884 at Katowice in Silesia—thirteen years before Theodor Herzl invoked the First Zionist Congress at Basel in Switzerland.

Herzl, an Austrian journalist, had attended the trial of Alfred Dreyfus in Paris and was moved by this revolting experience to write his famous *Judenstaat* ("The Jewish State"), one of those pregnant political pamphlets that make history. The Basel Congress called for a "publicly recognized and legally secured Jewish home in Palestine." The concept of minorities upon which the Austro-Hungarian Empire was based, motivated another Austrian, Count Kalergi, to conceive a Pan-European federation of European man; but Herzl's Jewish reaction was to affirm the "right to separateness" and build a narrow State around them. For him, the "Jewish question" existed wherever Jews lived in perceptible numbers: they had to be given "a portion of the globe" to satisfy their right to sovereign nationhood.

Aware of the difficulty of winning converts to the undisguised doctrine of a "Jewish nation" in emancipated Western Europe and the United States, the Basel platform (the first official pronouncement of modern Zionism) talks of a "home" and of "the Jewish people" rather than "nation."

An organized political movement had now replaced the Messiah in leading "the Jewish people back to Palestine." The Messianic coming, nurtured as it had been for centuries in the tribal life of the ghetto, had bred a deep national consciousness among the Eastern Jewry. The Zionist program could thus easily arouse the emotions of those who had for centuries been parts of both a religion and a national community.

In the meantime, Jewish strength had moved westward. Europe's persecuted had been arriving in the American colonies, and amongst them were of course Jews. At the time of the War of Independence, there were 2500 Jews in America (principally from the Iberian Peninsula), and the five synagogues of New York, Newport, Philadelphia, Charleston, and Savannah. Between 1830 and 1880, Judaist immigrants came mainly from Germany, and many American towns bear their names as they pushed on over the country.

Jewish immigration from Western Europe ceased with the granting of complete political emancipation in the western parts of the Old World. There were by then about 230,000 Judaists in the United States, strongly imbued with the philosophy of integration with America. Like most other early immigrants to

America, they had fled the religious bigotries of the Old World. Enjoying equal rights of personal citizenship, the early Jewish settlers in the United States were not concerned with group rights, nor had they any desire for a segregated cultural existence.

Reform Judaism freed religious practice from some outmoded encrustments to make Judaism again a faith rather than a separate way of life. As early as 1824, twelve members of the Charleston congregation, led by the journalist Isaac Harby, organized an abridged service, part of which was in English. They formed the congregation of Beth Elohem and built a new synagogue, in 1841, which used the first organ in an American Judaist service. In his dedicatory sermon Dr. Gustavus Poznaski announced: "This synagogue is our Temple, this city is our Jerusalem, this happy land our Palestine."[16]

In Germany, the movement for reform was led by Gabriel Riesser (who firmly avowed there was no such thing as a Jewish nation with its own corporate existence), and Abraham Geiger. The movement failed, suffocated by the dead hand of ancient European traditions. But it took hold in the United States where under the leadership of Isaac M. Wise, Reform Judaism became a major religious force. At the Pittsburgh Conference in 1885, eight basic principles of Reform Judaism[17] carried this solemn message: "We consider ourselves no longer a nation, but a religious community, and therefore expect neither a return to Palestine, nor the restoration of a sacrificial worship under the Sons of Aaron, or of any of the laws concerning the Jewish State."

Twelve years later, after Herzl's Zionism had begun to fascinate Europe, the Central Conference of American Rabbis passed a resolution which stated disapproval of any attempt to establish a Jewish State. "Such attempts show a misunderstanding of Israel's mission which from the narrow political and national field has been expanded to the promotion among the whole human race of the broad and universalistic religion first proclaimed by the Jewish prophets."[18] The reform congregations likewise voiced their "unalterable opposition to political Zionism," declaring themselves to be "a religious community." The declaration added: "Zion was a precious possession of the past . . . as such it is a holy memory, but it is not our hope of the future. America is our Zion." Zionism was regarded as a "philosophy of foreign origin" with little "to recommend itself to Americans."[19] The Reform paper, the *American Israelite*, was able to say that all Jewish newspapers edited or controlled by native Americans were "strongly anti-Zionist." In 1904, this paper noted that "there is not one solitary prominent native Jewish-American who is an advocate of Zionism."[20]

Between 1881 and 1924, the third wave of Jewish immigration brought two and a half million Jews from Central and Eastern Europe who settled in the larger eastern cities. Most of these new immigrants were Orthodox and inclined toward Zionism.

The concept of Jewish nationality was a product of Central and Eastern Europe, and of the Byzantine Empires, where ethnic and religious groups had received their rights as national minorities. Herzl's homeland, the Austro-Hungarian Empire, was a multi-national state, a kind of holding company of cohesive ethnic groups who possessed an acute sense of nationhood. ("Minorities" were represented in the legislature by their own political parties.) The United States Constitution, of course, is built on quite different political principles. Here, as Dorothy Thompson phrased it, "nationhood and statehood are conjoined."

The law of America knows no majorities, no minorities, and no special rights for any citizens. But Eastern Europeans, of all creeds, were accustomed to a complex minority status, even more deeply rooted in the Jewish mind by painful recollections of persecution. These East-European Jews had not only lived as a separate nationality but had voted as Jews for other Jews to represent them in governments. They mostly had spoken a language other than their environment's, and lived in a mental ghetto to "balance the physical ghetto around them."[21] The Jews from these countries had been a nation within a nation; so that, when they came to the United States as emancipated persons, the nation complex had come with them.

By sheer numbers these newcomers soon began to dominate their American coreligionists, taking over some older organizations and starting new groups of every variety. In 1918, with the creation of the nationalist-minded American Jewish Congress, the hegemony of the earliest Judaist settlers, the Sephardic and German Jews, had ended.

Reform Judaism continued to struggle in America against political Zionism. When Lloyd George granted the Balfour Declaration which called for the "establishment of a national home in Palestine," some Orthodox and Conservative segments of American Judaism opposed the a-religious and secularized methods of the return, but Reform theology refused the objective itself on the grounds that the call of Judaism (the call to carry to the world the universal message of the prophetic ethics) excluded a mass return. Reform leadership expressed a willingness to cooperate with Zionists in making Palestine a place of refuge, and a spiritual center, but Reform rabbis told a Congressional Committee in 1922 they could not concede that anything but the world was the Jewish homeland.[22] Their slogan, "Scrap Zionism and Build Palestine," led American Jewry to a growing emphasis on the latter aim and the emergence of a non-Zionist rather than an anti-Zionist position.

Until 1933, Zionism itself had made little progress in the United States. It had picked up certain momentum with the keen American interest in the plight of Russian Jewry before World War I, but this concern vanished with Czar Nicholas II and with the appearance of a new Russian regime which granted "equal rights" to all its citizens. But Hitler's drive against European Jews encouraged Zionists to transform American Judaist sympathies with oppressed coreligionists across the Atlantic into organizational strength. By 1943 there were in America 59,000 registered Zionists[23] whose total numerical periphery of affiliated and constituent organizations numbered some 207,000—less than 5 per cent of American Jewry.

The increasing concern over European Jewry drowned out scattered Judaist protests against Zionist nationalism. For, as Rabbi James Heller told the House Foreign Affairs Committee in 1944, "there is no religious duty more sacred than that of saving the sons of our people." That distressed compassion, and the resulting call for Jewish unity, brought to the side of Zionism hundreds of America's Jewish organizations.

But through the centuries, whenever the Jews faced trials and tribulations, there had been hardly a noticeable return to Palestine. At the end of the nineteenth century, Palestine's Jewish population was a little less than 50,000. Two years after the Balfour Declaration, there were 65,000 Jews in Palestine, about 7 per cent of the population which, in 1922, consisted of 78 per cent Moslems, 11 per cent Jews and about 10 per cent Christians. In the twelve years from 1920 to 1932, 118,378 Jews (or ¾ of 1 per cent of the world's Jewry) voluntarily returned to their reputed "home." In the first twenty years after the Balfour Declaration, Palestine received approximately 500 American Jews a year. Throughout the entire Christian era, the bulk of Palestine's population continued to be Arab. For 600 years these Arabs had conscientiously cared for the Holy Places, sacred to the parent religion and its two daughter faiths. These people and their neighboring coreligionists had never questioned for a moment that Palestine was theirs. They referred to the land as "that part of southern Syria which is known as Palestine."[24]

And then, in an emotional response to European barbarism, American Jewry suddenly staked its claim to a part of the Arab world. Political Zionists knew what they were doing. But thousands of non-Zionist American Jews supported them, totally unaware of the fact that they were thus being linked to a vibrant foreign nationalism—totally unaware of the mortal danger that such an emotional support of political Zionism could undo their efforts toward American integration.

CHAPTER II

Haven or State?

EARLY in World War I, some Zionist leaders, violently opposed to the Czarist regime, had attempted to work out a deal with Germany. The United States was not yet in the fight, and these Zionists hoped a victorious Germany would give Zionism Palestine. But the negotiations fell through and, in 1916, the World Zionist Organization began to look elsewhere. A memorandum was directed to the London Foreign Office urging support of Zionism on political and military grounds.[1]

It has been alleged that in the Balfour Declaration the British granted a Jewish foothold in Palestine as a *quid pro quo* for a secret agreement whereby world Jewry promised to support the Allies, even to the extent of trying to bring the United States into the war. Whether there was actually such a precise agreement is not verifiable. However, Lloyd George, then Prime Minister, and a strong supporter of Chaim Weizmann, was quoted by the Palestine Royal Commission, Report of 1937, as follows: "Zionist leaders gave us a definite promise that, if the Allies committed themselves to giving facilities for the establishment of a national home for the Jews in

Palestine, they would do their best to rally Jewish sentiment and support throughout the world to the Allied
cause. They kept their word."[2] This statement of the
British member of the "Big Four" alluded to a period in
1917 when the Allied position was most serious. The
Germans were reported to have been considering a similar gesture to woo Zionism.[3] Lloyd George, on his own
word, was also motivated by gratitude to Weizmann for
his ingenious process of developing trinitrotoluol needed
for the manufacture of cordite.[4] Yet Emanuel Neumann,
former President of the Zionist Organization of America,
stated that for all "his personal charm, persuasiveness
and skill, Weizmann would have failed but for the fact
that Britain, hard-pressed in the struggle with Germany,
was anxious to gain the wholehearted support of the Jewish people: in Russia on the one hand, and in America,
on the other. The non-Jewish world regarded the Jews
as a power to reckon with, and even exaggerated Jewish
influence and Jewish unity. Britain's need of Jewish
support furnished Zionist diplomacy the element of
strength and bargaining power which it required to back
its moral appeal."[5] And Lloyd George fully realized the
propaganda value the Declaration held: leaflets explain-
ing it were "dropped from the air on German and Austrian towns and widely distributed from Poland to the
Black Sea."[6]

There is much evidence that the British Government
issued the Balfour Declaration for more practical reasons than a mere belief in the justice of "Jewish rights."
The Suez Canal needed a protective base in a nearby
territory where, as Professor Temperley states in his
History of the Peace Conference,[7] "important elements
would not only be bound to (Britain) by every interest,
but would command the support of world Jewry." C. P.

Scott, the editor of the *Manchester Guardian*, who became a pillar of strength to the Zionist cause, spoke of the "national home" as a security measure for British Suez.[8] Weizmann himself describes an interview with Lord Robert (later Viscount) Cecil of Chelwood, the Assistant Secretary of State for Foreign Affairs, in which the Zionist pleader stressed the point that a "Jewish Palestine would be a safeguard to England, in particular in respect to the Suez Canal."[9] In July, 1937 Churchill, speaking of the Balfour Declaration in the House of Commons, said: "It is a delusion to suppose this was a mere act of crusading enthusiasm or quixotic philanthropy. On the contrary, it was a measure taken . . . in due need of the war with the object of promoting the general victory of the Allies, for which we expected and received valuable and important assistance."[10]

Whatever the motivation, the Government of Lloyd George gave the go-ahead signal for Jewish colonization of Palestine. The draft of the Balfour Declaration, as originally submitted by Weizmann, called for a recognition of "Palestine *as the* national home for the Jewish people"[11] and the "*re-establishment*" of the country. The Foreign Office, and the Prime Minister, accordingly submitted to the War Cabinet the proposal that "Palestine should be reconstituted as the National Home of the Jewish people." This phrase was changed to "His Majesty's Government view with favour the establishment *in* Palestine of a *National Home* for the Jewish people and will use their best endeavours to facilitate the achievement of this object." The alteration followed an impassioned anti-Zionist address by Edward Montagu, the Secretary of State for India,[12] who then accepted the rephrased Declaration merely as a "military expedient."

The obvious significance of the re-phrasing was not

lost on Weizmann. His memoirs note disappointment in the "painful recession" from "Palestine as *the* national home" to the limited character of "*a* national home *in* Palestine." Outstanding Jewish organizations in Britain, such as the Anglo-Jewish Association and the Board of Deputies, were led by Montagu, by Claude Montefiore, and David Alexander, who as Jewish Englishmen opposed Zionism as "traitorous disloyalty to their native lands." Concerning these opponents, Weizmann wrote: "The gentlemen of this type have to be told the candid truth and made to realize that *we* and not *they* are the masters of the situation."[13]

Moreover, on Supreme Court Justice Brandeis' insistence, the phrase "Jewish race," which Weizmann had won as a sop for concessions denied to him, was changed in the Balfour Declaration to "Jewish people." This was further restricted by the additional clause, "it being clearly understood that nothing shall be done which may prejudice the civil and religious rights of the existing non-Jewish communities in Palestine or the rights and political status enjoyed by Jews in any other country."

Ahad Ha-am (meaning "One of the People"), a close friend of Weizmann and the leader of the spiritual (as contrasted to political) Zionists, contended that in its final wording the Balfour Declaration was a rejection of Jewish historic rights to Palestine. He wrote (in June, 1920): "If you build your house not on untenanted ground, but in a place where there are other houses, you are sole master only as far as your front gate. National homes of different people in the same country can demand only national freedom for each one in the internal affairs and affairs of the country which are common to all are administered by all householders jointly. . . . Our leaders and writers ought to have told the people this."[14]

In other words, the Balfour Declaration was not a blank check but a conditional credit. There were no grounds for implying, as some have done,[15] that the intentionally obscure term "a national home" indicated the British had granted Zionists the right to develop a state in all, or part, of Palestine. "National home" and "political state" are not synonymous.

But even if the Declaration had been framed "in the Zionist interest"—the avowed Zionist interest was, at that time, anything but statehood. Nahum Sokolow, then President of the World Zionist Organization, declared in the introduction to his two-volume *History of Zionism*, written in 1918: "It has been said, and is being obstinately repeated by anti-Zionists again, that Zionism aims at the creation of an independent 'Jewish state.' But this is wholly fallacious. The 'Jewish state' was never a part of the Zionist programme. The 'Jewish state' was the title of Herzl's pamphlet which had the supreme merit of forcing people to think. The pamphlet was followed by the first Zionist Congress which accepted the Basel Programme—the only programme in existence."[16]

A week before the Balfour Declaration was issued, Lord Curzon, who was to succeed the Earl of Balfour as Foreign Minister, wrote Lloyd George an extensive outline of what he believed the grant to the Zionists should contain: "European administration (not Jewish) over the country"; machinery to safeguard and secure order and protection of Christian, Jewish and Moslem holy places; and "to Jews, but not to Jews alone, equal civil and religious rights with other elements of the population."[17] Lord Curzon added this comment: "If this is Zionism, there is no reason why we should not all be Zionists."

The Balfour Declaration and the Mandate cannot possibly be viewed as calls for a Jewish State. On the contrary, whatever the interpretation of "A National Home," the phrase was clearly and specifically intended to be *less* than what the Zionists had asked for—which had not been statehood. And even those English Jews who supported Weizmann (conspicuously the Rothschilds) were first and above all loyal Britons who had no intention of endangering their clear and undivided loyalty. Outside the synagogue, the word "Jew" had little meaning to them. "A national home" they understood as some sort of a "spiritual centre."[18] That much they indicated in a manifesto, answering their more conservative coreligionists who had opposed the Balfour Declaration in a strong letter to the *London Times* (May 24, 1917). And that some kind of "spiritual centre" was indeed the intended meaning of "national home" is emphasized by Lord Balfour himself who thus interpreted his Declaration: "National home meant some form of British, American or other protectorate to give Jews a real centre of national culture," the final form of government of which was a "matter for gradual development in accordance with the ordinary laws of political evolution."[19]

Churchill, in the 1922 White Paper, also talked of the "further development of the existing Jewish community" of Palestine "to become a centre."[20] As Colonial Secretary, he assured a deputation of Arabs that a Jewish national home did not mean a "Jewish government to dominate Arabs. We cannot tolerate the expropriation of one set of people by another."[21] Viscount Reading, Lord Chief Justice of England and at the time of the Declaration British Ambassador to the United States, could find no objections to the Balfour Declaration despite his profound opposition to the very idea of a Jewish nation; he believed that only a cultural home was being established. Before the Council of the League of Nations, Lord Balfour argued against those "who hope and those who fear that what, I believe, has been called the Balfour Declaration is going to suffer substantial modifications. . . . The fears are not justified, the hopes are not justified. . . . The general lines of policy stand and must stand."[22] And the British Mandate for Palestine, adopted in 1923 by the League of Nations, did not modify the Balfour Declaration.[23]

The Mandatory Instrument incorporated the British Palestine Policy Statement and did not enlarge the scope of the grant. All clauses safeguarding Arab and non-Zionist rights were specifically repeated. Emir Feisal, who represented the Arab Kingdom of the Hejaz, signed an agreement with Dr. Weizmann, representing the Zionist Organization. The Arabs accepted the Balfour Declaration and permitted the encouragement of Jewish immigration into Palestine, but only on the specific condition of acknowledged and guaranteed Arab independence.

True, some responsible members of the British and U. S. Governments believed that a Jewish majority might develop in Palestine in the course of time, and that a Jewish State might thus be the ultimate outcome of the Balfour Declaration. But in 1919, the Jews constituted not more than one tenth of Palestine's population. And the British Government accepted only one responsibility concerning any future population policy in Palestine—the solemn assurance given to the Arabs, through Sherif Hussein of Mecca, that nothing would be done which was not "compatible with the freedom of the existing population, both economic and political."[24] This commitment of the Foreign Office was delivered by

Commander D. G. Hogarth to the disturbed Arabs who at the time were being rallied by Lawrence of Arabia against their Turkish overlords. Hogarth, a famous scholar and archaeologist, was dispatched to Jedda, a few weeks after the passage of the Balfour Declaration, to reiterate for the future king of Hejaz, Hussein, what the British Government had officially communicated to him in January, 1916. (Britain had then promised "that so far as Palestine is concerned, we are determined that no peoples shall be subjected to another."[25]) Hogarth, in reporting on his mission to the British High Commissioner in Cairo, commented: "The King would not accept an independent Jewish state in Palestine, nor was I instructed to warn him that such a state was contemplated by Great Britain."[26] On the other hand Hussein, whose great-grandchildren now occupy the thrones of Iraq and Jordan, was reported to have agreed that "as far as the aim of the Declaration was to provide a refuge, he would use all his influence to further that aim."[27] And T. E. Lawrence informed the Cabinet that Hussein "would not approve Jewish independence for Palestine, but would support Jewish infiltration, if it is behind a British, as opposed to an international, facade."[28]

The text of what has come to be known as the Hogarth message was not published until twenty-two years later and was totally unknown outside of the Arab world.[29]

In 1919, President Woodrow Wilson sent the King-Crane Commission[30] to Palestine and other places in the Near East for an American survey of conditions in the former Ottoman Empire. On its return, the Commission declared that a "National home for the Jewish people is not equivalent to making Palestine a Jewish State" and that such a "State could not be erected without the gravest trespass upon the civil and religious rights of existing non-Jewish communities in Palestine." This report was the only official American study of the Palestine problem until 1946.

But the protective guarantees to the Arabs of Palestine (and to non-Zionist Judaists of the world), as contained in the Balfour Declaration and in subsequent agreements, were gradually whittled away. Finally in 1947, the United Nations acted just as if the original Weizmann draft had been fully embodied in the Balfour Declaration. And nothing contributed so much to this unprecedented breach of binding diplomatic promises as the political abuse of a staggering human emergency—the plight of Jewish refugees in Europe.

The end of World War II—if end it did—created in Europe that epitome of distress, the Displaced Person. These refugees from Hitler's gas chambers were actually, not theoretically, homeless. They came from many lands: Austria, Germany, Poland, Hungary, Roumania, the Baltic Countries. They were of all faiths: about 500,-000 Catholics, 100,000 Protestants, and 226,000 Jews.[31] Of these last, some 100,000 were in the assembly camps of Germany, Austria and Italy; 50,000 undetained in the United Kingdom; 12,000 in Sweden; 10,500 in Switzerland; the rest scattered over the Continent.

On August 31, 1945, President Truman wrote Britain's Prime Minister Clement Attlee that the issuance of 100,000 certificates of immigration to Palestine would help to alleviate the refugee situation. This letter was made public in the United States by Senator Guy Gillette of Iowa on September 13, 1945. In a policy statement of November 1945, the British Government declared it would not accept the view "that Jews should be driven out of Europe or that they should not be permitted to live again in these countries without discrimination, contributing their ability and talent toward rebuilding the prosperity of Europe." The Prime Minister invited a joint inquiry into these matters by representatives of the United States and the United Kingdom. This proposal was favorably received by President Truman. But Zionists called it "a fresh betrayal" to which they would never submit.[32]

The Anglo-American Committee of Inquiry on Palestine was set up on December 10, 1945, with six American and six British members. It was empowered to "examine political, economic and social conditions in Palestine as they bear upon the problem of Jewish immigration and settlement therein,"[33] and "to examine the position of European Jews" in terms of estimating the possible migration to Palestine or elsewhere outside of Europe. Among the Committee members were U. S. Federal Judge Joseph C. Hutcheson, (Chairman); Dr. Frank Aydelotte, Director of the Institute of Advanced Studies at Princeton; former American Ambassador to Italy, William Phillips; Bartley C. Crum; James C. McDonald (later to be the first American Ambassador to Israel); and R. H. S. Crossman, prominent Laborite member of Parliament. The first meeting was held in Washington early in January, 1946. Representatives of Jewish organizations as well as those who expressed the Christian and the Arab viewpoints were heard. Sessions were resumed in London in January, 1946 and several sub-committees carried on investigations in various countries of Europe. The full Committee held further sessions in Egypt, at which the Jewish Agency (the official liaison body between the Palestinian Jewish community and Jewry outside) and organized Arab groups were heard. Sub-committees also visited the capitols of Syria, Lebanon, Iraq, Saudi Arabia and Jordan. These exhaustive deliberations

were completed in Switzerland and a report, unanimously signed at Lausanne, was made public in London and in
Washington on April 30, 1946.[34]

The principal recommendation (No. 2 in the Committee report) called for the immediate issuance of entrance certificates into Palestine for 100,000 Jews "who
had been the victims of Nazi and Fascist persecution."
Had these 100,000 admissions actually been granted, the
overwhelming majority of Jewish Displaced Persons
whose situation required immediate action would have
been saved and the revolting D. P. Centers could soon
have been closed. The report went on to state that "Jew
shall not dominate Arab and Arab shall not dominate
Jew in Palestine, which shall be neither a Jewish State
nor an Arab State. . . . Palestine is a Holy Land, sacred
to Christian, to Jew and to Moslem alike, and because
it is a Holy Land, Palestine is not, and can never become
a land which any race or religion can justly claim as its
very own."[35]

But a Palestine which guarded "the rights and interests
of Moslems, Jews and Christians alike," to quote the
Committee, was never acceptable to Zionists. To the
leaders of political Zionism, nationalist politics were im-
measurably more important than humanitarian concerns.
For, indeed, Zionism has never been refugeeism and refugeeism never Zionism.

When the Kerensky government overthrew the Czarist regime in Russia, Weizmann minimized the effect an
emancipation of Russian Jewry would have on the Zionist cause: "Nothing can be more superficial and nothing
can be more wrong than that the sufferings of Russian
Jewry ever were the cause of Zionism. The fundamental
cause of Zionism has been, and is, the ineradicable national striving of Jewry to have a home of its own—a

national center, a national home with a national Jewish life."[36] This thought was later echoed by Mrs. Moses P. Epstein, national president of the American Jewish women's organization, Hadassah: "The Zionist movement is a revolutionary program organized to bring about a radical and fundamental change in the status of the Jews the world over. The sooner the world knows it, the better."[37]

The Anglo-American Committee had found that Palestine alone could never meet Jewish emigration needs and that the United States and British Government, in association with other countries, must endeavor to find new homes for displaced persons. And this, more than anything, doomed the Committee, so far as Zionism was concerned. The Jewish Agency rejected the humanitarian acts offered by the report because "the central problem of the homeless and stateless Jewish people had been left untouched."[38] That "central problem," of course, was the Zionists' need for a national state.

Organized Jewry was willing to endorse the Committee's plea for the admission of 100,000 Jews to Palestine, but opened fire against the report's other nine recommendations of which the accepted one was an integral part. The American Zionists in New York, the British Zionists in London, and the Jewish Agency in Jerusalem, insisted in the Committee hearings that nothing less than Jewish statehood would do. This was in accordance with the Biltmore Program adopted in New York four years earlier by Zionist groups.

Early in 1947, the British Government tried to make a last attempt to conciliate the Arab and the Zionist positions. The new proposal stipulated the admission into Palestine of 4,000 Jews per month for two years, and subsequent admissions depending on the future absorptive capacity of the country. This second offer for the rescue of almost 100,000 Jews was spurned, too: the Jewish Agency denounced it as incompatible with Jewish rights to immigration, settlement and ultimate statehood.

There were other lands, besides Palestine, to which the displaced persons could have gone. President Roosevelt was deeply concerned with the plight of the European refugees and thought that all the free nations of the world ought to accept a certain number of immigrants, irrespective of race, creed, color or political belief. The President hoped that the rescue of 500,000 Displaced Persons could be achieved by such a generous grant of a worldwide political asylum. In line with this humanitarian idea, Morris Ernst, New York attorney and close friend of the President, went to London in the middle of the war to see if the British would take in 100,000 or 200,000 uprooted people. The President had reasons to assume that Canada, Australia and the South American countries would gladly open their doors. And if such good examples were set by other nations, Mr. Roosevelt felt that the American Congress could be "educated to go back to our traditional position of asylum." The key was in London. Would Morris Ernst succeed there? Mr. Ernst came home to report, and this is what took place in the White House (as related by Mr. Ernst to a Cincinnati audience in 1950):

Ernst: "We are at home plate. That little island [and it was during the second Blitz that he visited England] on a properly representative program of a World Immigration Budget, will match the United States up to 150,000."

Roosevelt: "150,000 to England—150,000 to match that in the United States—pick up 200,000 or 300,000

32

elsewhere, and we can start with half a million of these oppressed people."

A week later, or so, Mr. Ernst and his wife again visited the President.

Roosevelt (turning to Mrs. Ernst): "Margaret, can't you get me a Jewish Pope? I cannot stand it any more. I have got to be careful that when Stevie Wise leaves the White House he doesn't see Joe Proskauer on the way in." Then, to Mr. Ernst: "Nothing doing on the program. We can't put it over because the dominant vocal Jewish leadership of America won't stand for it."

"It's impossible! Why?" asked Ernst.

Roosevelt: "They are right from *their* point of view. The Zionist movement knows that Palestine is, and will be for some time, a remittance society. They know that they can raise vast sums for Palestine by saying to donors, 'There is no other place this poor Jew can go.' But if there is a world political asylum for all people irrespective of race, creed or color, they cannot raise their money. Then the people who do not want to give the money will have an excuse to say 'What do you mean, there is no place they can go but Palestine? They are the preferred wards of the world.' "

Morris Ernst, shocked, first refused to believe his leader and friend. He began to lobby among his influential Jewish friends for this world program of rescue, without mentioning the President's or the British reaction. As he himself has put it: "I was thrown out of parlors of friends of mine who very frankly said 'Morris, this is treason. You are undermining the Zionist movement.' "[39] He ran into the same reaction amongst all Jewish groups and their leaders. Everywhere he found "a deep, genuine, often fanatically emotional vested interest in putting over the Palestinian movement" in men "who are little concerned about human blood if it is not their own."[40]

This response of Zionism ended the remarkable Roosevelt effort to rescue Europe's Displaced Persons.

On December 22, 1945, President Truman directed the Secretaries of State and War, and certain other federal authorities, to speed in every possible way the granting of visas and "facilitate full immigration to the United States under existing quota laws." Congress, which had often shown its vulnerability to Jewish pressure groups, did not implement the President's request regarding the application of unused quotas to uprooted Europeans. Finally, a bill was introduced by Congressman William G. Stratton in the so-called "Do-Nothing" 80th Republican Congress, in 1947, to admit Displaced Persons "in a number equivalent to a part of the total quota numbers unused[41] during the war years." Under the Stratton Bill, up to 400,000 displaced persons of all faiths would have been permitted admission into the United States. The Committee hearings on this legislation (HR 2910) lasted eleven days and covered 693 pages of testimony. But there were exactly 11 pages of testimony given by Jewish organizations. They seemed, in fact, profoundly uninterested. But in 1944, when the House Foreign Affairs Committee was considering the Wright-Compton resolution that called for the establishment of a Jewish Commonwealth, there had been scarcely a Zionist organization that had not testified, sent telegraphed messages, or had some Congressman testify in their behalf. In support of the Wright-Compton resolution, 500 pages of testimony were produced in four days, the vast bulk by Zionists and their allies.

Yet on the Stratton Bill, which would have opened

America's doors to 400,000 Displaced Persons, the powerful Zionist Washington lobby (otherwise most articulate) was virtually silent. Only one witness appeared for all the major Jewish organizations—Senator Herbert Lehman, then the ex-Governor of New York. In addition to Lehman's statement, there was a resolution from the Jewish Community Councils of Washington-Heights and Inwood, and the testimony of the National Commander of the Jewish War Veterans. Not a single word was volunteered in behalf of Displaced Persons by any of the Zionist organizations which were at that moment recruiting members and soliciting funds "to alleviate human suffering."

To a meeting at the Shoreham Hotel in Washington, Congressman Stratton expressed his surprise at the lack of support from certain organizations which normally ought to have been most active in liberalizing the immigration law. Obviously, the Illinois Representative (now Governor) had never heard the President of the Zionist Organization of America exhort his membership:

I am happy that our movement has finally veered around to the point where we are all, or nearly all, talking about a Jewish State. That was always classical Zionism. . . . But I ask . . . are we again, in moments of desperation, going to confuse Zionism with refugeeism, which is likely to defeat Zionism? . . . Zionism is not a refugee movement. It is not a product of the second World War, nor of the first. Were there no displaced Jews in Europe, and were there free opportunities for Jewish immigration in other parts of the world at this time, Zionism would still be an imperative necessity.

The generous admission of Jewish Displaced Persons to the United States, and other countries, would have eradicated the necessity for a "Jewish State." Yet the human flotsam in former concentration camps impressed the Zionist only in two respects—as manpower and as justification for Jewish Statehood.

This is what a Yiddish paper[42] had to say on the distressing subject: "By pressing for an exodus of Jews from Europe; by insisting that Jewish D. P.'s do not wish to go to any country outside of Israel; by not participating in the negotiations on behalf of the D. P.'s; and by refraining from a campaign of their own—by all this they [the Zionists] certainly did not help to open the gates of America for Jews. In fact, they sacrificed the interests of living people—their brothers and sisters who went through a world of pain—to the politics of their own movement."

And this is what the Jewish *Forward*, largest Yiddish newspaper in the world, had to say on December 11, 1943: "The Jewish Conference is alive only when there is something in the air which has to do with a Commonwealth in Palestine, and it is asleep when it concerns rescue work for the Jews in the Diaspora."

Dr. Louis Finkelstein of the Jewish Theological Seminary in Manhattan, one of the country's most renowned theologians, stated in an interview in 1951 it had always been his feeling that "if United States Jews had put as much effort into getting D. P.'s admitted to this country as they put into Zionism, a home could have been found in the New World for all the displaced Jews of Europe."

Speaking at the Eightieth Anniversary of the Miztah Congregation at Chattanooga, Tennessee, *New York Times* publisher Sulzberger pleaded that "plans to move Jews to Palestine should be but part of larger plans to empty these camps of all refugees, Jew and otherwise."

He called for a reversal of Zionist policy that put state-hood first, refugees last: "Admitting that the Jews of Europe have suffered beyond expression, why in God's name should the fate of all these unhappy people be subordinated to the single cry of Statehood? I cannot rid myself of the feeling that the unfortunate Jews of Europe's D. P. camps are helpless hostages for whom statehood has been made the only ransom."[43]

All these voices of reason and honest compassion were lost in the nationalist emotionalism of the day. Zionism's real objective was hidden behind the incessant denunciations of the British and anyone else who opposed Zionist aspirations in Palestine. The non-Zionist American of Jewish faith was engulfed by frenzied sentiment. A letter to the Editor of the *Washington Post*, pointing out that "it ill behooved Zionist sympathizers to shed crocodile tears over the displaced persons," resulted in a violent fist fight on Pennsylvania Avenue. Dissenting whispers against the partition of Palestine invariably were hushed by the stereotyped reminder: "How can you be so cruel as to prevent those poor refugees from finding a home?"

Only after Israel had come into being was a drastically limited Displaced Persons Bill enacted. The ensuing long fight by the Citizens Committee on Displaced Persons to liberalize this legislation was successful two years later. The devoted man who organized this Committee, and rescued thousands of homeless of all faiths, was Lessing Rosenwald, the most maligned Jewish American opponent of political Zionism.

As the Palestine crisis developed, unity and cohesive action amongst Jewish organizations in America was achieved through a virulent "Hate Britain" campaign.

Completely forgotten were the consistent British acts of friendship in Palestine, dating back to the Balfour Declaration and the Mandate.[44]

The Churchill White Paper of 1922 had disclaimed any intention of creating a Jewish State in Palestine. It defined the "National Home" in terms of a "culturally autonomous Jewish community" and looked toward an ultimate bi-national Palestine. The White Paper specifically denied that there would be any "imposition of a Jewish nationality upon the inhabitants of Palestine as a whole" or that there was any intent that Palestine should become "as Jewish as England is English."

Weizmann himself characterized the Churchill White Paper "as a serious whittling down of the Balfour Declaration."[45] Article 6 of the Palestine Mandate made Great Britain responsible for facilitating Jewish immigration under suitable conditions, while insuring that the rights and position of other sections of the population be not prejudiced. The Churchill White Paper construed this article to mean that Jewish immigration could not exceed whatever might be the economic capacity of the country to absorb new arrivals. These restrictions, accepted at the time by the Executive of the Zionist Organization, were the basis for the subsequent Passfield White Paper and for the British policy that followed.

As the population of the Palestinian community grew, Arab demands for independence began to harass the British Government. Successive Royal Commissions were unable to devise a workable plan for partition which would have been acceptable to both Arab and Jew. Two conflicting nationalisms in a territory as large as Wales were demanding sovereignty.

Increasingly serious disorders brought the Peel Royal

Commission to the Holy Land in 1937. The Commission recommended a tripartite division into Arab and Jewish states and a permanent British mandate to include Jerusalem and surroundings. This solution, resolving what the Commission declared were "irreconcilable obligations," was rejected by Arabs and Zionists.

The MacDonald White Paper of 1939 followed the lead of the earlier Churchill and Passfield documents and called for a unitary Palestinian state in which control was to be shared by Zionists and Arabs. In such a Palestine State, "Jews and Arabs would be as Palestinian as English and Scottish in Britain are British."

The British Government had found it necessary to limit Jewish immigration to Palestine in order to fulfill its protective guarantees given the Arabs in the Balfour Declaration. Seventy-five thousand Jews were to be admitted during the succeeding five years, further immigration depending on Arab agreement. But when the Germans invaded Poland, thousands of Jews were admitted to Palestine, far above and beyond the legal quota. And while the U. S. Congress was expressing its sympathy for persecuted Jewry in resolutions, tens of thousands of refugees from Nazi barbarism were being received in England and many of them supported with Government funds. During the war, when the English people were themselves hard pressed for shelter and supplies, thousands of other refugees were allowed to enter Britain.

And what other acts did the British commit to justify the charge of anti-Semitism? Under the administrative system established by Britain in Palestine, self-governing Jewish institutions were permitted to develop, a Jewish Agency was established, and Jewish immigration was facilitated. Almost 500,000 new Jewish immigrants had been brought into Palestine by the end of World War

II, despite the continued Arab unrest which the British sought to allay. (Palestine's Jewish population increased from 11% in 1922 to 32% in 1945.) The British gave arms and other equipment to the Jews in Palestine so that they might be prepared for their own defense. The British Eighth Army, under Montgomery, broke the back of General Rommel's Nazi forces and thus saved the Jewish Palestinian community from extermination.

Yet the British Government, of course, was unable to yield to the Zionist demand that Palestine be made a Jewish State, though it expressed its willingness to accept any reasonable settlement on which both the Zionists and the Arabs would agree. The conflict between uncompromising Jewish Nationalists and the Mandatory Administration led after World War II to illegal immigration, violence and sabotage. The Holy Land soon became an armed camp. The Arab Higher Committee was buying arms for its adherents. On the Jewish side, there was not only the Haganah (the more restrained and semi-official army of the Jewish Agency) but also the Irgun Zvai Leumi, the terrorist group which, since 1943, had been bombing Government buildings and installations.

The most vicious of the illegal bands was the Stern Gang[46] which had broken away from the Irgun. Throughout World War II, its members engaged in a series of outrages, climaxed by the assassination of the British Minister of State for the Middle East, Lord Moyne, in Cairo in November, 1944. Weizmann at this time wrote to Churchill: "I can assure you that Palestine Jewry will, as its representative bodies have declared, go to the utmost limits of its power to cut out, root and branch, this evil from its midst."[47] Two years after that

assurance, the Anglo-American Committee was still requesting the Jewish Agency "to resume active cooperation with the Mandatory Authority in the suppression
of terrorism and of illegal immigration and in the maintenance of that law and order throughout Palestine which
is essential for the good of all including the new immigrants."[48]

In Europe, a well organized movement, supported by
large financial contributions from Zionist sources, had
set up "the underground railway to Palestine." Jews
from all over Europe were moved down to ports on the
Mediterranean. There they were placed on ships, often
overcrowded and unseaworthy, under conditions of utmost privation and squalor. A very large proportion of
this human freight was brought from countries of Com-
munist-dominated Eastern Europe. For, indeed, the
Kremlin had begun to play its Middle Eastern game of
sowing unrest in the Arab world and pushing Britain
out.

To most Americans, however, the Palestinian struggle
was merely a drama of refugees fighting for homes—this
time against their new English oppressors. When the
British terminated all entry into Palestine, anti-British
feelings mounted in the United States.

Organized American Jewry exerted utmost pressures
on public opinion and politicians. This, everyone was
reminded, was the same kind of war the American Revo-
lutionists had waged against the very same imperialist
power. The tactics of the British in Palestine were compared with those used for a long time against Ireland's
fighters for freedom. The blowing up of the King David
Hotel in Jerusalem and the mob hanging of two British
sergeants brought this hussah from Hollywood's Ben

Hecht: "Every time you let go with your guns at the British betrayers of your homeland, the Jews of America make a little holiday in their hearts."

It was perhaps unfortunate that throughout this trying period Britain's Foreign Minister was Ernest Bevin. This onetime Welsh miner's temperament was hardly suited to reconcile two such intransigent forces as the Arabs and the Zionists. Nor was he able to demonstrate to public opinion, particularly in the United States, just how Britain was being squeezed between two flaring nationalisms. At Bournemouth, before a Labor Party gathering in 1946, Bevin charged that the United States was pressing Britain to allow more Jews into Palestine—because we did not want to allow them into America. While he meant to attack the political exploitation of human suffering, he brought down upon himself the totally unjustified charge of being anti-Semitic. His quick temper constantly handicapped his efforts to separate the problem of displaced European Jewry from the political question of Palestine.

By early 1947, events in Palestine clearly demanded international intervention. Zionists were more than ever insisting on a Jewish majority in Palestine in order to secure a Jewish Commonwealth. The British were resisting all efforts to force them into a new policy. The Arabs, fighting both the British and the Jews, were demanding an independent Palestinian state.

In the United States, audible public opinion supported illegal immigration. Such organizations as the American League for a Free Palestine, the Hebrew Committee for National Liberation, and the Political Action Committee for Palestine, were each raising funds for their own Palestinian terrorist group. Their competitive advertise-

ments defended terrorism and stressed the tax exempt-
ability of contributions for terrorist organizations. In
New York, Congressman Joseph C. Baldwin, scion of
one of the city's oldest families, and public relations adviser to the Irgun, defended the flogging of four British
soldiers and assured Menachem Begin, Irgun leader, that
he, Baldwin, would do everything to make his, Begin's,
position clear in this country. A confused public became
even more confused by the verbal barrages exchanged
between various Jewish factions. "Wise attacks Silver"
—"Ben-Gurion blasts the Hebrew Committee for National Liberation"—"American League for a Free Palestine assails the Jewish Agency"—"Haganah and Irgun
members clash."

And then the British decided to give up the Palestinian
ghost. The Anglo-Arab Conferences, which had started
in September 1946, and had adjourned to January, 1947,
proved a total failure. A total failure, too, was the so-
called Bevin Plan which, revising the earlier Morrison-
Grady Plan, suggested semi-autonomous Arab and Jewish cantons for a five-year period and the admission into
Palestine of 100,000 Displaced Persons. Both Parties ob-
jected, whereupon Britain announced it was not her intention to enforce any plan. At the same time, the Zionist Jewish Agency proclaimed its refusal to cooperate
with Mandatory authorities in any action against terrorists. Britain felt that there was nothing left but to place
the controversy before the United Nations. A special
meeting of the General Assembly was called by the U. N.
Secretary-General Trygve Lie.

Submitting the dispute to international adjudication,
Bevin let loose with a characteristic barrage of words.
He accused American politicians of wrecking any

chance for an amicable solution of the Palestine problem and, quite undiplomatically, pointed the finger at the White House. "I did reach a stage, however, in meeting the Jews separately . . . when things looked more hopeful," Bevin explained to the House of Commons. "There was a feeling . . . when they left me in the Foreign Office that day, that I had the right approach at last. I went back to the Paris Peace Conference, and the next day . . . —I believe it was a special day of the Jewish religion —my right honourable friend, the Prime Minister, telephoned me at midnight and told me that the President of the United States was going to issue another statement on the hundred thousand. I think the country and the world ought to know about this. . . . "[49] Bevin was referring to the Day-of-Atonement plea of President Truman to admit 100,000 refugees. The Paris Peace Conference was then in session and Bevin implored Secretary Byrnes to intercede with President Truman not to issue a statement which might upset current delicate negotiations. Whereupon the Secretary of State told him that "if the President did not issue a statement, a competitive statement would be issued by Dewey."

In the *New York Times* of October 7, 1946, James Reston disclosed that several Administration advisers had opposed the Truman statement in view of the fact that Britain was on the verge of reaching a truce with the Zionists. Attlee himself had asked the President to withhold the statement, but the President made it nevertheless. It was believed that Mead and Lehman, the Democratic candidates for Governor and Senator in New York, would be helped by the Truman declaration. On October 6th, Governor Dewey outbid Truman by declaring the British should admit "not 100,000 but several

hundred thousand Jews." Senator Taft also joined in
the fun of raising the ante. It was all part of the national
campaign which had elected what Truman was later to
call the "Republican Do-Nothing Congress."

Whether the British talks with the Zionists would have
been successful if domestic American politics had not
interfered, is questionable. But the whole episode was
extremely characteristic of the political pattern which
the U. S. Government was following whenever Israel
and the Middle East were involved.

The Arabs were as clearly inept in propaganda techniques as the Jewish Nationalists were masters. But
American national politics being what they are, the
chances of impressing this country with the Moslem
point of view were at best slim: there is a rather negligible
Arab vote in the U. S. Whatever the rights of Palestine's
indigenous inhabitants may have been, they were completely dismissed in the worldwide propaganda battle
between the Mandatory Administration and the Jewish
Agency.

The British were determined to maintain law and order, pending the United Nations decision over the ultimate fate of the Holy Land. The Zionists continued to
present their power play to the confused world in
terms of humanitarianism. Continuous clashes between
wretched would-be immigrants and the armed British
authorities were the only issue really discussed in the
American press. The S.S. "Abril," Ben Hecht's boat,
crowded with refugees, was seized by the British. Three
British were killed and several injured in an effort "to
rescue or capture" (as the U. S. press reported) refugees
who plunged into the sea. Terrorists blew up the Iraq
Petroleum Pipeline. The Irgun declared open warfare.

Dov Gruner and three other terrorists who had attacked a Palestine police station were hanged. The Stern Gang promised retaliation.

And all that time, the only contribution of the U. S. Government were words. There was much talk about Displaced Persons and human suffering, but no real effort to bring them into the United States. Everybody knew, and said, what Britain should or should not do. Every politician hurried to get in on the act, to exploit "humanitarianism" for votes. Everybody urged unlimited immigration to the Holy Land. Eleanor Roosevelt urged a luncheon meeting of the Women's Division of the United Jewish Appeal to tell Congress what to do on Palestine. "The time has come," she said, "when we have to stand up and be counted. You have not told Congress so they would hear one unmistakable voice."

Did organized Jewry really need such a reminder? Day in and day out the press carried such headlines as "The American Jewish Congress demands"—"Senator Lehman again renews his plea to open up Palestine"— "Congressman Javits of Manhattan suggests a Congressional junket to Palestine to foster the establishment of a Jewish commonwealth." The British Empire building in Radio Center was picketed while William O'Dwyer, not yet a refugee in Mexico, excoriated the British before the National Council of Young Israel. Zionists flooded the capitol with letters trying to link Palestine with aid to Greece and Turkey. "Tell the British," some letters said, "there will be no aid for the British policy in Greece and Turkey unless they follow the United States lead on Palestine."

The State and War Departments, it is true, were constantly cautioning the White House and Congress that an irresponsible vote-chasing policy for Palestine might irreparably damage the American position in one of the world's most strategic areas. But politicians, when following the scent of "blocs," seem to be beyond the reach of reason. At the climax of the Palestine crisis, at any rate, elections were just around the corner (they always seem to be in this blessed country of ours), and both parties were convinced that their eloquent support of statehood for Israel was a prerequisite for their conquest of pivotal states. There was, in fact, no need for the Zionists to refute the solemn warnings that were coming from the War and State Departments. All the Zionists had to do was to make sure that the politicians remained hypnotized by "the Jewish vote." Perhaps for the first time in history, a decisive battle could indeed be won with the tools of propaganda. It is to the credit of the Zionists' acumen that they grasped their chance. But it is perhaps less to the credit of America's non-Zionist Jewry that it permitted its self-appointed Zionist leaders to bet the future of American Judaism on the roulette of power politics.

CHAPTER III

The Unholy Partition
of the Holy Land

ON April 28, 1947, the Special Session of the General Assembly of the United Nations convened in New York to consider Palestine. Initial deliberations were comparatively brief, most of the time being consumed in procedural snarls. Permission to testify before a plenary meeting of the General Assembly was refused to the Jewish Agency. Hearings were held before the Political and Security Committee of the General Assembly, at which the position of both the Jewish Agency and the Arab Higher Committee were presented. No other Jewish factions were permitted to present their views, the requirement being that an organization, to be heard, should represent a considerable element of Palestine's population. A Committee was then appointed to investigate the situation in Palestine and report to the second regular session of the General Assembly in September, 1947.

Soviet Russia proposed to seat the Big Five on this fact-finding United Nations Special Committee on Palestine (UNSCOP), but the suggestion was rejected. The United States contended that the presence of the largest powers on the initial committee of inquiry would raise an "obstacle to a fair, impartial report." So the Committee was constituted of eleven smaller nations (Australia, Canada, Czechoslovakia, Guatemala, India, Iran, Netherlands, Peru, Sweden, Uruguay and Yugoslavia), with Justice Emil Sandström of Sweden as chairman.

Zionist pressures were incessantly exercised during the U. N. session and the Committee inquiry. The Chief Rabbis of Palestine jointly urged United Nations action favorable to the Jews. The C. I. O. pledged its support. The American Jewish Conference, the American Jewish Committee, Eleanor Roosevelt, the American Christian Committee for Palestine and the Jewish National Council issued simultaneous statements in the same tenor. The reputedly non-Zionist American Jewish Committee issued a statement that it "deplored" Ben Hecht's blood-thirsty statements. Dr. Israel Goldstein, later to become the head of the American section of the Jewish Agency, declared that efforts to create a Jewish State would continue regardless of what the United Nations decided. Additional religious sanction to Jewish nationalism was formally given by the Rabbinical Council of America, the organization of conservative rabbis. The Palestine Economic Corporation, a private American Company, added the business touch by announcing that the Negeb desert could be irrigated within one year. The *Nation* magazine associates, charging that the Arabs had been Axis aides, urged the General Assembly to establish two independent States in Palestine. Henry Wallace and the *New Republic* ran advertisements appealing for funds to aid Palestine terrorists.

Shortly after the Committee of inquiry arrived in Palestine, the case of S.S. "Exodus, '47" seemed to black out all other Palestine news. From the moment this old (renamed) Chesapeake Bay excursion boat had sailed from the French port of Sète, there was no question of what would happen: she carried illegal immigrants who would be intercepted by the British. But the Jewish nationalists had sagely mounted the props, brought in the players and solicited a world audience. If anyone was ultimately surprised, it can only have been the refugees whose misery was being exploited. They, at least, were really hoping to gain a haven.

As in the previous instances of the "Patria" (in 1940) and the "Struma" (in 1942), the British law required the detention of illegal immigrants. But the "Exodus" passengers were not simply interned in Cyprus (the established routine in most previous cases of the kind). They were bodily removed from the "Exodus" to three British transports, after a three-hour battle in which three persons were killed and 217 injured. There was no movie house in the United States that did not carry a newsreel shot of those distraught faces on "that long voyage home." The haven offered by the French Government was rejected by the refugees whom the British finally landed at Hamburg—not before a few swastikas, painted over the boat's Union Jack, and a hunger strike had made additional frontpage headlines.

The trip of the "Exodus" paid immediate dividends of almost insane Anglophobia. Swastikas were painted on British consulates in New York City and elsewhere. The garrotted bodies of the two British sergeants were found hanging near Nathanya[1] (named after one of its benefactors, the American philanthropist, Nathan Straus). But Judge Joseph Proskauer, head of the American Jewish Committee, attributed this Irgun action to the British White Paper of 1939, while Rabbi Silver stated it had been provoked by the British.

There was only one small Jewish voice that sounded out above all that physical and moral horror. While everyone else fell in line with ugliness, the conscience of Judaic ethics found expression alone through Dr. Judah L. Magnes, the President of the Hebrew University in Palestine. Dr. Magnes, as he had proved throughout his entire venerable life, was seeking, not political power, but a solution to a difficult and complex problem. He pleaded for a bi-national State that would not divide Palestine and would reconcile both nationalisms. The regenerated Jerusalem for which he prayed was to be gained only through "understanding and cooperation between Jew and Arab," never through a "moratorium on morality."

In opening the twenty-third year of the University, Dr. Magnes referred to "Zionist Totalitarianism" which is trying to bring "the entire Jewish people under its influence by force and violence. I have not yet seen the dissidents called by their rightful names: Killers—brutalized men and women." "All Jews in America," he added, "share in the guilt, even those not in accord with the activities of this new pagan leadership, but who sit at ease with folded hands. . . . If we raise the alarm, we do so with muffled voices. If our voices be raised, it is because of anxiety for the national discipline, not for anxiety concerning discipline to the spirit of Israel and the timeless values of Israel's tradition."

Not too long afterwards, Dr. Magnes came to the United States—never again to return to his beloved Jerusalem. He who had done so much to build Palestine, died in virtual exile: his family and friends did not permit him to run the risk of a Zionist terrorist's bullet.

Judah Magnes' commentary on the accomplishments of these terrorists will never be forgotten: "We had always thought that Zionism would diminish anti-Semitism in the world. We are witness to the opposite." And indeed, in England, where there never had been even social discrimination against British Jewry, prejudice flared. Anti-Jewish outbreaks rose with the succession of British casualties in Palestine. The police were forced to guard British synagogues. Three British police were killed by a bomb in London.

An article in the U. S. magazine on Jewish affairs *Commentary* (May 1947), entitled "British Jews in Heavy Weather," squarely faced the facts: British opinion was "hardening not only against the Jews of Palestine, but also against the Jews of Britain, who are felt, inevitably, to be in some kind of sympathy with these foreigners who are shooting British Tommies in cold blood. . . . The man-in-the-street cannot be expected to analyze all the facts; and while no violent reaction has yet occurred, it is quite certain that anti-Jewish sentiment is being stored up, with great potential danger to the Jewish community of Britain unless a satisfactory solution can quickly be found."

It was in this sickening atmosphere, and against this background, that the United Nations Special Committee On Palestine (UNSCOP) conducted its inquiry and reported its findings to the Second Session of the General Assembly. Between May 26th and August 31st, the day on which its report was signed, the Committee had held sixteen public and thirty-six private meetings at Lake Success, Jerusalem, Beirut and Geneva. Oral and written testimony had been received from governments, political organizations, religious bodies and individuals.

The Committee was unable to present unanimous

findings. A majority (Canada, Czechoslovakia, Guatemala, Netherlands, Peru, Sweden and Uruguay) proposed partition of Palestine. A minority (India, Yugoslavia and Iran) suggested a single state with a federal structure. Australia supported neither plan: her representative on the Committee, John D. L. Hood, contended that a committee of inquiry ought to present any suggestions in a form which did not prejudice judgment by the General Assembly—and this principle, he felt, had been violated by both sides in the Committee.

On September 3, 1947, the General Assembly designated an Ad Hoc Committee to consider the two suggestions. All member states of the U. N. were represented on this Ad Hoc Committee which elected the Australian Minister for Foreign Affairs, Herbert V. Evatt, its chairman. The new Committee held thirty-four meetings between September 25 and November 25, 1947. The Jewish Agency and the Arab Higher Committee were given an additional opportunity to be heard. The majority (partition) report was mainly defended by Garcia Granados of Guatemala and Rodriguez Fabregat of Uruguay, whose arguments were astonishingly replete with Zionist philosophy, data and symbols.

These two South American diplomats refused to join in an otherwise unanimous Committee recommendation that "it be accepted as incontrovertible that any solution for Palestine cannot be considered as a solution of the Jewish problem in general," a provision denounced by the Jewish Agency spokesman as "unintelligible." Granados later wrote a book, *The Birth of Israel: The drama as I saw it,* widely publicized and distributed by Zionists. Both he and Fabregat have lectured for Zionist groups, and in Israel today there are streets bearing their names, an honor these diplomats undoubtedly earned.

The United Kingdom representative, Arthur Creech-Jones, clarified at the outset that his Government had no intention of implementing any U. N. plan with British forces unless both sides to the contention accepted the plan. In the face of their already tremendous losses, in pounds as well as manpower, they'd "had it." The British stand placed an even greater responsibility on the other delegates: they had to arrive at some solution which could be implemented and would not further upset the disturbed peace. But while the delegates recognized the limited power of the U. N. to enforce a recommendation, and the grave lack of authority once the British withdrew, they refused to be unduly deterred. The United States representative, Herschel Johnson, said something about a recruited force of volunteers to carry out the partition decision. But if the implication was that his country was in any frame of mind to dispatch armed volunteers, it was obviously an insincere and politically gauged utterance.

Sir Mohammed Zafrullah Khan, Foreign Minister of Pakistan, bore the brunt of the Arab fight against partition. He emphasized that the right of Palestine's 1,200,-000 Arabs to choose the form of government under which they wished to live was guaranteed by the Charter of the United Nations. The United Nations could effectively prescribe, Sir Mohammed pointed out, the conditions which would secure for the country's 625,000 Jews complete religious, linguistic, educational and social freedom within the independent state of Palestine.[2] But the U. N. could hardly prescribe more.

The partitionists, influenced by the majority report and the Jewish Agency's brilliant argumentation presented by Rabbi Silver and Professor Weizmann, were not satisfied with such a solution. The international commitments with regard to the Jewish National Home, as provided in the Mandate, and the religio-historic ties of the Jewish people with Palestine were held strong enough to override all Arab objections.

One of the main props of the partition concept was the envisaged economic union between the Jewish and Arab States. The majority report had made that union an essential part of its final recommendations; and the plan adopted by the General Assembly of the United Nations in November, 1947, was not just for Partition, but for Partition *with Economic Union*. For no less than 60 per cent of Palestine's best territory and half a million of its inhabitants had been placed under the rule of one third of the people; consequently, at least the security of the Arabs was to be safeguarded through an economic union with that viable part of Palestine, under a Joint Economic Board. Even Mr. Shertok of the Jewish Agency stressed in his testimony the importance of the "closest economic ties between the states": the viability of both states was to depend on their economic oneness. But the very moment partition was resolved, this major justification for the U. N. surgery was completely forgotten.

The two working subcommittees of the Ad Hoc Committee were peculiarly constituted. For some inexplicable reason, Chairman Evatt refused to permit neutral delegates on these drafting committees, so that each subcommittee represented one monolithic and extreme view. No real contact between the two subcommittees was established. The so-called Conciliation group, headed by the Chairman himself, did nothing except write a letter to Prince Feisal of Arabia suggesting a meeting between His

Excellency and the U.S. Secretary of State, George Marshall. (Feisal agreed to such a meeting, but nothing further was heard of the proposal.)

According to the plan for partition with economic union, Jerusalem was to be an international city under United Nations rule. The only change requested by the Jewish Agency was the deletion of a clause that the governor of the city could "neither be a Jew nor an Arab," on the grounds that this could be discriminatory: the word "Jew," it was pointed out, had both an ethnic and religious connotation, whereas the use of the word "Arab" would permit a non-Arab Moslem to become governor.

Finally, in November 1947, everybody was talked out and the Ad Hoc Committee started voting. It first turned to the resolutions of Subcommittee Two which contained the Arab viewpoint. By a vote of 25 to 18, with 11 abstentions, the full Committee rejected the proposal that six questions concerning the Balfour Declaration and the Mandate be submitted to the International Court of Justice. By the even closer vote of 21 to 20 the Ad Hoc Committee dismissed the question of the competency of the U.N. to enforce, or recommend the enforcement of, partition without the consent of the majority of the people of Palestine. On both these issues Argentina, Brazil, Colombia, El Salvador, Greece, Haiti, Liberia and India supported the Arab states.

The Committee then adopted resolutions which requested all members of the United Nations to take back those Jewish refugees and Displaced Persons who belonged to them and desired repatriation, and to absorb others in proportion to the area and economic resources of each country. These were only recommendations, but they advocated absorption of refugees in countries other than in Palestine. So the United States voted against these resolutions.

On the next vote, which would have implemented these resolutions with a quota resettlement scheme, partition proponents defeated the idea 18 to 15. The establishment of a unitary Palestine was voted down 29 to 12 with 14 abstentions. The opposition consisted of the seven Arab states, Pakistan, Turkey, Afghanistan, Liberia and Cuba. At the concluding meeting, the partition plan itself easily passed by a vote of 25 to 13 with 17 abstentions. On every single resolution considered by the Committee, the United States and the Soviet Union had voted together. But despite that suspect harmony, the partition plan going before the General Assembly was actually a minority proposal. A majority of 32 had either voted nay, or abstained, or were absent (including three of the Big Five—France, China, and the United Kingdom).

The work of eighteen commissions and investigations over a span of 25 years, and of the United Nations for seven months, was nearing completion. The scene shifted from Lake Success, Long Island, to Flushing Meadows, Queens, where the partition proponents would have to meet their most formidable difficulty: while a bare majority sufficed in Committee voting, a two-thirds majority was needed in the General Assembly. And judging by the last vote in the Ad Hoc Committee, partition was one vote short of passage, if delegations did not change their mind. And the Philippine delegates, who had absented themselves on all Committee ballots, announced they still had received no instructions.

The General Assembly heard thirty-odd speakers. With the exception of the two gentlemen from South America, Granados and Fabregat, who presented the straight Jewish Agency line, and the delegates of the Soviet Union and the United States, the advocates of partition were full of doubts, regret and even apologies.

The delegate from Sweden, the country which had headed the Special Committee of Inquiry, admitted that the plan "has its weak sides and some dangerous omissions,"[3] but that Sweden was supporting partition because, if no decision were taken, this would have still more serious consequences.

The Canadian speaker supported the partition plan on the grounds that it was the "best of four unattractive and difficult alternatives."[4] He stated that the establishment of a well-rooted community of nearly 700,000 Jews in Palestine, the investment of $600,000,000 and "the devotion on the part of Jews all over the world to the idea of a Jewish national home in a country which, once at least, was a Jewish land," made the Palestine problem *sui generis* and unique; and that this set of circumstances constituted a vital flaw in the otherwise unanswerable Arab case. Then he added: "We support the plan with heavy hearts and many misgivings."[5]

New Zealand's Ambassador talked of the "grave inadequacies of the present proposal,"[6] while Belgium's Foreign Minister Van Langenhove said this of the partition plan: "We are not certain that it is completely just; we doubt whether it is practical; and we are afraid that it involves great risks. . . . But what is the alternative? The solution proposed or no solution at all; that is to say, still more serious troubles, if not utter chaos. We do not want to assume the responsibility for that, either by a negative vote or even by an abstention. That is why we are resigned to voting with the majority."[7] Of all delegates heard in this discussion, the Belgian alone hit at the very idea of Zionist segregation: "The Palestinian question is particularly disturbing for the Belgians. They have to make an effort to understand Zionism. The national home of our Jewish patriots is in Belgium. No one has treated them in such a way as to make them want to find another home in Palestine."[8] But still, Belgium voted for partition.

Herschel Johnson for the United States tried to contend that this was not partition in reality, because of the provisions for economic union and for the internationalization of Jerusalem. He naively envisaged that the boundary between the two new states "will be as friendly as the boundary which runs for three thousand miles between Canada and the United States."[9]

As in the Ad Hoc Committee, the oratory of Zafrullah Khan dominated the debate. He advised the Western powers to "remember that you may need friends tomorrow, that you may need allies in the Middle East. I beg of you not to ruin and blast your credit in those lands." He questioned the viability of the proposed Jewish State and the sincerity of the U.S. and the Western nations. They who gave lip service to humanitarian principles, he pointed out, were at the same time closing their doors to the "homeless Jew," and yet insisted on Arab Palestine providing not only "a shelter, a refuge but also a State so that he ('the homeless Jew') shall rule over the Arab." Sardonically, Pakistan's Foreign Minister referred to the proposal that unrepatriated Displaced Persons be allocated to Member States in accordance with their capacity to receive such refugees: "Australia, an overpopulated small country with congested areas says no, no, no; Canada, equally congested and overpopulated, says no; the United States, a great humanitarian country, a small area, with small resources, says no. This is their contribution to the humanitarian principle. But they state: let them go into Palestine, where there are vast areas, a large economy and no trouble; they can easily be taken in there."

The final vote was scheduled for November 26, following a night session at which the debate was to be concluded. But that night session was cancelled, and the balloting called off, after the Zionists had ascertained that they lacked positive assurance of the necessary two thirds. The move for adjournment skimmed through by a vote of 24 to 21. November 27 was Thanksgiving Day, so that the delay provided forty-eight additional hours in which to lobby. And November 27, 1947, may have been restful Turkey Day for the nation, but the United Nations quarters resembled the smoke-filled room of the most hectic National Convention. As a leading Zionist later wrote: "Every clue was meticulously checked and pursued. Not the smallest or the remotest of nations, but was contacted and wooed. Nothing was left to chance."[10]

General Carlos Romulo announced that the Philippine delegation, who had abstained from voting in the Ad Hoc Committee, had at last received word from home. The decision: not to vote in favor of partition. To add to the Zionists' shock, the General at the same time gave one of the most effective speeches against partition. He passionately defended the inviolable "primordial rights of a people to determine their political future and to preserve the territorial integrity of their native land. . . . As I pronounce these words 'without distinction as to race, sex, language or religion,' I think of our own United Nations charter; for these are words which occur in that instrument over and over again. And the reason is simple; they look forward rather than backward. . . . We cannot believe that the majority of this General Assembly would prefer a reversal of this course.

We cannot believe that it would sanction a solution to the problem of Palestine that would turn us back on the road to the dangerous principles of racial exclusiveness and to the archaic documents of theocratic governments. . . . The problem of the displaced European Jews is susceptible of a solution other than through the establishment of an independent Jewish state in Palestine."[11]

To compound the Zionist consternation, Haiti's representative, Antonio Vieux, had told the General Assembly that "the principle of sovereignty of states, which is a particular means of defense for small nations, was in opposition to the adoption of the special Committee's plan," and that Haiti, therefore, would vote in the negative. But Haiti, like the Philippines, was not impervious to American influence. Clearly, utmost pressures had now to be applied.

And so, while Macy's Thanksgiving parade was proceeding up New York's Great White Way, the Siamese Embassy in Washington got word that the credentials of the delegate who had voted against partition in the Ad Hoc Committee had been cancelled. And new credentials would not be forthcoming in time. Consequently, Siam's negative vote was simply invalidated in this "but-for-the-loss-of-a-shoe" story of the partition of Palestine.

Greece, too, had made known that she would join the opposition to the American-Soviet bloc. It was also considered likely that Liberia, who in previous tests had either abstained or voted with the Arab states would vote in the negative. The antipartitionists could count, even after the magic disappearance of Siam, on fifteen or sixteen negative votes; and this would have necessitated the mobilization of thirty or thirty-two votes for partition.

At this crucial moment the partition forces were able

to announce that Belgium, the Netherlands and New Zealand would vote a reluctant yes, and that Luxembourg was swaying in the same direction. These countries had previously abstained. The ever-absent Paraguay was still in neither corner, but her delegate was being closeted in secret conferences.

The General Assembly reconvened on Friday, November 28, and first listened to a few final speeches. Colombia's Dr. Lopez made a final bid for a peaceful solution by moving that the Ad Hoc Committee be reconvened and authorized to attempt conciliation for another three months. French Ambassador Parodi offered a substitute motion for a twenty-four hour adjournment. Venezuela, Luxembourg and Denmark supported the French proposal enthusiastically, in a spirit of "Where there is life, there is hope," and the Assembly was adjourned by a 25 to 15 vote. It is difficult to establish in whose interest this additional breather was proposed: supporters and opponents of partition were voting on both sides. But whatever the intention, the delay yielded satisfactory results for the partition forces.

On the morning of November 29, Dr. Oswaldo Aranha of Brazil, Assembly President, told reporters he was convinced that a two-thirds majority would be obtained for the majority report. As the session opened, the Zionists confidently announced partition was the absolute irreducible minimum, while the Arabs meekly indicated they might accept a cantonal state such as the Minority UNSCOP-Report had recommended.

After a few parliamentary maneuvers, the vote was taken and partition was decreed by 33 to 13 with 10 abstentions and 1 absent. Luxembourg voted aye. That Liberia should have shifted was astonishing enough; but truly sensational were the affirmative votes of Haiti and

the Philippines who only 24 hours before had been fiercely attacking the majority proposal.

When the vote was announced, a rabbi cried ecstat-
ically: "This was the day the Lord hath made. Let us
rejoice in it and be glad." Captain Bernard Marks, of the
S.S. "Exodus, 1947," burned a copy of the British Mandate to the delight of a jubilant crowd.

The *New York Times* commented editorially:
"Doubts of the wisdom of erecting a political state on
the basis of a religious faith must yield to the fact of a
decision made by a necessary two-thirds vote." A few
editors looked farther ahead and confessed to an appre-
hension that "the outcome may wreck the political world
as it stands."[12]

In the tumult and turbulence of the moment, the declarations of the Arab states that they would not be bound
by the decision of the U. N. were scarcely noticed. But
the breach between the West and the Arab-Moslem
world had commenced. Its repercussion was to be turmoil in the Middle East. From Marrakech in Morocco
to Karachi in Pakistan, American prestige, together with
that of her allies, has sunk to its lowest ebb in history.

Clearly, the two-thirds majority in favor of partition
did not express the unmistakable sentiment of the United
Nations. And yet, just as clearly, that decisive two-thirds
majority was somehow obtained. How? What had been
the pressure?

While the final vote was still in doubt, New York's
Congressman Emanuel Celler attacked the U. S. delega-
tion to the U. N. for having been restrained by the State
Department, specifically by Under-Secretary Robert
Lovett. And Zionist Celler's strange complaint was jus-
tified: neither the U. S. permanent delegation to the
U. N. nor the State Department had directly exerted un-

due pressures on any member of the United Nations. The compulsion and coercion came in much more refined ways.

While Senator Warren Austin, the Head of the U. S. delegation to the U. N., could express his sincere gratitude that at least the American anti-Zionists were presenting their views to foreign delegates exclusively through the proper channels of their own Government, the Zionists reached boldly into the chancelleries of foreign countries. "Operation Partition" was executed by a strategy board of immense international influence whose three American master minds were New York's Judge Joseph Proskauer, head of the American Jewish Committee, Washington economist Robert Nathan, and White House Assistant "for minority affairs," David Niles.

These three, speaking to foreign governments and diplomats always as "mere private citizens," were men of impressively good connections in public affairs. Robert Nathan, for instance, knew precisely how to weaken Liberia's objections to partition. The Liberian delegate, Mr. Dennis, was simply told that Nathan would go after his good friend Stettinius, former Secretary of State, who at that time was attending to his enormous business interests in Liberia. The Liberian diplomat considered this to be attempted intimidation and so reported to the Department of State. Finally, however, by some strange coincidence, Liberia's vote was cast in favor of partition. And informed hints to various South American delegates that their vote for partition would greatly increase the chances of a Pan-American Road project, then under consideration, seem to have improved traffic in the General Assembly.

Eleanor Roosevelt, too, inexhaustibly worked on the

many friends she had among the foreign delegates to the U. N. And she was incessantly prodding her husband's heir, Harry S. Truman, to put pressure on the State Department, whose officers were properly limiting their efforts to peaceful debates with foreign delegates.

When partition prospects looked particularly grim, Bernard Baruch was prevailed upon to talk with the French who could not afford to lose Interim Marshall-Plan Aid. Other important Americans "talked" to other countries such as Haiti, Ethiopia, the Philippines, Paraguay, and Luxembourg, all dependent on the United States. Drew Pearson, an old friend of the Zionists, told in his "Merry-Go-Round" column how Adolph Berle, legal adviser to the Haitian Government, "talked" on the phone to Haiti's President, and how Harvey Firestone, owner of vast rubber plantations in Liberia, "talked" with that government.

In discussing the partition vote at a Cabinet luncheon on December 1, 1947, Robert Lovett said that "never in his life had he been subjected to as much pressure as he had in three days beginning Thursday morning and ending Saturday night. Herbert Bayard Swope and Robert Nathan were amongst those who had opportuned him."[13] The Firestone Tire and Rubber Company, according to Lovett, made use of its concession on Liberia and had transmitted "a message to their representative there, directing him to bring pressure on the Liberian Government to vote in favor of Partition." Lovett remarked that Jewish zeal was so intense that it "almost resulted in defeating the objectives" sought.

And no pressure was sadder, or more cynical, than that put on the Philippines. General Romulo left the United States shortly after delivering his fiery speech against partition. Ambassador Elizalde had spoken by telephone to President Roxas and told him of the many pressures to which Romulo and the delegation had been subjected. The Ambassador's own view was that, though partition was not a wise move, the United States was determined on partition. It would be foolish to vote against a policy so ardently desired by the U. S. Administration at a time when seven bills were pending in the U. S. Congress in which the islands had a tremendous stake. The Ambassador and President Roxas agreed (this was all subsequently reported in a lengthy cable from the U. S. Ambassador in Manila to the State Department) that the Philippines must not risk the antagonism of the United States when support could be gained so easily by a proper vote on Palestine. A joint telegram from twenty-six pro-Zionist U. S. Senators, drafted by New York's Robert F. Wagner, was a particularly important factor in changing the Philippine vote.

That senatorial telegram, sent to twelve other U. N. delegations, changed four votes to yes, and seven votes from nay to abstention. Only Greece risked antagonizing the United States Senate, and stuck to no.

Sir Mohammed Zafrullah Khan was speaking for many of his fellow U. N. delegates when he declared in a post-vote statement: "In the words of the greatest American 'We have striven to do the right as God gives us to see the right.' We did succeed in persuading a sufficient number of our fellow representatives to see the right as we saw it, but they were not permitted to stand by the right as they saw it. . . . We entertain no sense of grievance against those of our friends and fellow representatives who have been compelled under heavy pressure to change sides and to cast their votes in support of a proposal the justice and fairness of which do not commend themselves to them. Our feeling for them is one of sympathy that they should have been placed in a position of such embarrassment between their judgment and conscience, on the one side, and the pressure to which they and their Governments were being subjected, on the other."[14]

A few months later, Dean Rusk, then Director of the State Department's Office of United Nations Affairs and now President of the Rockefeller Foundation, admitted to a meeting of representatives of national organizations that, while the U. S. "never exerted pressure on countries of the U. N. in behalf of one side or another, certain unauthorized officials and private persons violated propriety and went beyond the law" to exert such pressure. As a result, Mr. Rusk pointed out, partition was "construed as an American Plan" in the eyes of certain countries, and the decision was robbed of whatever moral force it might otherwise have had.

In many instances, no pressure was necessary. Certain delegates quite consciously permitted moral considerations to override the legal. Through these diplomatic representatives, Christendom was determined to expiate what it recognized as the long persecution of the Jewish people. Not a few were influenced by their upbringing in the Old Testament. There was a strong appeal in helping the "return to Zion" and a very romantic excitement in recreating a State which had existed 2000 years ago. This biblical sentimentality, a factor in the thinking of Earl Balfour and General Smuts, accounts for the manner in which such men as Carl Berendsen of New Zealand, and other astute students of international law, permitted their grave misgivings to be allayed.

"The historical connection of the Jewish people with Palestine," words which first appeared in the preamble of the League's Mandate in 1922, were a hypnotizing phrase in the battle for partition. Rabbi Silver, in his masterful presentation to the Ad Hoc Committee, placed great emphasis on this phrase and its counterpart, "*re-constituting* their national home." This wording, rejected in the Balfour Declaration, bolstered the claim to the continuity of the "Jewish people." The majority of the United Nations Assembly anxiously grabbed such ringing statements, rather than inquire into the factual support for the contention of Jewish historical continuity. It seemed to matter little that the term "a national home in Palestine"—used, but never defined, in the Balfour Declaration and the Mandate—was obviously not equivalent to "the Jewish State in Palestine" (which words should have been employed had that been the intended meaning). Nor did it make any difference that, whatever this promise to the Zionists implied, an inconsistent promise had been made to the Arabs even earlier.

The Zionist apathy toward the Stratton Displaced Persons Bill, and Zionist opposition to the negotiations of the Freeland Organization for the transfer of 30,000 Jewish refugees to Netherlands Guiana, in South America,[15] had illuminated the real motivation of Zionist leadership. But the alliance of American- and Soviet-dominated delegations acted as if they were supporting Zionism for "humanitarian" reasons.

These diplomats were not unaware that the "national home in Palestine" did not require partition: under a British mandate, a desert had been made to bloom, and clean new cities had arisen out of age-old sand dunes, wonders that had come to pass while only a few fanatics were talking of statehood.

The 600,000 Palestinians, and the 200,000 additional

Jewish Displaced Persons, could have been guaranteed adequate protection under a bi-national unitary state, or a federal state such as Switzerland. Within the Swiss Republic, four diverse ethnic groups, speaking four different languages, live in separate cantons, are all afforded equal rights, and are all harmonious parts of the same political entity. If Swiss of Italian, French and Germanic origin could live peacefully side by side, through two world wars within the framework of their republic, Arab and Jew, who both speak a Semitic tongue, could have done likewise.

So long as it appeared that statehood was demanded by "all Jews," the conscience of Christendom could feel that by creating Israel, all sins committed against Jewry could be fully expiated. The Ambassadors of Argentine, Colombia, Peru, and Norway admitted in private conversations with the author that a manifestation of real Jewish opposition to Zionism would have gone a long way towards weakening the plea. Ambassador Muniz, of Brazil, and many other delegates felt that the Zionist movement was a "regression from a universal spiritual force to a national political faction," and that the establishment of the Jewish State might "encourage the tendency toward non-integration shown by those of Jewish faith in my country" (as the Peruvian Ambassador to the United Nations put it). But these were arguments that could not be effectively advanced by "non-Jews." Such doubts could have been turned into effective conviction only by a militant Jewish opposition to partition. Instead—fearful lest they emulate the pressure tactics of the nationalists which they were condemning—the anti-Zionist followers of Lessing Rosenwald kept their case practically to themselves. They submitted a single lengthy memorandum which, of course, soon disappeared among the thousands of pieces of paper presented to the United Nations.

As to the U. S. pro-Zionist pressure lobby, Weizmann himself found words of the highest praise for the lobbying assistance given to him, not only by Zionist leaders and the non-Zionist American Jewish Committee, but by Bernard Baruch and Herbert Bayard Swope. Yet these two gentlemen scarcely fit into the picture. Baruch enjoyed then—as he does today—the nation's undivided confidence, and could gain little additional prestige, while risking a great deal. He was far removed from Jewish organizational life. Churchill had told Weizmann in 1944 that his "friend Bernard" was opposed to Jewish statehood. And the adviser to Presidents had publicly declared, only the year before the U. N. debate, that he was no political Zionist. Baruch's parents worshipped as Jews, but he does not now practice the Jewish faith. Had he, in his own way (as had nations), found expiation in the Palestine controversy? Was his conscience upset by a guilt feeling that he had deserted the faith of his forefathers?

One week before the U. N. vote was taken, Weizmann visited President Truman to reinforce the Zionist position and to make sure that the Bay of Akaba, gateway to the Indian Ocean, was not sliced away from the "Jewish State." Close contact had been maintained at all times between the White House and the Zionists through David Niles and Edward Jacobson, the President's old Kansas City business partner, to whom the Israeli chieftain acknowledged a deep debt of gratitude. At the U. N., just as Ambassador Herschel Johnson and Major General John H. Hilldring were giving Jewish Agency representatives some sad news concerning Akaba Bay, the telephone rang. It was the President, conveying instructions that the Bay be handled exactly as Weizmann desired.[16]

The partitioning of Palestine was the first and only major issue on which the U. S. and the U. S. S. R. had worked together in the closest harmony since the formation of the United Nations. This fact alone should have cautioned against the policy the United States was pursuing. But like the Venezuelan delegate, Sr. Zuloaga, who naively declared that this Russian-American amity on Palestine was "the most important historical event in the life of the U. N.," the U. S. Government demonstrated once more a complete lack of comprehension of Communist tactics. Why was the Kremlin permitting, and even encouraging, the emigration of Jewish refugees to Israel from satellite countries? Why would the Kremlin allow the concentration of 30,000 immigrants for Palestine in Black Sea ports (as reported by the *New York Times* on October 15, 1947) if this did not somehow serve Soviet ends and fit into their plans for the Middle East? These and other implications of Soviet pro-Zionism were stressed in reports sent home by U. S. diplomatic representatives in the field, but their warnings remained completely ignored in Washington.

Soviet Russia had pressed the United Nations for the earliest possible withdrawal of the Mandatory Power, and for obvious reasons: the earlier the evacuation, the sooner the collapse of law and authority; and the greater the chaos in the interim period between the two administrations, the better the chances for Communist scheming in the area. January 1, 1948, was the date advanced by the Soviet Union for British departure but she was finally satisfied with May 15.[17]

Why did no one in America pay attention to the transparent objectives of the pro-Zionist Soviet gambit? Because no portion of the globe has been concealed from American view by a thicker veil of ignorance and misinformation than the Middle East. Americans have some knowledge of Europe and even of the Orient. But the Middle East, Americans customarily envision as a land mass inhabited by glaucoma-ridden, shiftless Bedouins who neither could nor would ever be of importance to the United States. A powerful propaganda machine consciously nurtured the widespread misconception that basic needs of the people of this region could be sacrificed without jeopardy to the national security of the United States. And as there was, thus, no danger for the U. S. in a partition of Palestine, well-meaning Americans could afford making amends at the expense of those inconsequential Arabs, to the Jews who had suffered so many injustices. This was so obviously a most convenient course to pursue that nobody wanted to be bothered by the ominous Soviet policy.

Yet Christian support of partition came also from less well-meaning sources. The Zionist position was welcomed and accepted by some Americans because it seemed to vindicate their bias. The establishment of the new Jewish state seemed a good way of getting rid of the Jews in America. In this sense, Israel became the anti-Semite's Mecca. The bolder the Zionist pressures, the stronger the ties between Israel and American Jewry, the broader the grin on the face of the American anti-Semite. His charges of a "nation within a nation," of "the dual loyalties of Jews," were now being given a grade of authenticity by the very objects of his spleen.

To summarize, the United Nations dealt a severe blow to the prestige of international law and organization by its hasty, frivolous and arrogant treatment of the Palestine question. The General Assembly turned down the only two reasonable suggestions—a referendum in Palestine and submission of the legal problems to the International Court of Justice. The Displaced Persons Problem was handled with outrageous thoughtlessness. For persons displaced by World War II, whatever their faith, were surely a responsibility of international welfare organizations—not pawns in a whimsical power play of Jewish nationalists.

The nearly unanimous recommendation of the U. N. Special Committee, that no settlement of the Palestine problem could be considered a solution of the Jewish problem, was ignored. The U. N. flouted the protective injunction of the Balfour Declaration, the Mandate and the recommendations of the Anglo-American Committee of Inquiry, that Jewish statehood was not to be granted so long as hostility existed between Jews and Arabs. It was under this same provision that Judah Magnes, Ahad Ha-am, Louis Brandeis and Albert Einstein had lent their support to varied cultural activities in the Holy Land.

The United Nations tied the establishment of Jewish and Arab States to the acceptance of an economic union and the internationalization of Jerusalem. But six years after the fateful decision, there is no Arab Palestinian State; there is no economic union; there is no internationalized city of Jerusalem; there are no boundaries; there is no peace and stability in the Holy Land.

There is an independent State of Israel, deep in economic distress. There are armistice lines. There is a Holy City divided in two by a 50 foot strip of noman's land. There are almost one million new refugees—Arabs, scattered throughout the Middle East, who have become dangerously infested with vermin and Communism.

CHAPTER IV

A State is Born

I N THE Holy Land, after the fatal U. N. vote of November 29, 1947, confusion turned into pandemonium and bloodshed. Seventeen hundred persons were killed in Palestine during the first 100 days that followed the partition recommendation.

The General Assembly had prescribed the "what" for Palestine but had not given the remotest idea as to the "how." The Arabs abided by their pledge to ignore the U. N. decree, and were intransigent. The United Kingdom stuck to its decision not to enforce any plan for Palestine that did not have the joint approval of the Jews and the Arabs. The United States kept optimistically hoping that the Jews and Arabs of Palestine would miraculously get together and arrive at some genuine agreement. Consequently, lawlessness in the Holy Land increased so much, and so fast, that some international action could no longer be evaded. The proponents of partition were urging armed intervention—if not by the United Nations, then by the United States alone. Mrs. Roosevelt, Sumner Welles, and Senators Herbert Lehman and Elbert Thomas called for the use of force, while Senator Taft specifically suggested a Palestine Army.

74

The U. N. Security Council was meeting at Lake Success when the American Ambassador to the United Nations, Warren Austin, went to Washington to confer with Secretary Marshall. On his return to Lake Success, Ambassador Austin expressed the view that the Council was not empowered by the Charter to enforce partition, and could act only if deciding that a breach of the peace had been committed in the Holy Land. The U. S. policy, it seemed, was to distinguish between permissible use of force to keep the peace and non-permissible force to compel partition—a strictly legalistic interpretation, obviously thought up to evade the decision which had to be faced. As an unofficial diplomatic observer caustically remarked, the United States was saying, "Let's do nothing at once."

The new United States approach had been under discussion in Washington for several weeks. A movement for a bipartisan policy on the Holy Land was reported underway, motivated by a growing military concern over the oil shortage and the political fear that Zionism would go to any length in enlisting the support of pro-Zionist groups in the U. S. For days before the Austin statement, United Nations headquarters had been seething with rumors about a new U. S. plan for a Palestine truce.[1] The press of the nation kept reporting that the President was under great pressure from New York's political leaders to take a stronger pro-Israel stand.[2] The normally Democratic 24th Congressional District in the Bronx, with a heavily Jewish population, had been carried by a Labor Party candidate, Leo Isacson, who advocated repeal of the arms embargo and the dispatch of U. S. troops to enforce the partition. Once more, the White House was caught between the machine bosses who wanted "the Jewish Vote" and the State Department that wanted to avoid both bloodshed in Palestine and the necessity of committing U. S. troops. President Truman was very mindful of public objections to a unilateral military American commitment in Palestine and perfectly aware of the fact that a U. N. intervention would require an international force with Soviet participation. His National Security Council and his Defense Department were vigorously opposed to any step which would have opened the Middle East to Soviet military penetration under U. N. sanctions. Caught in such dilemmas, the Truman Administration picked on the extremely fine point of "legal limitations of permissible remedies."

The Big Five were split wide open. The British were neutral and remained aloof from the discussion. Soviet Russia was not dissatisfied with things as they were: chaos in Palestine was the Soviets' aim, and chaos they had. The French wished to bring about some kind of conciliation. The Chinese were demanding an immediate political-military truce and equal treatment of Jews and Arabs. Only the U. S. and the U. S. S. R. were willing to ascertain that a threat to peace existed in Palestine. Under these circumstances, the Security Council could not possibly resolve economic sanctions or some other affirmative action to enforce an Arab-Zionist compromise: Seven votes were needed in the Council, but no propartition policy had ever aligned more than six.

On March 19, 1948, Ambassador Austin called in the Security Council for suspension of all efforts towards partition, for a truce in Palestine and a special session of the General Assembly to approve a U. N. trusteeship for Palestine. This seeming change of U. S. policy was dictated by the total failure of the U. N. Commission on Palestine to secure order in Palestine. Of equal importance was, unquestionably, a report of the National Security Council which warned that the Palestine turmoil was acutely endangering the security of the United States. A report of the Central Intelligence Agency stressed the strategic importance of the Middle East and its oil resources. The President, who had just asked the nation to support the draft legislation, could not possibly ignore such military warnings.

The shift of U. S. policy—from partition to trusteeship—had been sudden. Only the day before, the United States was still supporting partition and had gone so far as to propose consultations of the great powers with the U. N. Military Staff Committee. There was talk, the next day, that Ambassador Austin had acted without direct knowledge of the White House. In point of fact, Austin's statement had been sent to the White House for clearance and Robert McClintock, a top-ranking officer in the Department of State's U. N. Liaison Division, was told by one of Truman's assistants that it was O. K. Mc-Clintock noted on the statement that it had been cleared in the White House.

But no sooner had Mr. Austin finished reading the statement of the new U. S. position to the Security Council than there began the conventional "bombardment" of the White House. The President immediately asked for the text. It was produced from a pile of papers on his desk. A member of the White House staff had taken for granted that, as no objection had been raised, it had been cleared. The State Department, accordingly, authorized the announcement of a vital change in U. S. policy.

While Secretary Marshall issued a statement endorsing trusteeship as the only way to prevent bloodshed, Democratic Congressman Arthur Klein, of Brooklyn, labelled the move "as the most terrible sellout of the common people since Munich," and Republican Governor Thomas E. Dewey of New York attacked the bungling of the administration. The President of the Zionist Organization of America, Dr. Neumann, threatened that any U. N. abandonment of partition would only revive Jewish claims to *all* of Palestine. The *New York Times* and other papers added to the confusion by disclosing that President Truman "would deliver a strong statement paving the way for the recognition of the Jewish state." But Charles Ross, Presidential Press Secretary, retorted, "This is news to me." Rumors and counterrumors flew as pressures and counterpressures were exerted. Senator Carl Hatch of New Mexico quoted the President as saying he was "casting aside politics and will do what is right without regard to political consequences." Two days later, the President himself spoke up. He urged a temporary trusteeship, but denied that the partition plan had been abandoned.

This seemed to imply a retreat from the Austin declaration of a new U. S. policy. Ambassador Austin, Dean Rusk, and other spokesmen for the American U. N. delegation, re-echoed the Truman theme that the proposed trusteeship was not a substitute for the partition plan, but just a temporary measure to comply with the vacuum which must develop in Palestine upon the withdrawal of the British Mandatory Administration: Had not the majority report of UNSCOP, supporting partition, foreseen an initial period of trusteeship until an agreement could be reached between the Arabs and the Jews? But neither this explanation, nor any other voice that endorsed trusteeship as a means for saving the Holy Land from becoming a tinderbox for World War III, abated the wrath of U. S. Zionism and its allies. Even the *New*

78

York Times, heretofore extremely cool to the Zionist program, now joined the critics of the trusteeship proposal.[3]

On April 20, 1948, the U. S. informally submitted to the Second Special Session of the General Assembly a working paper, entitled "Draft Trusteeship Agreement for Palestine" (US Press Rel. 411), that embodied trusteeship proposals similar to those previously presented to the Security Council. The proposal failed to obtain the required two-thirds majority. A combination of political pressures in this country, and early military successes of the Jewish Army (the Haganah) had made a convincing case for the feasibility of partition.

The Truman Administration was assailed for its "betrayal of humanitarianism" by the preponderantly Republican press which could not resist the temptation of profiting from Democratic blunders. In the large cities, organized Jewry once again mobilized public opinion. The story of the courageous fight of the Palestinian Jews crowded newspapers and radio. In New York City, Communist and left-wing labor leaders ran a "Palestine Protest Rally" in Madison Square Park, attended by 10,000, at which "oil politics" was attacked. On April 8th, special services were held in more than 8,000 Jewish houses of worship throughout the nation, in protest of the U. S. stand on Zion.

Invaluable support was given the Zionists by the American Association for the United Nations, a key group for swinging U. S. public opinion—not alone because of its own affluent membership, but also because it was in a position to mobilize other influential national organizations. Clark Eichelberger, the head of the Association, was a determined supporter of partition. Sumner Welles, Mrs. Eleanor Roosevelt and other distinguished Association members blocked Mrs. Kermit Roosevelt's attempt to prevent the organization from alloting funds for such propartition advertisements as the full-page Association ad in the *New York Times*, "Program To Save The U. N. and Settle the Palestine Crisis."[4] Teddy Roosevelt's daughter-in-law fought hard, but it was a losing battle.

In the Association's contention, the prestige of the United Nations demanded that the partition plan be carried out. But the U. N. General Assembly had merely *recommended* the partition of Palestine—it had neither decided, nor ordered, nor enacted anything. The General Assembly was not then—no more than it is today— either a legislative or a judicial body. It possessed no machinery for implementing proposals. If the partition plan was unworkable, as it then seemed, to take a new course might have been less damaging to the world organization than to insist on the execution of unreasonable and cruel plans. It was particularly ironic that the American Association for the United Nations, which had fought any revision of the U. N. Charter, should claim for the Charter, as it stood, in the Palestine issue the very power which they refused to grant in general amendments.

As the date approached on which the British were to yield the mandate, armed conflict in Palestine and public hysteria in the United States increased. Dr. Judah Magnes was refused permission to bring his views of bi-nationalism before the U. N. General Assembly: the Jewish Agency alone was to be recognized as spokesmen for the "Jewish people." Albert Einstein, in supporting the position of Dr. Magnes, made this public declaration: We appeal to the Jews in this country and in Palestine not to permit themselves to be driven into a mood of despair or false heroism which eventually results in suicidal measures.[5] Of course, the Zionists, who had previously exploited Einstein statements for their publicity purposes, ignored these wise words.

"Americans for Haganah," the "Palestine Resistance Committee," and the "Red Mogen Doved" continued to raise funds for partition propaganda—always, of course, in the name of the "Displaced Persons." New York's Republican Representative, Jacob K. Javits, told Zionist women, "We'll fight to death and make a Jewish State in Palestine if it's the last thing that we do." The non-Zionists, led by Judge Proskauer (who had previously performed services in "putting the squeeze" on some smaller U. N. nations), added to the clamor by insisting that the U. S. sell arms to the Haganah ("those who are defending the decision of the United Nations"). A National pilgrimage to Washington of the "United Committee to save the Jewish State and the United Nations" visited Congressmen and picketed the White House.

Against this organized hue and cry, voices recommending reason, moderation, and compromise were lost. But there were such voices. William Tuck, executive secretary of the International Refugee Organization, tried to explain why Palestine cannot be considered a haven of any importance for D. P.'s. On May 5, the *New York Times* reported from "unimpeachable sources" that, whereas in 1947 a vast majority of Jewish D. P.'s wished to go to Palestine, 80 per cent of them now were saying they wanted to go to the United States and were specifically adding that they "do not want to go to the Holy Land." Yet it was too late for such truthful statements to make any impression. The appointment of General John Hilldring as Special Assistant for Palestine, to the Secretary of State, was an indication of the turn U. S.

policy was taking: two days before he was appointed, the General, in a speech before the Jewish Welfare Board, stated that he unmistakably favored partition.

The Mandate had but a few more days to run when, as Weizmann said, "I strengthened our contacts with *our friends* in Washington, and affirmed my intention of going ahead with a bid for recognition of the Jewish State as soon as it was proclaimed."[6] Then, on May 13, 1948, he wrote a personal letter to President Truman asking that the United States "promptly recognize the Provisional Government of the new Jewish State." Up to that day, the General Assembly had neither revoked nor reaffirmed the partition resolution of November, 1947, and was still wrestling with the problem of how to save lives in Palestine. The Arab armies were threatening an invasion of the Holy Land. The United States Government was still committed to "truce and temporary trusteeship," the policy dictated by the military security of the United States. But on the morning of May 14, 1948, Clark Clifford, the President's Counsel (who had been in constant touch with Democratic leaders as well as Zionist spokesmen), persuaded the President that something must be done at once to get the Democratic Party off the election hook. The political bosses had convinced Clifford that the U. S. shift to trusteeship would defeat Truman, adducing as evidence the special Congressional Election in New York and sentiment in other pivotal states. A serious political revolt threatened the President within his own Party.[7] The Jewish vote had to be kept in line, Clifford felt. On May 14, the President was closeted with his intimate advisers. One of the few callers he received that day was Frank Goldman, President of the B'nai B'rith, an organization whose membership prominently included

Mr. Truman's intimate friend and old Kansas City partner, Eddie Jacobson. Congressman Sol Bloom of New York, Chairman of the House Foreign Affairs Committee, had wired the President that the U. S. had better take the lead in recognizing the new Jewish State in order to "help keep Palestine and the Near East from Soviet influence and domination." All during the day, the White House maintained rigid silence on the developments in Palestine.

Around eleven-thirty that morning, Eliahu Epstein (later, as Eliahu Elath, the first Israeli Ambassador to the U. S.) was called to the White House. Epstein, then representative of the Jewish Agency in Washington, was told that the U. S. would like to accord *de facto* recognition immediately upon the declaration of Israel's independence, but that, obviously, a request for such recognition would have to be received first. Epstein pointed out, quite reasonably, that the new State could not send such a request prior to its birth (which was not expected before midnight, *i.e.*, 6 P.M. Washington time). He also promised that he would advise Tel Aviv at once of Truman's desire and haste.

At this morning session of May 14, it was also decided that the President would not inform Secretary of State Marshall, or anyone else in the Department of State, of the contemplated recognition until fairly late in the afternoon, to avoid a news leak and any objections General Marshall might raise. For Niles and Clifford wanted to make absolutely sure that the President would not be persuaded to delay the recognition. Sometime between three and four that afternoon, General Marshall was told that the President would release a statement recognizing Israel shortly after 6 P.M. that evening. The General was instructed neither to impart this information to anyone else in the State Department nor to send it in any form to New York City where the United Nations, at that very moment, was debating the question of trusteeship. Specifically, Ambassador Austin was not to be notified over the Department's direct wire to the American U. N. Delegation.

Shortly before six, Secretary Marshall told a few of his immediate aides what was about to happen. At six o'clock, Washington Eastern Daylight Time, the British mandate expired. At 6:01 P.M. the new State of Israel came into existence. And at 6:11 P.M. the United States accorded recognition. Charles Ross, Presidential Press Secretary, had summoned reporters to his office in the White House shortly after six and read, at 6:11 P.M., the two-paragraph announcement of President Truman that accorded *de facto* recognition to the new state of Israel. Coupled with the announcement was an expression of hope for peace. But as the Administration was in Washington, recognizing the sovereignty of Israel, United States representatives at the United Nations were still proposing trusteeship for Palestine!

Around six o'clock, Dean Rusk, Director of the State Department Office of United Nations Affairs, was requested to inform Ambassador Austin of the Presidential step. At that hour, Austin was not at the General Assembly where members of his staff were devotedly debating trusteeship. He received the incredible Washington news in his rooms at the Waldorf-Astoria Hotel. He was outraged.

A variety of wild rumors had been circulating at Flushing Meadow where the 135th Plenary Meeting of the General Assembly was in session to receive a report of its First Committee. The General Assembly did not convene until 4:30 P.M. With Dr. Arce of Argentine in the chair, the delegates were considering the question of the internationalization of Jerusalem. The appointment of a U. N. Commissioner for the Holy City had just been voted, and it was approximately six o'clock when the Colombian delegate, Mr. Gonzalez Fernandez, asked the U. S. representative whether he was in a position to confirm the information given to the press that a Government of a Jewish State had been recognized by the United States.[8] Francis B. Sayre, former Assistant Secretary of State, and one of the three U. S. representatives on the Permanent Mission to the United Nations, replied that for the time being he had no official information on that subject. Betty Gough, one of the Assistants from the International Organization Division of the State Department, was sent out for the latest news. The discussion continued with Cuba's Ambassador, Dr. Guillermo Belt, expressing his surprise that the U. S. representative had no information. It appeared to the Cuban delegate "that the representatives of the USSR and Poland were better informed on events in Washington," and that further consideration of the resolution under debate was pointless since the "U. S. Government had recognized the new Jewish State."

Some time later, a rather confused and embarrassed Professor Philip C. Jessup, Deputy U. S. Representative, arose to announce that the "U. S. delegation was now able to communicate to the Assembly the text of the statement by the President of the United States." Holding in his hand the clipped-off portion of press-ticker tape Miss Gough had handed to him, Professor Jessup read as follows: "This Government has been informed that a Jewish State has been proclaimed in Palestine and recognition has been requested by the provisional Government thereof. The United States recognizes the provisional Government as the *de facto* authority of the new State of Israel."

This is how the American delegation to the United Nations received word of the President's historic decision. To be sure, the Presidential statement that "recognition has been requested by the provisional Government thereof" was hardly the truth. The only communication the President had before him at the time his statement was issued, was a letter, dated May 14, 1948, and written on the letterhead of the Jewish Agency for Palestine, saying that such a State "*will* be set up at midnight." It was signed by Eliahu Epstein as Agent of the Provisional Government; but there was then no such Government. The only legal authority over Palestine, at the time the letter was written and received, was the British Mandate. It was only after the ink had dried on the Presidential signature that the Provisional Government of Israel came into being. Almost twenty-four hours after the President's indecently hasty action, the Department of State received a cable from the Provisional Government of Israel requesting recognition.

At what was one minute past midnight of May 15, 1948, in Palestine, the first flag of Israel was unfurled at the Washington headquarters of the Jewish Agency for Palestine. In Israel, British High Commissioner General Sir Alan Cunningham's departure from Haifa was bringing to a close twenty-six years of the Mandate. At that precise moment, Zionists were proclaiming the new State of Israel in these words: " . . . This recognition by the United Nations of the right of the Jewish people to reestablish their independent state may not be revoked. It is moreover, the self-evident right of the Jewish people to be a nation, as all other nations, in its own sovereign state. Accordingly, we, the members of the National

Council, representing the Jewish people in Palestine and the Zionist movement of the world, met together in solemn assembly, by virtue of the national and historic right of the Jewish people and of resolution of the General Assembly of the United Nations, hereby proclaim the establishment of the Jewish state in Palestine, to be called Israel. Our call goes out to the Jewish people all over the world to rally to our side in the task of immigration and development and to stand by us in the great struggle for the fulfillment of the dream of generations—the redemption of Israel."

And people danced in the streets of Tel Aviv, Washington, New York, and elsewhere. On the capitol's Massachusetts Avenue, Americans wept, sang the Jewish national anthem, danced the Palestinian Hora, cried "Mazeltov" (good luck) and waved small Israeli flags. Yet the mood was not entirely happy everywhere. The Pittsburgh (Pa.) *Post Gazette*, in an editorial, "Laughter at Lake Success," noted: "The Administration's handling of the Palestine problem has been so inept that the American delegation has become a laughing stock in the United Nations. The President's precipitous decision to recognize Israel left our allies in the dark, plunged the State Department into confusion and in general made us look wholly irresponsible." The Richmond *Times* pointed to New York's momentous electoral votes in the coming election, while the St. Louis *Post Dispatch* said: "The White House says it (recognition) is not a snap judgment, but the United Nations delegation bitterly thinks otherwise. They cannot avoid taking it for what it seems—shameless junking of international interests to regain the Jewish votes the recent Bronx election showed had been lost."

CHAPTER V

Wooing the Jewish Vote

THE British Mandate over Palestine was issued by the League of Nations in 1922. Though the United States was not a member of the League, and therefore not a party to this act, a Joint Resolution of Congress formally sanctioned, the same year, the idea of a "Jewish National Home."[1]

Similar resolutions were thereafter introduced in a number of State legislatures and passed in a routine manner, without opposition. Several Presidents paid lip service to Zionist aspirations. The sixty-seven ambiguous words in the Balfour Declaration, carried over into the Mandate, made it simple for the vote-hungry politicians in league with Jewish nationalists to embroider each consecutive White House endorsement. As elsewhere in the story of Zionism, loose semantics played an important part.

In the hearings before the House Committee on Foreign Affairs on the Wright-Compton Palestine Resolutions[2] in 1944, Chairman Sol Bloom quoted this alleged statement of President Woodrow Wilson: "I am persuaded that the Allied Nations, with the fullest concur-

88

rence of our Government and our people, are agreed that in Palestine shall be laid the foundations of a Jewish commonwealth."[3] This alleged declaration of Wilson has been repeated *ad infinitum* in Zionist propaganda. But Woodrow Wilson never did make that statement.

In March 1919, President Wilson had momentarily returned from the Paris Peace Conference to the United States. The Egyptian press published a copy of a telegram dated Washington, March 4, as an official American communique from the American Diplomatic Agency in Cairo:

A Jewish Delegation headed by Judge Julian Mack of Chicago interviewed the President regarding the future of Palestine. The President expressed his sympathy with the principle of the incontestable right of the Jewish people everywhere to equality of status and recalled that he had previously expressed his personal approval of a declaration to the British Government respecting the historic claims of the Jews regarding Palestine. He said he was persuaded that the Allied Nations with the fullest concurrence of the American Government were agreed that the foundations of a Jewish Commonwealth should be laid in Palestine.[4]

At one of the daily meetings of Commissioners Plenipotentiary in Paris, at which Secretary of State Robert Lansing represented the U. S., the question of the authenticity of that statement was raised. The official minutes of this meeting of April 12, 1919, read as follows:

The Commissioners very much doubt whether the President had ever made any such statement, but requested that it be sent to the President with the statement as to its source. They desired that the President be asked whether this quotation were correct, and that it be added that in case it were not correct, they were of the opinion that it should be denied at once.[5]

On April 13, Mr. Lansing submitted to President Wilson, who had returned to Paris, a copy of the telegram published in Egypt, asking "whether the quotation contained therein is correct."[6]

On April 16, President Wilson sent the following note to Secretary Lansing who was staying at the Hotel Crillion:

My dear Lansing:
Of course I did not use any of the words quoted in the enclosed and they do not indeed purport to be my words. But I did in substance say what is quoted, though *the expression "foundation of a Jewish Commonwealth" goes a little further* than *my idea at the time.* All that I meant was to corroborate our expressed acquiescence in the position of the British Government with regard to the future of Palestine.

Faithfully yours,
(s) Woodrow Wilson.[7]

So much about the accuracy of Zionist propaganda.

Although the Wright-Compton resolutions were shelved (out of deference to the considered judgment of Secretary Stimson and the War Department that "such action would be prejudicial to the successful prosecution of the War"),[8] the propaganda value of the hearings was to be fully exploited. At Congressman Bloom's suggestion, a 512-page volume of testimony was published and widely distributed. The many Congressmen who had testified in behalf of Zionist groups back home were only too happy to put themselves on record as firm supporters of President Wilson's manipulated declaration.

In 1945, another Congress resolution endorsed the free entry of "Jews" into Palestine "to the maximum of its agricultural and economic potentialities . . . so that they may freely proceed with the upbuilding of Palestine as *the* Jewish national home." By substituting "the" for "a", Congress in effect had broadened the obligation contained in the Balfour Declaration and the League Mandate (to which the United States was not a party).

President Roosevelt, always the adroit politician, had the great knack of seeming to say "Yes" to everyone. He told Weizmann in 1942 that he wanted the Palestine problem settled. To Ibn Saud, the President sent a confidential message in May of 1943, stating that there would be no change in Palestine "without full consultation with both Arabs and Jews." At Malta in 1945, en route to Yalta, the President revealed to Winston Churchill his desire "to bring about peace between the Arabs and the Jews," and spoke of his plan to visit Ibn Saud. James Byrnes relates in his autobiography[9] the British Prime Minister's pessimism on this score: "Churchill wished him good luck, but didn't seem very hopeful that the President would meet with success."

Following the Yalta Conference, F.D.R. held his colorful meeting—goats and all—with Ibn Saud aboard the heavy cruiser *U.S.S. Quincy* in the Eastern Mediterranean. Roosevelt assured the ruler of Saudi Arabia that he "would sanction no American move hostile to the Arab people." As Elliott Roosevelt phrased it,[10] the President later admitted to Bernard Baruch that "of all the men he had talked to in his life, he had got least satisfaction from this iron-willed Arab monarch." Pro-Zionist British Parliament member Crossman sarcastically noted that the President then hurried back from the Crimea to Washington to assure Zionists that his attitude toward them was the same. But a week before he died, the President confirmed by letter to Ibn Saud his promise of fair treatment for the Arabs.

The Zionists, it is interesting to note, felt that during Roosevelt's Administration they had made little headway at the White House. The story of their relationship with Presidents Roosevelt and Truman is frankly expounded in a revealing tribute to Dr. Silver by Emanuel Neumann entitled "Abba Hillel Silver: History Maker."[11] Roosevelt's friendship toward Jews was indisputable, but for the Zionist cause "we had little time and less thought," says Dr. Neumann.

The American Zionist Emergency Council formed the American Palestine Committee, numbering hundreds of U. S. Senators, Representatives, cabinet members, Governors and influential personalities from all walks of life. In December 1942, 63 Senators and 181 Congressmen called on Roosevelt, in a joint statement, "to restore the Jewish homeland." But the President, the Zionists now relate, had a "deep-seated skepticism about Jewish Palestine and a cool indifference," which Silver described as an attitude of "uninvolved benignancy." He was "unwilling to act," and the Zionist leadership dared not oppose his views for reasons Dr. Neumann admitted quite frankly:

"To the Jewish masses in America and throughout the world, Roosevelt loomed as the great friend and champion of their people. Now could such a friend oppose or ignore Jewish national aspirations? Not only was it difficult to accept such a painful thought—there was a strong psychological need to reject it. In a tragic hour and a hostile world there simply had to be a champion and protector. If it was not Stalin or Churchill, it had to be Roosevelt. This emotional dependence on Roosevelt was reinforced by eminently practical considerations. He might be re-elected, and he was re-elected for a fourth term. His would be the power to shape the postwar settlement. To cross him, to offend him, to alienate his affection was to court disaster for the Zionist cause."

The "going became easier" after Harry Truman took office. The successor to F.D.R., we are told, "was a far less complex personality than his illustrious predecessor —less adroit and sophisticated, simpler and more straight-forward. He accepted the Zionist line reluctantly and under pressure, at first, but having accepted it, he followed through honestly and firmly. In the end he found himself in direct conflict with Britain's Bevin. He did not shrink from the encounter, but, supported by popular opinion, he stuck to his guns and forced the State Department to acquiesce in his pro-Zionist policy."[12]

Organized nationalist Jewry could count on a strong link in the Executive Office of the White House to keep the President interested in Zionism. As the national press noted when he passed away in the fall of 1952, David K. Niles was a key factor in the drive for Israel's statehood. The protegé of Harry Hopkins, Niles became an executive assistant to President Roosevelt after the 1940 elections. He was a member of a select group of confidential advisers with an often-quoted "passion for anonymity." Niles, at any rate, though occasionally publicized as "Mr. Truman's Mystery Man,"[13] remained totally unknown to the public.

First, Roosevelt assigned certain problems relating to minority groups to Niles for briefing; but gradually the

President, weighed down by war responsibilities, turned such problems over to Niles for action. Niles, in fact, developed into what amounted to the first Jewish Ambassador to the White House. When Truman succeeded Roosevelt, the Palestine issue was placed in Niles' lap.

The President's old Kansas City partner, Eddie Jacobson, very active in B'nai B'rith and a passionate believer in Jewish nationalism, gave Zionism no less valuable service. What the combination Tinkers to Evers to Chance was to baseball, Jacobson to Niles to Truman was to Israel. Niles was the "pivot" man, with direct access to the President, Jacobson and Truman were partners again, this time in the more serious pursuit of creating a new State.

There were many ways in which Niles served the State of Israel after partition, too. Early in 1950, when the United States first awoke to the Soviet danger in the Middle East, our Government requested the various Arab countries for information regarding troops, equipment and other confidential military data. These statistics were necessary in order to plan possible assistance under the Mutual Security Act. The Arab nations were naturally assured that the figures, supplied for the Chief of Staff, would be kept secret.

Late that year, military representatives of the Middle East countries and of Israel were meeting in Washington with General Riley, who headed the United Nations Truce Organization. Trouble had broken out over the Huleh Marshes, and charges and countercharges of military aggression were exchanged between Israel and the Arab countries. The Israeli military representative claimed that Syrian troops were employed in a certain manner, and General Riley remarked: "That's not pos-

sible. The Syrians have no such number of troops."
Whereupon the Israeli representative said: "You are
wrong. Here are the actual figures of Syrian military
strength and the description of the troops." And he produced the confidential figures, top secret Pentagon information. General Riley himself had not been shown the
new figures given by the Syrian War Ministry to his
superiors.

When the question of Egyptian military strength was
raised, a similar security leak appeared. It was obvious
that top-secret figures had been passed on to the Israeli
Government. Both the Central Intelligence Agency and
Army G-2 investigated the security breach but discovered only that these figures had been made available to
the White House. How and through whom they leaked
out of the White House remained forever obscure. However, the Chairman of the Joint Chiefs, General Omar
Bradley, reportedly went to the President and told the
Chief Executive that he would have to choose between
him (Bradley) and Niles. Not too long after this reported intervention, David Niles resigned from his post
as Executive Assistant to the President and went on a
visit to Israel.

Thirty-two of the nations which voted for the partition of Palestine could possibly justify their position in
terms of humanitarian considerations. But the thirty-
third, the United States, so responsible for the votes of
many of the other U. N. members, can not. The true
motivation of U. S. Palestine policy was correctly stated
by Ernest K. Lindley in the *Washington Post:* "The
policy and tactics of the United States in the Palestine
controversy were, of course, influenced greatly by
American Zionists. Domestic politics rather than a con-

sidered analysis of the interests of the United States had been the predominating factor in our policy concerning Palestine."

Any doubts that American decisions on Palestine were determined by the calculating consideration of domestic politics, rather than the good Samaritan's concern for refugees, were dispelled with the publication of the *Forrestal Diaries*.[14]

At a cabinet luncheon, on September 4, 1947, Postmaster General Hannegan briefed the President on the necessity of making a statement in favor of the entrance of 150,000 Jews into Palestine. As reported by Forrestal, Hannegan said, "he didn't want to press for decision one way or the other. He simply wanted to point out that such a statement could have a very great influence and great effect on the raising of funds for the Democratic National Committee. He said that very large sums had been obtained from Jewish contributors and that they would be influenced in either giving or withholding by what the President did on Palestine."[15] Forrestal reminded Hannegan that the President's remarks a year ago (which had brought forth the attack against Truman in the House of Commons by Foreign Secretary Ernest Bevin), did not have the expected effect in the New York election—a reference to the 1946 campaign in which Governor Dewey had matched Truman's offerings to "the Jewish Vote" and had emerged victorious.

Forrestal was determined to obtain an agreement of both parties to lift the Palestine question out of the political contest. But the Democratic National Chairman, J. Howard McGrath (later U. S. Attorney General), did not like the idea. He stressed the fact that a substantial part of the contributions to the Democratic National Committee came from people who "wanted to be sure to have an opportunity to express their views and have them seriously considered on such questions as the present Palestine question."[16] And a national election, for which the party coffers had to be filled, was just around the corner. McGrath insisted that, furthermore, there were two or three pivotal States which could not be carried without the support of people who were deeply interested in the Palestine question, some of whom felt that the United States was not doing all it should "to solicit the votes in the U. N. General Assembly"[17] for partition. McGrath could not understand Forrestal's reasoning that he "would rather lose those states than run the risks which, he felt, would ensue from that kind of handling of the Palestine question," and that "no group in this country should be permitted to influence our policy to the point where it could endanger our national security."[18] Even when the report on Palestine, prepared by the Central Intelligence Agency, was read to McGrath, the politician would not change his mind.

Forrestal tells of his talks with the former Secretary of State, James Byrnes, "who recalled the fact that he had disassociated himself from President Truman's decision a year ago to turn down the Grady report which had recommended a federated state for Palestine or a single Arabian state."[19] The ex-Secretary of State described how the President's political criticism of the British "for their conduct of Palestine affairs had placed Bevin and Attlee in a most difficult position." Byrnes attributed the chief responsibility to David Niles and Sam Rosenman, both of whom had warned Truman of Dewey's impending endorsement of the Zionist position on Palestine and the loss of New York state to the Democrats unless Dewey's move was anticipated. Mr. Byrnes cast a damper on Forrestal's hope that the Republican leadership would ever agree to a non-partisan handling of the Palestine question because "of the fact that Rabbi Silver was one of Taft's close associates, and because Taft followed Silver on the Palestine question."

However, the growing antagonism of the Arab countries made Forrestal redouble his efforts toward bi-partisanship. He sought to win from both parties an accord that future decisions would rest on the sole consideration of what was in the best interests of the United States as a whole. He suggested that Dewey, Stassen, Taft, McGrath and General Bradley be briefed on the strategic importance of the Middle East and the danger of Soviet penetration.[20] Forrestal labored for months, but his efforts to persuade such Republicans as Governor Thomas E. Dewey, John Foster Dulles, Winthrop Aldrich, and even Senator Arthur H. Vandenberg, the father of bi-partisanism in U. S. foreign policy, remained fruitless.

One of the staunchest advocates of a strong pro-Israel policy was at that time the newly elected Congressman, Franklin D. Roosevelt, Jr. Forrestal told young Roosevelt of his present efforts and of the "methods used by people outside of the executive branch of the Government to bring coercion and duress on other nations of the General Assembly which bordered closely on to scandal."[21] F.D.R. Jr. said it was impossible to get the two parties to agree not to press the issue and that "the Democratic Party would be bound to lose and the Republican gain by such an agreement."[22] Forrestal's significant answer was: "I think it is about time that somebody should pay some consideration to whether we might not lose the United States."[23]

These were the motivations of Forrestal who was soon to be vilified as the favorite whipping boy of the Zionist-dominated press. From Bernard Baruch, his good friend, Forrestal received a warning not to become too active in this matter as he (Forrestal) was already identified to a dangerous degree with the opposition to the U. N. policy on Palestine. Forrestal ignored Baruch's advice. He sensed the immense strategic importance of the Middle East. His military advisers were agreed that the withdrawal of the British from Palestine would result in serious trouble, which could only help the Soviet Union. It was this fear that prompted Forrestal's lonely attempt to retain a modicum of Arab friendship for the U. S.

An ardent pro-Zionist was later to write of Forrestal: "He was in no sense anti-Semitic or anti-Israel, nor influenced by oil interest. He was convinced that partition was not in the best interests of the U. S. He certainly did not deserve the persistent and venomous attacks on him which helped break his mind and body; on the contrary, these attacks stand out as the ugliest examples of the willingness of politicians and publicists to use the vilest means—in the name of patriotism—to destroy self-sacrificing and devoted public servants." These words were written by the first Ambassador of the United States to Israel, James G. McDonald, in his "My Mission to Israel."[24]

Forrestal, in short, was perspicacious enough to look ahead and realize that Middle East would replace the Caribbean resources as the West's most important oil repository in the forthcoming world battle against Communism. What hurt this sensitive man so deeply and contributed to his taking his own life was not his failure to achieve a bi-partisan Palestinian policy, but the fact that his motivation should have been impugned with the smear, "tool of the oil imperialists." The facts surrounding the Palestine Affair, as they have now been unearthed, and the subsequent events in the Middle East have formidably increased the stature of James V. Forrestal.

Two weeks before the Democratic Convention of 1948, President Truman ordered the State Department to announce the appointment of James G. McDonald as Minister to the new nation of Israel. McDonald had been long active in behalf of Jewish nationalism and the United Palestine Appeal. When Under-Secretary of State Lovett questioned the choice of McDonald "because of his close identification with the Zionists," he was told by Clark Clifford that the "President did not want any discussion of the matter but to have action followed at once in the form of an announcement that afternoon from the State Department."[25] The appointment had been decided, according to McDonald himself, only the day before at a meeting at which David Niles, Clark Clifford and General Hilldring were present. Secretary of State Marshall resented the appointment as well as the fact that it was made without even consulting the responsible Cabinet member.

McDonald's position was singular. More than being American Ambassador to Israel, he was from the outset the Democratic Administration's Ambassador to the nationalist Jews. His unprecedented pro-Zionist conduct was meant to produce ammunition for the President and the Democratic Party in their fight for the control of the so-called "Jewish Vote." In a letter wishing McDonald "God speed in your important mission," written July 21, 1948, Truman said: "I shall expect you to keep me informed on such matters as relate to the Arms Embargo, *the appropriate time* for full recognition and the types of assistance as may be required by and can properly be granted to the new State."[26] But the very moment the President thus promised full recognition,

Under-Secretary Lovett, and other State Department officials, were instructing the new Ambassador on the tremendous complications in the way of *de jure* recognition. The State Department was properly concerned with assurances of stability and representativeness of the Israeli Provisional Government, while the White House was subordinating such essential concerns of international policy to the whims of party politics.

The new Ambassador proceeded to Tel Aviv via London, Geneva and Rome—stop-overs in which he revealed early symptoms of a peculiar conditioning that was later to be viewed as too pro-Zionist even by the Israeli Government. McDonald was an Ambassador *from* Israel before he had been accredited as Ambassador to Israel. Accompanied by the American Ambassador to the Court of St. James, Lewis Douglas, McDonald called upon Ernest Bevin to inquire why the British Government had not recognized the State of Israel. When the American Ambassador to Israel hinted gently to the British Foreign Secretary "that it would be helpful for me to have a British colleague in Tel Aviv," "Bevin flushed, the color mounted to his cheek."—"This is something which I can't discuss," was Bevin's retort.—"I'm sorry, I wasn't asking a leading question. I merely wanted to state a fact," was McDonald's inept parting shot.[27]

Before leaving London, the U. S. Ambassador to Israel expressed his desire for British recognition to other members of the Foreign Office. In Rome, McDonald worked on Count Carlo Sforza, Italy's Foreign Minister, who was hesitant about "a pro-Israel announcement which might cause disturbances amongst the Moslem population of the former Italian colonies."[28] But it was, of course, inconsiderate of the Italians and the French to worry about the Moslems of North Africa, and of the

British to fret about the Arabs, instead of helping Truman to the "Jewish Vote" in the United States.

Ambassador-designate McDonald stopped in Geneva to see Chaim Weizmann, President of the Provisional Israeli Government, who was ill and begged McDonald "to remind his colleagues at home to write to him." Apparently he was not receiving information from the Government he was supposed to head. And indeed, McDonald did on his arrival in Tel Aviv intercede with Golda Myerson, Israeli Ambassador to Moscow, who told him that Weizmann's grievance stemmed from the refusal of his colleagues to accept his ideas of a strong presidency.

In the Holy Land, McDonald continued to fill the extraordinary role of Ambassador *for* rather than *to* Israel. He reported not to the Department of State, but to the White House.

On August 24, 1948, McDonald wrote to Washington: "My conclusion is that since the President and the Department want peace, they should concentrate on getting peace negotiations started. . . . On this issue I do not think the U.S. should be overly influenced by the views of either the mediator or the British. The former, so far as I can judge, is almost completely discredited not only among the Jews but among the Arabs. His inability to enforce decisions and his wordy pronouncements have left him neither substantial moral authority nor dignity."[29] The American Ambassador was burying Count Bernadotte even before the U. N. mediator was killed by Zionist terrorists.[30]

The task of Niles *et al.* was considerably facilitated by the peculiar fact that Americans are the world's most eager joiners. The success of any extremist movement in this country can, at least in part, be traced to the weakness of "prominent" Americans to join promiscuously any organization smart enough to pick a sweet-sounding name. The Reception Committee for Mr. Menachem Begin was just such an organization.

It was dreamed up by the American League for a Free Palestine. Its leading figures were author Louis Brom-field, writer Ben Hecht, and U. S. Senator Guy Gillette. On its National Committee (In Formation) were such dignitaries as Senators Arthur Capper of Kansas, Theo-dore Green of Rhode Island, Herbert O'Conor of Maryland, a score of Governors, men of letters, and clergymen of all faiths. The invitations, calling upon the recipient to add his name to the list of distinguished Americans welcoming Menachem Begin to the United States, said:

As Commander-in-Chief of the Irgun Zvai Leumi, he led one of the most glorious and successful resistance move-ments in history. A little defenseless community, a people who, in the course of almost two thousand years of disper-sion, had lost the art of military defense, was transformed under the miracle of his leadership into a fighting and heroic nation. It was through the Hebrew Underground under his command that the hitherto parish people of the world, the Jews, won back their dignity and self-respect and the respect of the civilized world. It was because of the valiant fight waged by the Irgun that the whole struc-ture of the British regime in Palestine collapsed, making possible the proclamation of Hebrew sovereignty and the establishment of the State of Israel.

The two-page letter neglected to mention that Mr. Begin had publicly claimed credit for such deeds as the blowing up of Jerusalem's King David Hotel, placing a time bomb in the British Colonial office in London, the garrotting and hanging of the two British Sergeants at

Nathanya, and the massacre of Arab women and children at Deir Yassin. But according to the Reception Committee, Begin was the hero of Israel and the Freedom Movement's candidate for Prime Minister. This, coincidentally, was the Fall of 1948—the time of an important national election in the United States. And, as a member of the House Foreign Affairs Committee remarked, "Put any petition with the name Jew on it before a candidate in an election year, and you can get anyone to sign anything!" At any rate, within a few weeks the Welcoming Committee had grown to include eleven Senators, twelve Governors, seventy-odd Congressmen, seventeen Justices and Judges, and educators, public officials, and mayors by the scores. These more or less celebrated names emblazoned a huge advertisement in the *New York Times* under the headline: "The Man Who Defied an Empire and Gained Glory for Israel.—Menachem Beigin,[31] former Irgun Commander-in-Chief, arrives on Good-Will Mission Today." The usual Waldorf-Astoria Dinner was to follow, also an official welcome at City Hall. The main object of the visit was to obtain funds for electing Begin as Prime Minister of Israel. His political platform called for the incorporation of most of Jordan and other adjacent territories into Israel so that the new State would include the original boundaries of Canaan (or Eretz Israel).

Begin's record was well known in the State Department. Consequently, his visa application was rejected by two intelligent and competent officials—the Director of the Office of Near Eastern, South Asian, and African Affairs, and the Chief of the Visa Division. But from Key West, where President Truman was vacationing after his election victory, came a presidential order to grant the visa.

Some of the violence and lawlessness during the last months of the British Mandate was at least emotionally understandable, but the premeditated hanging of the two British Sergeants could justify no conceivable defense. Yet the arrival in the United States of the man who planned this crime, and avowedly aimed to overthrow the United Nations-United States partition proposals, was exuberantly heralded by U. S. officialdom. It was only some time after Dr. Henry Sloane Coffin, Father John La Farge and Rabbi Morris Lazaron had publicly warned the duped U.S. politicians and called for the repudiation of Begin that the Welcoming Committee disintegrated.

Senator Arthur Capper claimed he did not know how his name happened to appear in a newspaper advertisement concerning the Begin affair. Senator Herbert R. O'Conor, Democrat of Maryland, asserted that he had never approved acts of terrorism and that the only possible connection he had with the Begin shindig was his concern with "the general Palestinian problem in furthering the United States policy on the new State of Israel." Congressman (later U.S. Senator) John F. Kennedy from Massachusetts wired Louis Bromfield: "Belatedly and for the record I wish to withdraw my name from the reception committee for Menachem Begin, former Irgun Commander. When accepting your invitation, I was ignorant of the true nature of his activities, and I wish to be disassociated from them completely." The office of Congressman Joe Hendricks of Florida revealed that the Congressman had been out of town and thus his name "had been given" to the Begin Committee. Several other Congressmen could not recall later whether they, or their office, had ever authorized the use of their names. Dr. Harry C. Byrd, President of the University of Maryland, said: "Some people I know asked me if they could use my name as a member of the reception committee and I said they could. I didn't know who he was. I am not going to New York."[32] Hugh H. Bennett, Chief of the Soil Conservation Service of the Agricultural Department, told the *Washington Evening Star* that he "occasionally is asked to sponsor various functions and sometimes authorizes the use of his name because this seems the easiest out."[33] And so it went—after the damage was done.

Professor Albert Einstein, Professor Sidney Hook, and others, denounced the Begin-Freedom-Party as an "admixture of ultranationalism, religious mysticism and racial superiority. . . . They have pressed for the destruction of Free Trade Unions." This made Philip Murray, then President of the C. I. O. and one of the original members of the Welcoming Committee, suddenly realize that he had never authorized the use of his name— after his name had appeared for weeks, on thousands of letters and a great number of advertisements.

Meanwhile, Mr. Begin was touring the United States, meeting with financial advisers and holding sensational press interviews. Questioned about the bombing of the King David Hotel, the Irgun leader laid the responsibility squarely on the shoulders of the British Palestine Administrator, "who," he declared, "had been warned of the bombing and had refused to evacuate the hotel." (To Walter Deuel, of the Chicago *Daily News*,[34] Begin confided that the British had all of thirty minutes in which to evacuate their headquarters). Mr. Begin also belittled the charge that he had been a deserter from the Polish Army and a Soviet agent in Spain and China before going to Palestine. While in the United States, and later in his book,[35] Begin ridiculed the accusation that 250

Arab inhabitants of Deir Yassin had been massacred. (This slaughter had brought forth, at the time, an apology from Premier Ben-Gurion to King Abdullah and a statement from the Jewish Agency that it deplored "the commission of such brutalities by Jews as utterly repugnant.") He claimed that "this atrocity charge" was a combined Zionist-Arab propaganda story—quite a trick for warring nations. But throughout *The Revolt,* Begin boasts of the daring deeds he committed. He refers to "the military victory at Deir Yassin" and admits that the subsequent wild tales of Irgun butchering resulted in the "maddened, uncontrollable stampede of 635,000 Arabs. . . . The political and economic significance of this development can hardly be overestimated."[36]

While the American Zionist Organizations did not officially participate in the Begin parade—they had their own candidates for Israeli Premiership—neither did they repudiate him. In his memoirs, Begin tells how the Zionist Emergency Council was urged from many quarters to denounce the "dissidents" and how Abba Hillel Silver rejected these proposals and prevented their adoption. The Cleveland Zionist Rabbi is quoted as having said, "the Irgun will go down in history as a factor without which the State of Israel would not have come into being." From his pulpit, another nationalist Rabbi took up the defense of the Irgun. Dr. Neumann, holding the post of official observer for the Central Conference of American Rabbis at the United Nations, labelled the Coffin-LaFarge-Lazaron letter as "only another attempt to sabotage the progress of Palestine Jewry . . . in direct succession to the other anti-Jewish monuments of the last several years organized by Lazaron." (Morris Lazaron is an anti-Zionist Rabbi.)

The one voice that would not have been stilled by the Zionist clamor was now quiet forever. Dr. Judah Magnes was dead, and there was no one else to awaken the conscience of Jewry. No one had the courage to throw at Bloody Begin what the late President of the Hebrew University in Jerusalem had written months before to the *New York Times:* "It is very easy to join in the cry that Jewish terrorists are responsible for this atrocious crime. But who has been responsible for the Terrorists? We all bear some responsibility. Certainly the large number of American supporters do—the Senators and Congressmen, the newspaper publishers and writers and the large number of Jews and others who have supported terrorists morally and financially."[37]

Attorney General Tom Clark, now Supreme Court Justice, was called upon to investigate Begin's activities in the United States and the tax-free status of the organizations sponsoring him in this country: though money contributed to Begin's activities was obviously for political, and not humanitarian, purposes, the Begin group (as so many others) was permitted to collect such money as tax-free donations. But the Attorney General of the United States refused to intervene.

Menachem Begin has since achieved the honorable position of membership in the Knesset (the Israeli Parliament). He and Nathan Friedman Yellin, the leader of the Stern Gang (released from jail in time to be sworn into office), sit side by side. From the Knesset, Begin directs the extreme right-wing Herut Party which promotes a vast expansion of the borders of Israel. Should he ever wish to pay another visit to the United States, undoubtedly as glittering an array of political names could again be rounded up to welcome this man with blood on his hands.

CHAPTER VI

The Magic and Myth
of the Jewish Vote

NONE of the many powerful political lobbies in Washington is better entrenched than the brokers of the "Jewish Vote." The Zionists have managed to frighten the politicians, but there is little to back up their threats. With the possible exception of its response to the Hitler terror, American Jewry has been as divided on basic issues as have been other religious denominations. Yet the mythical unity attributed to the "Jewish people" by Zionist propagandists caused the American politician's surrender to Jewish nationalism. For the professional politician is too cowardly to call the bluff of the "professional Jew," and the individual Jew will not take the Zionists to task for usurping his voice and peddling his vote. Thus, the happy alliance between American politicians and Zionists.

It would, of course, greatly simplify the American politician's life if he could purchase what is claimed to be a group vote rather than sell himself to a multitude of individuals. That is why the American melting pot is replaced in national campaigns by separate national and religious frying pans—the "Polish Division," the "Negro Division," the "Jewish Division," the "Catholic Division." And the politicians are particularly fascinated by the fact that 75 per cent of the American Jewry live in fourteen cities, and more than 42 per cent in the city of New York. The Empire State, with its 45 electoral votes, remains a top prize in every national election.

Though there is little evidence that a "Jewish Vote" exists and is deliverable to any party, or a particular candidate, the myth survives. It is easy to believe in it, particularly if one is paid for doing so. And indeed, financial compensation has been an additional incentive to U. S. officialdom's activities in behalf of Jewish nationalism. Under the Truman Administration, Vice-President Barkley, several Cabinet Members, innumerable heads of federal agencies and members of Congress helped fill the air with Zionist speeches, mostly for a fee. (Mr. Barkley received as much as $1500 per speech.) And it is of course quite pleasant politicking—not only with vote potentials, but with hard cash too.

The only bipartisan policy developed in things Jewish is the firm resolution of both major parties to grab the "Jewish Vote" with sacrificial offers to Israel. When the Senate Foreign Relations Committee needed a study of Palestine and the Arab States, the job was turned over to Senator Guy M. Gillette, Democrat from Iowa, an avowed pro-Zionist who had headed the American League for a Free Palestine (the sponsors of Begin). When the House Foreign Affairs Committee required a similar report, the task was assigned to Republican Congressman Jacob K. Javits of New York, a staunch advocate of Jewish Nationalism. His views were well known, but Javits requested and received this assignment as a tacit acknowledgment by his Republican colleagues that objectivity on this subject was impossible as well as undesirable.

In this unprincipled quest for the "Jewish Vote," the Republican Party has been as arduous as have been the Democrats. Doris Fleeson, commenting upon the defeat of Republican Senator Owen Brewster in the Maine primaries of 1952, alluded in her syndicated column to certain foreign interests Brewster had openly supported: "The flag is flying at half mast over the Spanish Embassy and Pan-American Airways." Miss Fleeson, perhaps significantly, forgot to mention that the flag ought also to have been flying at half mast over Zionist headquarters: Brewster was one of the fiercest Congressional advocates of Jewish nationalism. Through him, Senator Taft, and Governor Dewey, the Republican Party was committed to Zionism.

The two major parties have continually attempted to outbid each other for the "Jewish Vote" with favorable planks in their national platforms. In 1944, the Democratic platform spoke of a "free and democratic Jewish commonwealth," while the Republican plank used the phrase "a free and democratic commonwealth," omitting the word "Jewish." In the ensuing campaign, Candidate Dewey declared his party stood for the "reconstitution of Palestine as . . . a Jewish commonwealth." The Zionist key word was speedily restored.

In 1948, Israel had already been accorded *de facto* recognition when the Republican Convention met in Philadelphia. The platform committee, headed by Senator Henry Cabot Lodge of Massachusetts, heard representatives of the anti-Zionist American Council for Judaism who argued against inserting what they called another obvious bid for the "Jewish Vote." The State Department, too, had advised Senator Vandenberg not to adopt a stand which would further alienate the Arab world. Consequently, the first draft of the Republican foreign policy plank merely extended greetings to the new State of Israel, but omitted support of Israel's boundary claims and her admission into the United Nations.

The Zionists immediately went to work and, within twenty-four hours, corrected the situation. Governor Dewey, the candidate-to-be, and an old hand at playing the minority-group angle, used his influence with John Foster Dulles and other architects of Republican foreign policy. Rabbi Abba Hillel Silver went into conference with Senator Taft and made clear, in unmistakable words, that he would not deliver his scheduled invocation and would publicly walk out of the Republican Party, unless a more pronounced pro-Israel commitment was inserted. New York Senator Irving Ives criticized the original draft for "saying less than a New Year's greeting card." And under the guidance of the New York Senator, the Resolutions Committee rewrote the original Republican Palestine plank, making it perfectly suitable to the most ardent Jewish nationalist.

The Democrats, for sixteen triumphant years masters in the art of exploiting minority-group consciousness (Roosevelt and Truman had an assistant specifically assigned to the task), were from the start free of their rival's indecisiveness. The Democratic platform of 1948 went beyond the G.O.P. policy promises by offering "financial aid" for Israel and a repeal of the U. S. arms embargo: the Truman Administration did not intend to let the electorate forget just who had been the best friend of the "Jewish people."

During the campaign itself, Governor Dewey tried hard to reduce the Truman handicap. Secretary of State General Marshall supported at the September session of the United Nations a compromise Palestine plan as proposed by Count Folke Bernadotte (who had been assassinated that very month). The Bernadotte Plan would have altered the original partition proposal by giving the Negeb area in Southern Palestine to the Arabs. John Foster Dulles, Governor Dewey's chief adviser on foreign policy, was a member of the delegation. Members of official U. S. delegations are normally bound by the decisions of the delegation, but this time there was an understanding that Dulles could publicly clarify his own decision whenever it had any domestic political significance. And Dulles immediately issued a statement that he—and Governor Dewey, by implication—were not bound by Marshall's approval of the Bernadotte Plan. On October 22, Candidate Dewey declared himself in favor of giving the Negeb area to Israel. A few days later, President Truman declared that no change in the original United Nations partition plan should be made unless acceptable to Israel—a considerable step beyond what Dewey had advocated.

John Foster Dulles, the first Republican Secretary of State since 1932, had built a curious record on the Israel issue. His personal views, influenced by his lasting affiliation with the National Council of Churches, should have left him unaffected by Zionism, but his close ties to New York politics often balanced the scales.

The Christian Churches have been understandably intent on the provisions of the U. N. resolution which call for the internationalization of Jerusalem. When Dulles was a candidate in 1949, to succeed himself as New York State's Senator in a contest with Lehman, he rejected the request that he support the administration of Jerusalem by the Israeli Government. Dulles courageously announced his position at a luncheon arranged by 200 Jewish civic, business and professional leaders in "tribute to his contributions toward the creation of the Jewish State and in support of his candidacy for the Senate." Although obviously on the spot, Dulles endorsed the internationalization of the Holy City, twice decreed by the United Nations.

But Dulles' refusal to change his views in regard to Jerusalem seem to have contributed to his losing the New York election by a margin of 197,000 votes; and ever since he seemed anxious to remember the painful lesson. He certainly remembered it while he was building the foreign policy plank of the 1952 Republican National Convention.

During the open hearings on that plank, a representative of the American Council for Judaism urged the Republican Party not to make any special promises to Israel but rather to treat the entire Middle Eastern area from only one point of view: What was in the best interests of "all American people and the entire free world." Congressman Javits, voicing the position of the American Zionist Council, advocated special preference for Israel. At the end, and with Mr. Dulles' at least tacit consent, the 1952 Republican plank outbid any previous Democratic platform in its hunger for the "Jewish Vote."

After devoting an entire sentence to the Middle East and Africa, the platform discussed in three paragraphs the necessity of aiding Israel and went on:

The Republican Party has consistently advocated a national home for the Jewish people since a Republican Congress declared its support of that objective thirty years ago. In providing a sanctuary for Jewish people rendered homeless by persecution, the State of Israel appeals to our deepest humanitarian instincts. We shall continue our

friendly interest in the constructive and inspiring under-
taking. We shall put our influence at the service of peace
between Israel and the Arab states and we shall cooperate
to bring economic and social stability to that area.

While the Dulles platform did not entirely follow the
Javits-Zionist formula, which was calling for the resettlement of the Arab refugees in neighboring Arab countries, it simply failed to mention, even in a single word,
the existence of hundreds of thousands of wretched Arab
refugees.

Two weeks later, the Democrats nominated Governor
Adlai Stevenson. This time, the Democratic plank on
the Middle East properly treated the area as a whole
and spoke of the "people of the Middle East." What aid
was promised to Israel and her refugees was equally assured to the "Arab states and the Palestinian refugees."
This represented a considerable toning down of past
Democratic commitments to Zionism and an awareness
of the real forces in the Middle East.

Political platform promises, like international treaties,
are not necessarily worth more than the paper they are
written on, but the change of Democratic tone from
Roosevelt-Truman Zionism to Stevenson aloofness was
in itself significant. The latest Democratic plank on the
Middle East had not been dictated, as usual, by a White
House open to political expediency, but by Department
of State personnel trained in foreign affairs. Stevenson
had served with the U. S. delegation to the United Nations and was fully aware how policy decisions, wherever Israel and the Arab States were concerned, were
invariably denied to the Secretary of State. Byrnes had
complained that the State Department's sole authority
in regard to the Palestine problem was to transmit mes-

sages for and from the President. Marshall had not even been advised on the forthcoming Presidential decision to leave the Negeb to Israel. Both Secretaries of State were several times on the verge of openly breaking with their Chief on Palestine policies.

The nomination of Adlai Stevenson ended, so far as the Democratic Party was concerned, this complete domination of U. S. Middle East policies by party hacks. Had he been elected, he would hardly have yielded to the political pressures that persuaded President Truman to neglect the best interests of the nation. Throughout his campaign, Stevenson refrained from making any special bid to the "Jewish Vote" and declared his complete independence from minority pressure-groups of all kinds. In fact, this frankness may have contributed to the size of Stevenson's defeat. On his 1953 visit to the Middle East there was some indication, however, that the former Governor of Illinois may change his tactics and that any new policy for the area by the Eisenhower Administration might be met with the usual Democratic play to the "Jewish bloc."

In his vituperative whistle-stop campaign President Truman, however, was true to form by injecting his conventional appeal to the "Jewish Vote." In a letter to the Jewish Welfare Board's National Mobilization for G.I. and Community Services, the President charged General Eisenhower with a willingness to accept "the very practice that identified the so-called master race." The President was referring to the aid Republicans had given to the Immigration Act of Democratic Senator McCarran and charged that General Eisenhower's failure to repudiate these members of his Party indicated his support of their views. Within thirty-six hours of the publication of the Truman letter, Rabbi Abba Hillel

Silver had met with General Eisenhower at his Columbia University home and letters previously exchanged between the Zionist leader and the Republican Presidential nominee were immediately released. Rabbi Silver had written to thank the General for the inclusion in the Republican Party platform of the strong endorsement of the State of Israel; and the General, in turn, indicated how deeply he was concerned with Israel's problems and how "vigorously and effectively Republican Senators and Congressmen, Governors and State legislatures had supported the cause [of Israel]."

On the whole, Eisenhower's campaign followed much more closely than Stevenson's the "bloc vote" pattern which Presidents Roosevelt and Truman had set and Governor Dewey had previously tried to emulate. (In Eisenhower's headquarters at New York's Commodore Hotel there were office rooms reserved for the "Jewish Division of the Republican National Committee.") In the past, such campaign emphasis has resulted in obligations which required a pay off. Yet it is too early to speculate whether the new Republican Administration will maintain the traditional White House alliance with Zionism. Secretary Dulles' tour of the Arab world and the facts he reported to the President have caused considerable consternation in Zionist circles.

President Eisenhower, if he wants, can call the bluff of the Jewish nationalists and give the lie to the contention of a "Jewish Vote." For the General's overwhelming victory can hardly be credited to any one vote bloc.

In 1948, of the twenty-odd million votes cast in the five largest states where "the Jewish Vote" is claimed to center, only 150,000 votes (three fourths of one per cent!) separated the two parties. What did this prove about the "Jewish Vote"? Obviously, if it existed, it would have much more weightily supported an Administration which had so well served, in deed and word, Jewish nationalism. Yet despite all the favors they had done for Zionism, the Democrats carried, of the four pivotal states, only Illinois and California, and lost the larger electoral votes of Pennsylvania and New York. Nor was Rabbi Silver able to deliver Ohio, the fifth state, to the G.O.P. candidate he supported. In short, the election statistics disproved the myth of the "Jewish Vote" even in 1948—at the peak of Zionist hysteria.

These same five pivotal States gave Eisenhower, in 1952, an approximate plurality of 2.7 million votes out of some 23.5 million votes cast—a differential of better than 10 per cent. The swing from the Democrats to the Republicans was so tremendous that it is difficult to separate the details of the landslide. But there can be no doubt that innumerable formerly Democratic Catholics must this time have voted Republican. And there is every reason to believe that tremendous numbers of Jewish votes went to Eisenhower.

A study Columbia University made for *Life* magazine in 1952 revealed that 37% of the Catholics, 36% of the Jews and 23% of the Protestants are affiliated with the Democratic Party; and only 6% of the Jewish Voters are registered Republicans, as compared to 22% of the Catholics and 45% of the Protestants. But the most significant revelation of this study is that 58% of Jewish Americans are affiliated with neither party. Consequently, neither party has a first mortgage on the votes of Jewish Americans.

Indeed, all past statistical election analyses have shown that the factors determining the choice of so-called minority groups were never different from those which influenced the vote of all other socially comparable groups. For if there ever has been any noticeable bloc voting, it always followed economic division lines cutting through religious affiliations. The strong democratic majority for Stevenson in New York's Lower East Side was a working-class vote rather than a "Jewish Vote": this is where the effectively organized needle workers live. But in the economically more substantial and almost equally Jewish West-End-Avenue-Manhattan districts of New York, Eisenhower received close to 45% of the total vote.

There is, of course, an indeterminate number of voters who, in the past, have supported a candidate because "he is good for our people." Yet, interestingly enough, this type of thinking has been much more prevalent in a negative sense, i.e., when a "minority group" felt uneasy about one of its own members. For example, when Albert Ottinger ran as Republican candidate for the New York Governorship, in 1928, against Roosevelt, he was the victim of a whispering campaign concerning the quality of his "Jewishness" which undoubtedly resulted in his defeat (by an extremely narrow margin in an election which otherwise swept Herbert Hoover and the rest of the Republican ticket into office). On the other hand, considerably more New York Jews voted in 1945 for the Catholic Democrat William O'Dwyer than for the Jewish Republican, Judge Jonah Goldstein. Where there is a Jewish candidate running against a non-Jewish opponent, certain Jews will no doubt be influenced in favor of "one of their own," but this die-hard Jewish vote is only as large as is Jewish nationalism itself.

All things being equal, and neither candidate "of the faith," there has never been conclusive proof that the votes of Jews can be delivered, as a bloc, to any candidate. In 1948, when he was supporting Dewey for President,

Rabbi Silver's Ohio home county, Cuyahoga (which in-cludes Cleveland), went to Truman by 43,000 votes. In the same county Stevenson trailed Eisenhower in 1952 by some 5200 votes. There is evidence that this large shift represented the failure of labor to deliver for the New Deal rather than Dr. Silver's sudden ability to de-liver "the Jewish Vote" to the Republican ticket. The Korean issue, if any one factor, seems to have been the responsible factor for the Anti-Truman revulsion in Cuyahoga County, as most everywhere in the U. S.

From the synagogue, there came in 1952 one voice of the rabbinate which made particularly good sense. Rabbi Joseph Lookstein, of Manhattan, pointed out that the "grave error" of his colleague Dr. Silver "might have been avoided had he on that morning (Saturday) been where a rabbi should be—in the synagogue. . . . When a religious teacher enters the arena of a political campaign he does a candidate little good and religion much harm. . . . "[1]

CHAPTER VII

Smears and Fears

"I BELIEVE," wrote Learned Hand, the retired Chief Judge of the Second Federal Court of Appeals, "that the community is already in the process of dissolution where each man begins to eye his neighbor as a possible enemy, where non-conformity with the accepted creed, political as well as religious, is a mark of disaffection; where denunciation, without specification or backing, takes the place of evidence; where orthodoxy chokes freedom of dissent; where faith in the eventual supremacy of reason has become so timid that we dare not enter our convictions in the open lists to win or lose."[1]

This concise statement of a noble man's dreads can be applied, without the slightest change, to the precarious position of the anti-Zionist American Jew within American Jewry.

At the end of World War II, when the partition of Palestine began to look feasible, it became virtually impossible to raise doubts as to the merits of the proposition. Since the State of Israel was created, its policies, and the activities of U. S. organizations assisting the new sovereignty, have been placed beyond the pale of criticism.

Christian would-be critics were speedily silenced with the smear-word "Anti-Semitism"; and any latent Jewish opposition to Zionist nationalism has been throttled by the fear of being labeled "treason to Jewry." Crushed between the smear and the fear is American foreign policy in the Middle East.

There has developed within American Jewry—as, indeed, throughout our entire civilization—a horrible readiness to bow before the fetishes of words, to surrender personal thought to group jargon, individual responsibility to group emotionalism. People (and American Jews *are* people) seem to abhor nothing so much as the apparently unpleasant process of personal rationalizing. Rather, they accept cleverly manufactured catchwords as self-evident truths which must not be, ever, exposed to intellectual analysis. And no tragedy in the long and tragic history of Judaism could have been more appalling than the meekness with which the religious community that gave Monotheism to a pagan world seems to be yielding to the savage paganism of word fetishes.

Zionism, in short, won its *blitzkrieg* over American Jewry simply because it was permitted to put the label "Humanitarianism" on the power politics of Jewish nationalism. There are tens of thousands of American Jews who detest rabid nationalism, Jewish or otherwise; but there is hardly an American Jew who would want to be thought "antihumanitarian." Consequently, Zionism did not waste time or energy on proving its extreme program to be morally and historically sound. All it had to do was to equate it with man's compassion for the victims of history's most cruel pogrom. And this, Zionism did extremely well—with unprecedented aggressiveness, and with the help of an easily frightened American press.

The capture of the American press by Jewish nationalism was, in fact, incredibly complete. Magazines as well as newspapers, news stories as well as editorial columns, gave primarily the Zionist views of events before, during and after partition. And there was little incentive to resist the Zionist pressure exerted on the U. S. press. Arab readership was negligible, and latent Jewish opposition to Zionism remained inarticulate. If the Zionist story could not be presented straight, it could always be smuggled in under humanitarian disguise. Even the most objective story on Displaced Persons carried a Zionist propaganda message.

The American press, to be sure, was happy to comply with the Christian desire of making at least partial amends for the persecution of European Jewry; and its special contribution was obviously to handle news in a manner the articulate (i.e., Zionist) Jews would consider sympathetic. If voluntary compliance was not "understanding" enough, there was always the matter of Jewish advertising and circulation. The threat of economic recriminations from Jewish advertisers, combined with the fact that the fatal label of "Anti-Semite" would be pinned on any editor stepping out of line, assured fullest press cooperation.

A modicum of newspaper space was occasionally given to such anti-Zionists as the American Council for Judaism or the Christian Group headed by Dean Virginia Gildersleeve and Bayard Dodge. But each time a New York newspaper published a news item unfavorable to Zionism—even a reader's critical letter to the editor—the pressure was applied: innumerable telephone calls to the editor, the news desk and the advertising department, and a flood of protesting letters. Newspaper offices are not overly sensitive to that type of pressure; but in this particular case, their power of resistance was greatly reduced by the unnerving fact that the ugly charge of "Anti-Semitism" was accompanying the coercive acts.

In the lobby of the *New York Times* hangs a plaque with these words inscribed: "To give the news impartially without fear or favor, regardless of any party, sect or interest involved." And the *Times*, of all papers, has most nearly lived up to that maxim, even when under Zionist pressure. In November 1946, the *Times* publisher, Arthur Hays Sulzberger, said publicly: "I dislike the coercive methods of Zionists who in this country have not hesitated to use economic means to silence persons who have different views. I object to the attempts at character assassination of those who do not agree with them." This, coming from an American of the Jewish faith and the publisher of the most influential and, thus, most vulnerable American newspaper, was courage indeed. The *Times* was then opposing the partition of Palestine and feeling the whip lash of the pressure group who had declared a virtual boycott of the *New York Times*. The details of that boycott action remained one of the guarded secrets on Times Square. There is a heavy file tucked away in Mr. Sulzberger's safe and no one will today talk about *the* frightening experience. Yet the *Times* continued to report the news impartially and, on the whole, it still endeavors to be as objective as it can *vis-à-vis* the State of Israel. (Personally, Mr. Sulzberger is a non-Zionist rather than an anti-Zionist.)

The big Republican rival of the *New York Times*, the New York *Herald-Tribune*, was not slow in taking advantage of the difficult position in which the non-Zionist but Jewish-owned *Times* had been placed by the Palestine controversy. In New York City, there were over 2 million Jewish readers at stake, and the *Herald-Tribune* did its best to cut into the *Times* circulation. The paper went overboard in its support of partition. Its "reporting" of Palestine news outslanted[2] even the New York *Post's* Jewish nationalism. Chaim Weizmann's diaries were serialized. For the first time in its history the *Herald-Tribune*, in fact, threw aside its Anglophilia to replace it with Zionism's evaluation of Britain's "colonial policy."

When Dr. Harry Gideonse, the President of Brooklyn College, warned that an exclusive preoccupation with Israeli concerns, and a disregard for legitimate American Jewish national interests in the Middle East, could be a dangerous stimulant to the growth of bigotry and intolerance, he was furiously attacked in the New York press. The New York *Post* called Dr. Gideonse editorially "an apologist for encouragement of Arab aggression against Israel" and refused to publish his reply to the slander. In the New York *Jewish Day*, Dr. Samuel Margoshes pilloried the Brooklyn educator with wild references to Wall Street, the house of Dillon, Reed and Company and the "pro-Arab cabal" in the State Department, topping it all off with an appeal to Brooklyn students not to permit Dr. Gideonse to get away with his impudent frankness.

In other parts of the country, the press was similarly knuckling down. The National Public Opinion Research Center of Denver, Colorado, interviewed a representative group of daily and weekly newspaper editors at the height of the public debate over Palestine (October, 1947). *Opinion News,* the official publication of the Research Center, reported that 50% of the editors opposed partition and favored a unitary Palestine; 30% went along with the UNSCOP majority; and 10% favored a federalized State. But these personal opinions of the editors hardly showed in their papers. The news coverage of the Palestine story carried a clear pro-Zionist slant throughout the country. And by November, 1947, more than 57% of surveyed national papers had refrained from any editorial comment on the Palestine question.[3]

Since summer 1948, one million distraught Arab refugees had been exposed to hunger, privation and the "happy talk" of the Communists. But because these people were Arabs, the U. S. press had little space for their problems. This indifference may have been due, to some extent, to the belief that American readers would not be interested in this far-away story. But, alas, there can be no doubt that U. S. editors wanted, above all, to avoid a "sticky" humanitarian problem that contained embarrassing political connotations. And whenever they were mentioned in the U. S. press, the Arabs were somehow depicted as tools of the Grand Mufti of Jerusalem, as Pro-Nazi Falangists, or as desert marauders.

Volume after volume espousing the Zionist position from every possible angle inundated the book stores. More important, the books by James McDonald, Bartley Crum, Richard Crossman, William Ziff, Sumner Welles, Robert Nathan, Robert Capa, Pierre Van Paassen, Walter Lowdermilk, and Herbert Evatt, received enthusiastic national press attention. Even Carlson's *Cairo to Damascus*, a veritable hatchet job, enjoyed glowing reviews. But less pro-Zionist books, like the one Willie Snow (Mrs. Mark) Ethridge wrote, met a vastly different reception. Mrs. Ethridge, the wife of the publisher of the Louisville *Courier-Journal*, had accompanied her husband to his post in the Holy Land as U. S. member of the United Nations Conciliation Commission. In *Going to Jerusalem*, she not only gave an account of Jewish suffering in Israel, but also described the misery of the Arab refugees. And just for that, a *Washington Post* review written by the publisher himself, called her "wide-eyed" and accused her of giving a "distorted, if different view of the situation." Particular exception was taken to the perfectly fair remark Mrs. Ethridge attributes to her husband: "The Arabs are not lily-white and neither are the Jews. It is a confused, complex situation." The review in the New York *Herald-Tribune* took even more violent exception to Mrs. Ethridge's description of the contentious land in which more than 900,000 Arabs were forced to relinquish beautiful orchards and villages.

Mrs. Ethridge, by the way, was invited to address the Maryland Teachers Association in Baltimore and chose, several weeks in advance, *Going to Jerusalem* as the subject of her speech. Four days before her scheduled talk, the secretary of the Maryland Teachers Association informed her that she must not give that particular speech. Despite her willingness to submit its full text beforehand, the secretary would not change his mind; so much pressure had been brought to bear on him, he explained, that he would lose his job if Mrs. Ethridge insisted on the delicate subject. Mrs. Ethridge, a lady of compassion, changed it finally to "The Balkans Balk."

Other expressions of plain sympathy for the new Displaced Persons of the Middle East were similarly received. Professor Millar Burrows of the Yale School of Divinity, a distinguished Bible student and archaeologist, has always enjoyed an unchallenged reputation for scrupulous objectivity in his scholarly pursuits—until 1949, when the Westminster Press published his book, *Palestine Is Our Business*. And his case is indeed a frightening example of Zionist tactics.

In *Land Reborn*, the house organ of the American

Christian Palestine Committee, Professor Burrows was promptly accused of "careless writing, disjointed reporting and extremely biased observation." The publishing firm, according to the *Land Reborn* reviewer (a Christian minister) "should have rejected the manuscript of this shoddy piece of work which ill becomes a distinguished Bible scholar." (The same magazine had described Mrs. Ethridge's work as "cloying and tiresome.") The American Zionist Council really gave full treatment to Professor Burrows' book. In an interpretative survey of Arab propaganda, prepared and distributed by the Zionist Council,[4] Dr. Burrows was labeled an "out and out anti-Zionist" and his book "an anti-Semitic opus." Everyone who had ever dared to raise his voice against the one-sided presentation of the Middle Eastern picture was accused in this same pamphlet of being part of a "pro-Arab campaign in America, stretching from the intellectual and philanthropic circles at the top, through various religious groups and into the cesspool of anti-Semitism." Dorothy Thompson, Vincent Sheean, Professor William E. Hocking, the Presidents of the American Universities in the Middle East, *Reader's Digest*, *Time*, *Atlantic Monthly* and Stewart Alsop were all lumped together with Gerald L. K. Smith and Merwin K. Hart in this "propaganda ring" allegedly after Israel and the Jews in this country.

In a protesting letter to the Zionist Council, Professor Burrows pointed out that he had been one of the organizers, and for some time a vice-president, of the National Committee to Combat Anti-Semitism; that he had been active in the inter-faith movement in New Haven; and that "strong differences in political convictions are compatible with personal respect and honesty." The executive director of the Zionist Council, Rabbi Jerome Unger, admitted in his reply to Dr. Burrows: "You most certainly should not be charged with anti-Semitism." Then, with argumentative finesse, the Rabbi added: "You will readily admit, of course, that in the make-up of many anti-Zionists—indeed, some of the leading ones —anti-Semitism is a strong component part. It is always very difficult to sift out one from the other but I feel certain that, in your case, it requires very little sifting." But beyond this ambiguous admission, in a letter, there was no apology and of course no public retraction to undo the harm that had been done to Dr. Burrows.

In the fall of 1949, the Holyland Emergency Liaison Program was organized to bring the plight of the Arab refugees to the attention of the American public. The organization was headed by the former President of the Union Theological Seminary, Dr. Henry Sloane Coffin, and assembled on its National Council thirty prominent clergymen, judges, college presidents, philanthropists, diplomats and writers. In its initial statement of September 12, 1949, H.E.L.P. (as the group came to be known) called for an immediate solution of the Arab refugee problem. Lest the intent of the organization be construed as political, or aimed against Israel, H.E.L.P. explicitly stated that "our concern is not with how or why the Arab refugees came into being. They exist, and the Holyland Emergency Liaison Program intends to focus public attention on their plight."[5]

The general press of the country (where was now its humanitarian purport?) devoted a ludicrously small amount of space to the activities of H.E.L.P., but the Yiddish press assailed the organization with furor. When Dorothy Thompson joined the group, the headlines of the *Jewish Examiner* screamed: "Miss Thompson heads Pro-Arab Hate Group." Her previous support of Zionism and her leadership in the country's mobilization against Nazism were wiped out by Miss Thompson's impudence to sympathize with human suffering even when the sufferers were Arabs.

Throughout its brief existence, H.E.L.P. persisted in its non-political objective and never blamed Israel for the creation of the Arab refugee problem. But the very existence of H.E.L.P. was anathema to Zionism: it exposed the guilty conscience of Jewish nationalist leaders. Men and women in public life were advised not to join this movement; and those who had already done so, received more than mere advice to get off. Governor Christian Herter of Massachusetts, for instance, had accepted the post of Vice-Chairman of H.E.L.P. when he was a Congressman from Boston. Less than three weeks after H.E.L.P.'s statement of objectives had been released, Herter sent a letter of resignation to Dr. Coffin. In this letter, the Congressman stated that "my own position on the Council (of H.E.L.P.) has already given the erroneous impression that I have chosen to take sides against Israel."[6] On the telephone, and in conversation with officers of H.E.L.P., Mr. Herter indicated that pressures from constituents were tremendous and that his political career was in the balance. A delegation headed by a rabbi from Herter's Congressional district had come to Washington to demand that he resign. His mail had been heavy with letters, including one from the Jewish War Veterans, accusing him of selling out to the Arabs. An editor of the Jewish Telegraphic Agency had informed the Congressman (without giving him a copy of the alleged monitorings) that Arab radio broadcasts had boasted H.E.L.P. "was going to drive the Israelites back into the Sea." Herter was finally impressed by a Hebrew broadcast which asserted that "the task of the new institution (H.E.L.P.) . . . is to exercise pressure on Congress to fulfill Arab demands." In such manner, a pressure group drove a politician to cover. On resigning, Congressman Herter issued a press statement taking a critical view of the "political objectives" of H.E.L.P.— after he had assured the organization that there would be no press release on his withdrawal. A quiet resignation, of course, would scarcely have satisfied those who wished to destroy H.E.L.P.

Trouble Makers,[7] a book sponsored by the Anti-Defamation League (whose avowed task is to fight "the causes and effects" of prejudice), tells of a secret meeting between Azzam Pasha, then Secretary General of the Arab League, and members of H.E.L.P. who conspired with Azzam Pasha in his anti-Jewish propaganda. No such meeting ever took place: at the time of the alleged meeting, H.E.L.P. had ceased to exist for more than three months.

Volume VIII of *The Facts*, published in May, 1948, by the Anti-Defamation League's Civil Rights Division, dealt with "Anti-Semitism and the Palestine Issue"— and listed under that title the activities of Dean Virginia Gildersleeve, Kermit Roosevelt, Bayard Dodge, and Max Thornburg. "Their espousal of the Arab cause in opposition to Zionism has been marked by an increasingly hostile attitude towards the Jewish people themselves. While anti-Zionism and sympathy for the Arab cause are not necessarily indications of anti-Semitic prejudice, there are many whose pro-Arab utterances and activities have contained sufficiently expressed or implied anti-Semitism to give cause for genuine alarm."[8]

Was there ever a weaker case of "guilt by association"

or, rather, guilt by juxtaposition? The evaluation of these men and women whose motivation the Anti-Defamation League concedes might be sincere is intermixed with an analysis of Coughlin, Gerald L. K. Smith, and others patently insincere.

The Committee for Justice and Peace in the Holy Land, to which many opponents of the partition proposal belonged, was attacked with similar insinuations and the double-bottomed "concession" that "on the other hand anti-Semitism has been read into some anti-Zionist attitudes, which stem from ostensibly sincere opposition to the establishment of a Jewish State." Final conclusion: "They and the Committee have aligned themselves with the official Arab propaganda line in this country (both opposed partition) which sometimes has gone beyond bounds. . . . They may be contributing wittingly or unwittingly to an increase of anti-Jewish sentiment in the United States."[9]

"While there has been no evidence that Dean Gildersleeve or any member of her Committee has been deliberately anti-Semitic (We all have intimate Jewish friends, Dean Gildersleeve explained in her letter,)[10] it is an unquestionable fact that less scrupulous endorsers of the Arab cause have taken advantage of the Committee's propaganda activities," the Anti-Defamation League asserted. Intolerance was charged to Miss Gildersleeve because of her claim that "Palestine Jews are capable of doing very wicked things"—a contention in which she has the support of Sulzberger, Einstein, and Magnes (amongst other "anti-Semites"): Miss Gildersleeve had been appalled by the Israeli burnings of George Antonius' *The Arab Awakening*, a historical exposition of Arab nationalism.

The Anti-Defamation League's evidence against Kermit Roosevelt was that the Arab office in Washington had suggested his name as a speaker who would be friendly to the Arab cause.

The Anti-Defamation League's proof of the un-American nature of Dr. Bayard Dodge consisted of the fact that he had been the President of the American University of Beirut and had stated: "I am not anti-Jewish, but Americans must study carefully the consequences of aggressive support of extreme Zionists."[11]

The Anti-Defamation League's study of the Palestine issue, and its subsequent "Survey of the Reaction to the Establishment and Recognition of Israel," attributed anti-Semitism to any portion of the press which dared to point out that the Administration had backed the partition of Palestine primarily to get Jewish votes at home. Editorials of the Richmond *Times* and St. Louis *Post Dispatch* were singled out on this score, as were the *Evening Record* of Jersey City and the Tucson (Arizona) *Daily Star* which pondered editorially that the creation of Israel might raise the question of dual loyalties. The *Saturday Evening Post* came under fire for a brief editorial, "Let's Suppose Partition Came Home to Roost," in which the question was asked how the U. S. would react if the U. N. proposed an all-Negro state. Dr. Peter Marshall, the universally respected chaplain of the U. S. Senate (whose sermons were posthumously published in the best-selling *A Man Called Peter*) was attacked for a sermon given in the Church of the Presidents. Dr. Marshall spoke of "The Paradox that is America" and noted that the British were out of Palestine and we were in. "Our President," he then said, "put us in by his immediate recognition of the Jewish State of Israel and it is going to cost us something, you may be sure of that." This moderate, correct and perfectly sensible statement gave Dr. Marshall the complexion of an untouchable.

*   *   *

However harsh the treatment the Zionists were giving non-Jewish opponents of a Jewish State in Palestine, it was sheer tenderness compared to the fate of Jewish non-Zionists.

Rabbi Louis Finkelstein, President of the Jewish Theological Seminary was only a non-Zionist. But when he refused to allow his students to sing the Israel National Anthem at commencement in 1945 (on the ground that a political song had no place at a religious ceremony), a storm of resentment descended upon him throughout the organized Jewish community in the U. S. (At least one large contributor to the Seminary tore up his annual check.)[12]

From the outset, even the U. S. rabbinate was determined to silence all who disagreed with Zionist tenets.

When the Biltmore Program (calling for the establishment of a Jewish State) was publicly opposed by a small Jewish organization, four rabbis branded the opposition statement, before a meeting of the American Jewish Conference, as "impertinent attempt to sabotage," "outrageous action," "treachery to the cause of Israel" by men "who placed themselves outside of the pale of Israel."

The Central Conference of American Rabbis not only rejected the assertion that Zionism was incompatible with Reform Judaism, but tried to eliminate all organized opposition to the prevailing Zionist sentiment. When the American Council for Judaism was organ-

ized to represent the Judaists who reject Jewish nationalism, the Central Conference adopted, by 137 to 45
votes, a resolution which ended with these words:
"Therefore without impugning the rights of Zionists
and non-Zionists to express and to disseminate their convictions within and without the Conference, we, in the
spirit of amity, urge our colleagues of the American
Council for Judaism to terminate this organization."[13]

The record of Zionist pressures exerted against Jews
who shared the views of the American Council for Judaism is long, sad and continuous. This writer, no matter
how hard he would try, could never present that record
in its massive entirety—for the good and forceful reason
that the more submissive victims of Zionist pressures are
usually too ashamed or too afraid to publicize their experience. I have therefore decided to confine the rest
of this chapter to my own experience—not because I
consider it extreme (I know of worse case histories), and
certainly not because of any pride in martyrdom, but
simply because I know that story particularly well and
can tell it freely.

In 1949, I grew tired of the self-appointed spokesmen
who purported to speak for me. I did not feel that a yen
for Jewish Statehood was a necessary component of either
my Jewish faith or my compassion for Hitler's victims.
And I sincerely resented the Zionist propaganda which
wanted to make my Christian fellow citizens believe that
all American Jews, in a fictitious "unity," desire a political separation of "the Jewish people." I wrote an article to express my attitude (which, I felt, must be that
of innumerable other Americans of the Jewish faith)
and sent it to the *Saturday Evening Post*.

Several years before, the *Saturday Evening Post* had
published a provocative article by Milton Mayer, en-

titled "The Case Against the Jews," in which Mayer criticized the self-segregating habits of many American Jews but showed his authentic devotion to the universal tenets of his Jewish faith. (The editors also gave the floor to two other American Jews, Judge Jerome Frank and author Waldo Frank, to present divergent views on the same subject.) The publication of Mayer's article exposed the *Saturday Evening Post* to what was perhaps the worst ordeal in the magazine's venerably long history: tremendous and quite often venomous mail flooded the editorial offices, subscriptions were cancelled and advertising was withdrawn in an obviously organized drive. *L'affaire* Mayer, still nervously remembered in the publishing world, was to establish once and for all the rule that no national magazine must dare present an article which, even remotely, attacks Jewish nationalism—unless the magazine was courageously prepared for a serious and prolonged battle. The *Saturday Evening Post* evidently was not. Its editors returned my manuscript with these kind remarks: "Let us promptly concede that this is a good and eloquent article, but it is not one we can use. The pity is that, if all Jews were as broad-minded as this author, there would be no Zionist problem."

The piece was later rejected, with similar explanations, by other national magazines—until it reached the *Reader's Digest* whose editors wanted it. The *Digest*, with its colossal circulation, could run the risk of publishing a controversial article, because the magazine's U. S. edition carries no advertising. But even the *Digest* had to protect itself. Though the Jewish nationalist story had appeared in print a thousand times, the *Digest* editors decided to present the two opposing views in the same issue. So Rabbi Abba Hillel Silver's "The Case for Zionism" appeared in the September, 1949, issue of the *Read-*

er's Digest with my "Israel's Flag Is Not Mine." But even that impartiality was not deemed sufficient protection against the displeasure of Zionism. Twelve prominent Americans of the Jewish faith were invited, and agreed, to testify in that *Digest* issue: "We feel that presentation of both sides of the Zionist Question by the *Reader's Digest* is an important public service." All twelve were anti-Zionists, but the magazine could at least show some impressive Jewish support for the publication of both articles.

One of those who declined to join this group endorsement was Rabbi Isadore Hoffman, Counselor to Jewish Students at Columbia University. Dr. Hoffman wrote William L. White, the *Digest* Editor in charge of the two articles, that he resented "the efforts of some extreme Jewish Nationalists to intimidate or silence those of the Jewish faith who differ with them," but because of the position he held, Rabbi Hoffman had to refrain from publicly approving that an American of the Jewish faith received a chance to express his non-conformist views on Zionism.

These unprecedented safeguards in publishing a simple and in itself anything but "explosive" article did not, however, save its author from an ordeal of considerable magnitude. From the Synagogue pulpits and from the Anglo-Jewish and Yiddish press, throughout the nation, the heaviest barrages were fired against the article and its author.

The *Jewish Post* of Louisville, Kentucky, announced gravely that it was time for United States Jewry to take action against those who charge dual loyalty. The Denver, Colorado *Intermountain Jewish News* called on the Anti-Defamation League, and other defense agencies, to recognize that "Jews can be anti-Semitic and crack down on those who carp about dual loyalty in the public press." What hurt and enraged these papers particularly was that the huge Christian readership of the *Digest* was for the first time informed that "Jewish unity" (whatever that is) was fictitious. As the *B'nai B'rith Messenger* of Los Angeles, California, put it: "When they (anti-Zionists) go to the non-Zionists, go to the non-Jewish press with lies, false logic and implied appeal for them to destroy the American Jewish community, then it becomes a serious menace, not only to the Jewish but to the general community."

The *Digest* came in for such accusations as "snide remarks—twisted attitude toward Israel and Zionists—profascistic editorial position in general." In an open letter, the *Jewish Times* of Philadelphia insisted that the "publication of such stuff presents a case for organizations which fight anti-Semitism," while the *Jewish Floridian* charged that an alliance of traitors and anti-Semites had made the publication of the vicious article possible. The *National Jewish Post* of Indianapolis and the Detroit *Jewish Chronicle* called for a holy war against, and excommunication of, the American Council for Judaism for distributing free reprints of the *Digest* article. The National Community Relations Advisory Council (which is the co-ordinating body for the American Jewish Committee, the American Jewish Congress, the Anti-Defamation League, the Jewish War Veterans, Jewish Labor Committee of 25, Hebrew Congregations, and 27 local Community Councils) passed this resolution: "The Executive Committee is directed to take appropriate measures with the American Council for Judaism looking toward the discontinuance by the American Council of its false and unwarranted charges impugning the loyalty of American Jews." Neither the accused organization (which had never sponsored my article) nor the man whose article was so attacked were given an opportunity to challenge the accusation and to prove that not the *Digest* article but Jewish nationalism had raised the very real issue of dual loyalties. They were condemned, instead, in star-chamber fashion that would have done justice to the combined efforts of a Cromwell, a Hitler, and a Stalin.

Moreover, I was excoriated from some fourteen pulpits in various parts of the country. No rabbinical attack was more bitter than that by Rabbi Abraham Feldman of Temple Beth Israel in Hartford, Connecticut, delivered on the evening of September 30, 1949. Now Hartford, a wonderful town, has always been very close and dear to me. A good part of my family comes from there, including an uncle from whom I was inseparable throughout his life. I had known a boy's happiness in this humid city on the Connecticut River. And in Hartford, of all places, at the momentous Friday night service before the Day of Atonement, Rabbi Feldman took for the title of his sermon "Israel's Flag Is Not Mine." The Rabbi had his sermon printed and distributed, with the compliments of a Zionist leader, throughout Hartford.

Using the pulpit of God, and high office, the Rabbi distorted my view. Just as his colleague, Rabbi Silver, had done in the *Digest*, Rabbi Feldman presented Zionism as a purely philanthropic, not at all nationalist, movement. I was depicted as a kind of monster, completely callous to the needs of suffering fellow Jews, rather than merely opposed to a political machine which was selling extreme Jewish nationalism. But the *Digest* article had centered on the serious issue whether the new State had created "a collective Jewish nation with its center in Israel," to which all members of the Jewish faith owe obligations and unswerving political aid; and this central question Dr. Feldman did not even try to answer. Rather, the Rabbi advised me to "pray penitently and fervently for Divine forgiveness for the cruel and reckless injury" I had done "to all American Jews."

The powers of propaganda and emotion being what they are, most of his audience that Friday night readily accepted Rabbi Feldman's interpretation of what I had actually written. In the Jewish community of Hartford, I was adjudged guilty of the heinous crime of treason to the new State of Israel by proclaiming the indivisibility of my American citizenship. For months thereafter, some members of my family would not talk to me (including a relative who, though Protestant, allowed emotionalism to sweep aside her usually sound judgment). Ten months later, when I visited Hartford for the first time since the "*cause celèbre*," some old friends would still have no part of me. A few sidled over to me and whispered that they shared my views; but they only whispered.

A written request was submitted to let me, consonant with the American tradition of fair play, present my side of the quarrel to Rabbi Feldman's congregation who, for years, had been indoctrinated in Jewish nationalism. The request resulted merely in a bitter exchange of correspondence which, for all practical purposes, netted the answer Dr. Feldman was reputed to have previously given to an intermediary: "It will be over my dead body." And indeed his Hartford community has remained solidly in the Jewish nationalist camp. In passing, an ironic "switch" occurred several months later when Rabbi Feldman visited the State of Israel. Because Israeli law has given complete control of religious life to the Orthodox Rabbinate, Conservative or Reform Judaism was not then, and still is not, permitted in the new State.[14] Consequently, on his return to the United States, Dr. Feldman bitterly attacked Israel and its practices in a statement, published throughout liberal Judaist circles, which far outdid any known criticism of the new State by anti-nationalists. Criticism of Israel, wherever an American Zionist vested interest is involved, is of course permissible.

There was, however, one servant of God who demonstrated his belief in the American tradition of free speech. Rabbi William F. Rosenblum of the Temple Israel in New York City, where I had taken my vows to universal Judaism at the age of thirteen, made the pulpit available for me to answer my critics. When it became known that, for the first time, a pulpit in the United States was being given, during Friday evening services, to a sermon on the anti-nationalist point of view, the Zionist steamroller started moving. Dr. Rosenblum was approached by the Executive Director of the American Zionist Council who, by persuasion and other means, tried to get my privilege cancelled. But the Rabbi of Temple Israel, who is neither a Zionist nor an anti-Zionist, indignantly rejected coercion when he introduced me to his synagogue audience on March 3, 1950.

Three days later, the American Zionist Council director, Dr. Jerome Unger, wrote a letter to Rabbi Rosenblum in which he said: "I yield to no one in my devotion to a free pulpit and to the right of freedom of speech. It is a nice question, however, which is giving many Americans serious concern today, as to just how far liberalism must go in providing freedom for those who would attack and undermine the very foundation of a free society (of course, I don't put Mr. Lilienthal in this latter class)." Dr. Unger noted that the *New York Times* had reported my speech and expressed fear that encouragement had been given me "to seek opportunities in other places equally receptive to his remarks." "I repeat what I said to you over the telephone—that it is too bad you had to let this come to pass. Somebody suggested that a good text for Mr. Lilienthal's address, since last Friday night was still Purim, might have been 'Esther, Chapter 3, Verses 8-9'. Maybe you would like to suggest to your confirmant his perusal of these verses and study of their implication." I took the hint and read: "And Haman said unto King Ahasuerus, There is a certain people scattered abroad and dispersed among the people in all the provinces of thy kingdom; and their laws are diverse from all people; neither keep they the king's law: therefore it is not for the king's profit to suffer them. If it please the king, let it be written that they may be destroyed: and I will pay ten thousand talents of silver to the hands of those that have the charge of the business, to bring it into the king's treasuries." (Esther 3:8-9.)

Here at least was a frank and open declaration of Zionist dogma for which I was grateful. The obvious implication to be drawn from the recommended passages is the inevitability of the persecution of Jews, and the lasting necessity of Jewish segregation and separateness: Because some 2350 years ago a cruel Persian ruler, Ahasuerus, was almost persuaded to destroy the Jews of that country, it must follow, contend the Zionists, that fully emancipated Jews, related to those Judaist Persians only in Zionist fancy, can never become integrated today and can live happily only in Israel!

At any rate, the sermon on "Israel's Flag Is Not Mine," delivered in New York's Temple Israel in spite of Zionist attempts to prevent it, was reprinted in *Vital Speeches of the Day* (April 15, 1950), together with addresses of Dwight D. Eisenhower, Bernard Baruch, and J. Howard McGrath, and it seemed that the truth, if not yet on the march, was at least beginning to toddle along.

It had been an up-hill struggle since that early Sunday morning two years earlier in Washington. The phone had startled me from a sound sleep, and a voice with a slightly foreign accent said:

"Are you the rat who wrote that letter to the *Post* which appeared this morning?"

"Who is this?"

"This is Joseph Halutz of the Haganah. If you don't stop, we will have you killed because you are undoing everything that we have been struggling for. You are killing innocent people."

"What did you say your name was?"

"It doesn't matter—just lay off what you are doing."

The Zionists, who had fought so hard to stifle any public suspicion that no one group could speak for all American Judaists, only intensified their activities.

A tremendous problem (at that time, and ever since) in need of public attention in America was the plight of the Arab refugees. The U. N. General Assembly was told by its Palestine Relief and Works Agency in 1952 that 880,000 Arab refugees from Palestine were placing a huge social and economic blight on the entire Middle East.[15] Why had this humanitarian question, loaded with momentous political implications for America, remained virtually unreported to the American public? A letter written in 1949 by the press adviser to Israel's Washington Embassy perhaps supplies part of the answer: it advised that anyone interested in the Arab refugee problem was to be considered "pro-Arab oriented" and hence "anti-Semitic."

As far back as 1949, this writer was anxious to tell about the Arab refugees in a national publication. The

Saturday Evening Post and *Collier's* were simply not interested. The *Reader's Digest*, as its editor-in-chief wrote to me, felt the situation was "so many-sided and provocative of violent opinions that it is particularly hard to handle." And not before the spring of 1952 did the otherwise so alertly edited *Digest* run an instructive article on the Middle East (by Dr. Stephen Penrose of the American University in Beirut), part of which was devoted to the Arab refugees. Mrs. Ethridge, by the way, had written a first-hand account of the Arab plight even prior to the publication of her book; but although practically everything she has ever written was readily published, this one piece was rejected by every U. S. magazine to which it was sent.

In the summer of 1952, the *Freeman* magazine returned an article which had been previously commissioned. The managing editor explained that the publication was simply too crowded for "Why We Are Losing the Middle East." Attached by sheer accident to the manuscript was a chit from one of the members of the staff to the editor saying that if the article was to run, "you must know of the powerful Zionist bloc against the *Freeman*. . . ."

The same article was then sent to *Esquire* and bounced back with these six words penned in explanation: "Not for us for one second."

Most of whatever I myself have managed to get into print on the subjects of Zionism and the Middle East has appeared in what "liberals" call "reactionary" publications.[16] And Willie Snow Ethridge once expressed her sincere regrets that "these articles did not appear in liberal magazines." But she is by now certainly aware that the terms "liberal" and "reactionary" have been reduced to empty slogans, meaningful only as emotional stimuli, particularly in the area with which this book is concerned. When a reactionary and repressive movement of fanatical nationalists wrapped itself in "liberal humanitarianism," it could immediately command the liberal press, exploit its venerable clichés and ensnare its unthinking audience. Even worse, the traditionally liberal press of this country has, at least in the Palestine controversy, sinned more than anybody else against the very essence of liberalism—the appeal to the reasoning and open mind in an honest debate of opposing views.

My accusation is *not* against the liberal press support of the creation of a Jewish State. As a *Herald-Tribune* editor once reminded this writer, it has been indeed an old and liberal tradition of this country to extend a helping hand to struggling small nations. Yes, it is only natural that American editors have been led to give warm encouragement to a new country, many of whose settlers had escaped the gas chambers, a country whose desert pioneering had been widely admired. But the terrible shame of American liberalism is that it has ferociously suppressed, at least within its own orbit, even the most moderate and most sympathetic opposition to high-pressure Zionism.

Who, I ask, are the liberals? The *Nation* Associates, Freda Kirchway, Henry Wallace, Clark Eichelberger, Alben Barkley, William O'Dwyer, Ludwig Lewisohn, Abba Hillel Silver, all of whom have intolerantly and ardently supported Zionism? Or Norman Thomas, Arthur Garfield Hayes, Morris Ernst, Leo Cherne, Vincent Sheean, Willie Snow Ethridge, Henry Sloane Coffin, Dorothy Thompson and Virginia Gildersleeve, who have fought this (as any other) extreme nationalism with an honest appeal to reason and with a burning compassion for the persecuted? If those who practice Voltaire are eliminated from the ranks of the liberals, only those who give lip service and refuse to shuck liberalism of its blind dogmatism will remain.

I have started to tell my own experience, and I cannot finish that story without mentioning another writer —a writer of considerably greater fame and merits than I can ever hope to achieve. Herman Wouk, the author of *Caine Mutiny*, and I sat next to each other in New York's Townsend Harris School. In those days, our disputes were about the Yankee who deserved to win the year's Most Valuable Player Award. Quite a few years later, I saw Wouk's stirring play *The Traitor* on Broadway. In that play, my old schoolmate expressed his passionate devotion to freedom of thought and warned of the dangers resulting from attempts to curtail it. I wrote Herman an enthusiastic congratulatory note. Some time later, I sent him a copy of my article, "Israel's Flag Is Not Mine." And I got an entirely unexpected answer.

Commencing with a flat statement that he was not a Zionist, Wouk wrote: "In my opinion you have committed a terrible personal blunder, probably the worst of your life . . . , by carrying your private opinion against the Jewish party called Zionists into the potent American forum of the *Digest*. I'm sure you acted in good faith. Hitler acted in good faith—he believed in what he did. You haven't committed murder, of course. But your error of judgment has been magnified to a stupendous scale, at the cost of your co-religionists." Then Wouk went on to say that there was no point in discussing the argument I had advanced. "*The better your case, the worse your error would have been.* Your proper course, if you felt so strongly about this, was to dedicate your days to spreading your view in Jewish circles, as the Zionists do." (Wouk significantly ignored the incessant propaganda Zionism carried before the general American public; and just as significantly, he axiomatically assumed the inherent separateness of the Jew.) Then Wouk cited *l'affaire* Mayer, noting that in the ensuing furor "the Editor of the *Post* was replaced, the *Post* apologized, and Mayer vanished into a vague infamy." And this is how Wouk closed his long, angry, and remarkable letter to me: "Recantation would do no good. ... I don't think you're evil or a traitor. But I think you have been a fool and have blared out your folly irreparably. The American Jewish community will survive the occurrence, but I cannot think your reputation will. ... I always thought of you kindly. Though I have spoken bluntly, I feel sorry for you. I hope you will in the painful aftermath find some way, that I can't see, to restore in some measure the damage to yourself and to Americans of Jewish faith."

In defense of my old schoolmate, I hurry to admit that obvious space limitations prevented my *Digest* article from giving Herman Wouk, the Pulitzer Prize winner, the full measure of the issues under discussion. This book, a fuller treatment, will help him in recovering his celebrated judiciousness. Or so I hope. That I am not necessarily "evil or a traitor," Wouk has generously understood from the start. Perhaps he will now learn to understand that my position is simply this: American Jews should no longer be forced, by smears and fears, to have a foreign policy separate from that of Methodists or Episcopalians. Their country cannot afford such a dichotomy.

CHAPTER VIII

There Goes the Middle East

THE Middle East—the junction of Europe, Asia and Africa—commands the world's airways. And in that strategic area, pregnant with decision, forty-five million Arabs, supported by two hundred and fifty million Moslem coreligionists throughout the world, are seething with hatred of the West. Their antagonism endangers the vital interests of the United States.

For the Russian Empire, whose westward expansion has been stopped on the Elbe, the Middle East must constitute a temptation of first magnitude. A thrust southward over the border to Azerbaijan, the northwesterly province of Iran, or down the Caspian Sea to Teheran, would secure wealthy oil lands. A Soviet penetration of the Middle East would force our position in Greece and Turkey. Russian strategy would then undoubtedly call for a further drive, through Egypt, into North Africa. The Soviet envelopment of Europe, in short, presupposes the conquest of the Middle East.

The Kremlin has long been interested in this part of the world. In November 1940, Molotov proposed to the Nazi Ambassador in Moscow an agreement between

148

Berlin and Moscow whereby the USSR would be assigned the sphere of influence "south of Batum and Baku in the general direction of the Persian Gulf, as the center of the aspirations of the Soviet Union."[1] At the end of World War II, the Soviets renewed their old claim for a direct share in the control of the Turkish Straits. When this was rejected by the Western powers, a Red coup flared up, in 1946, with the assistance of the Iranian Tudeh Party in Azerbaijan. It failed. But the Soviet aspirations have never been shelved.

After her temporary failure in Iran, Soviet Russia waged a war of nerves against Turkey, made demands for a trusteeship over part of Italy's African colonies, and otherwise started stirring up the Arab caldron. The aim of the Soviet vote in favor of the partition of Palestine was simply to drive the British out—the first step towards the larger goal of creating a vacuum throughout the entire Arab world and of forcing total Western withdrawal from the Middle East and North Africa. The creation of Israel could not fail to multiply the havoc in the area and, consequently, satellite Czechoslovakia was permitted to arm the infant state of Israel to insure the continuance of such a happy situation. Also, a disruptive wedge could be driven between the American and the British people by sharpening the Palestine issue.

Only recently has the U. S. government begun to appreciate that James Forrestal was six years ahead of his time. The Arab Land contains between 50 and 55 per cent of the estimated crude oil reserves of the world. Even today, some 1.9 million barrels of oil are produced daily in Saudi Arabia, Iran, Iraq, Kuwait, and Bahrein, while Russian production of oil, in the Soviet Union and the satellite countries, hardly exceeds a million barrels per day. This fact alone explains why the Soviets keep looking so enviously southward across the Caspian Sea. It is this Arab oil upon which Western Europe has been increasingly relying for its recovery and rearmament. In 1938, Western Europe imported 25% of its oil from the Middle East. By 1948, this figure had reached 62%; in 1950, 85%; and it is estimated that, in 1953, Western Europe will draw 97% of its requirements from the Arab world.

The area's strategic importance is tremendous. The air bases at Habbaniya (Iraq), Shu'aiba (Iraq), Dhahran, Bahrein and Heliopolis (an old American base on Payne Field, outside of Cairo), provide a crucial check to Soviet expansionism so long as they remain in anti-Communist hands: vital Soviet industries are within easy flying range of these Arab air bases.

Britain's capitulation in the Palestine dispute was a public confession of her declining power in the area. "If the Israelis can push the British out, why can't we?" became the theme of Iranian and Egyptian politics. The events in the Middle East encouraged the North African uprisings against French rule. There, the demands for "liberation from colonial oppression" were carried to such extremes that an amicable compromise seems inconceivable. The United States no longer commands enough respect to serve as a conciliator. The inhabitants of Tunisia and Morocco have been so thoroughly incited that their leaders are reluctant to accept a status within the French Union comparable to that enjoyed by the new sovereign states in Southeast Asia. And this area impinges vitally on the North Atlantic defense community. (Morocco contains five decisive U. S. strategic air bases.)

The triumph of Zionist nationalism in the Holy Land has awakened the Arab World. At first, the Arab states, completely disunited in their fight against Israel, were routed. But their hatred of the new State, combined with fear of its possible aggressive designs, drove them together. The Arab League was strengthened, and a collective-security pact signed by the seven Arab States.

An exclusively Islamic bloc, stretching from Turkey to Indonesia, had not emerged as Secretary General of the Arab League, Azzam Pasha, had hoped.

However, fifteen African and Asian nations are in the process of building a powerful "neutral" group, which includes the Philippines, India, Burma and Ceylon. This bloc tries to keep out of the gathering East-West conflict, but it dreads the further expansion of Communist influence. The "bloc" is still an informal affair, but has considerably solidified. By 1952, it was showing a great deal of cohesiveness, standing closely together on the Tunisian and Morrocan questions as well as the controversies over "apartheid" and the treatment of Indians in South Africa.

Not so long ago, the United States was in a promising position to upset Soviet strategy. The ancient Arab animosity against the West (against the "infidels") had been gradually dissolving over the years. American missionary enterprises, and generous educational, health, and social institutions in the area were beginning to pay off. The Boston Jesuit College in Baghdad, the Aleppo College,[2] the American universities at Cairo and Beirut, were educating Arab leaders well-disposed to Western ideas. Missions, the YMCA and YWCA, and the Near East Foundation were building good will, and the innate Arab suspicion of the West was dying out.

But virtually everything that private philanthropic effort had accomplished was swept away by the U. S. Government's Palestine policy: the United States completely disregarded the Arab viewpoint in the Palestine controversy and forced partition down the throats of all smaller nations. Friendly U. S. mediation could have quelled the extreme nationalist outbreaks, but the U. S. Government chose precisely the role the Soviets wanted it to play—the role of the Zionist strongman.

The bitterness of the Arab states toward Israel is expressed in the fanatical saying one can currently hear throughout the Arab world: "We would rather have a Russian alliance than countenance a Jewish state on Arab soil." The United States never took this threat seriously, but the Soviets did. They are drawing closer to the Arabs and driving the West farther away. The violence which engulfs the entire Moslem world in a virtual holy war has been encouraged by an increasing number of Communist agents; indeed, the Party is evident in every street fight.

Arab nationalism would have flowered eventually, even without the partition of Palestine. But the U. S. partisanship in favor of Israel made it impossible to moderate the nationalistic movements of the Middle East. And what the partition policy left undone in arousing the Arab world's anti-Western passions, the U. S. has finally accomplished with its callous neglect of the Arab refugees from Palestine.

Almost one million Arabs were displaced from their homes or totally impoverished by the Holy Land War of 1948, scattered throughout the hills of Judea and Samaria, in the Gaza region of Philistia, in the Jordan Valley, in the highlands of Ammon and Gilead. The United Nations, which had in two solemn resolutions guaranteed the return of these refugees, first provided seven cents a day per refugee, and then recommended a program of combined relief and work projects. At the U. N.

session of 1951, another relief program was voted—but nothing effective has been accomplished to this day. Meanwhile, the Arab refugees are being subjected to anti-Western propaganda which argues, with great effectiveness, how generously America has customarily treated refugees who had not been her responsibility— and how terribly she neglects those Arab refugees who are a direct American responsibility: are they not victims of U. S. pressure on the United Nations?

Officially, the Communist Parties are outlawed in the Arab states, but they operate underground and, on many fronts, publicly. They have deeply infiltrated the nationalist movements, perhaps beyond any chance of separation. But with some help and encouragement from us, they could have been checked. Instead, the U. S. Government did everything to encourage the marriage of convenience between the Communists and the extreme nationalists.

Charles Malik, Ambassador to the United States from Lebanon, and Chairman of the Human Rights Commission of the U. N. (a true statesman and a profound philosopher), wrote in the *Foreign Affairs Quarterly* (January, 1952): "If the present arrogance, defiance and ambition are to persist, and if Israel is to be again and again confirmed in her feeling that she is to be favored—just because the U. S., owing to the position of the Jews in this country and to certain well-known peculiarities in the American political and social system, to widespread ignorance in the United States of real conditions in the Near East and also to a certain genuine, well-meaning goodness of heart on the part of American people, will at the crucial moment always decisively side with Israel against her immediate world—then I am afraid there will never be peace in the Near East and the U. S. cannot be altogether innocent of responsibility for that situation." There has seldom been a more complete diagnosis of a complete mess.

Between November 1948 and June 1953, the new State of Israel received from this country, in governmental grants, loans, Point Four assistance, and U. S. surplus agricultural commodities, some 295 million dollars.[3] This, of course, is over and beyond the more than 600 million dollars contributed by private American sources, and the revenue from the sale of Israel Bonds (a three-year program of an additional 500 million dollars). After the 1950 Washington Conference of Jewish groups, Israel's financial influx from the U. S. for 1950-1953 was set at one billion dollars. This is the aid given a country of 1,600,000 inhabitants, a country of approximately 7,800 square miles, or about three quarters of the size of the State of Vermont.

The seven Arab countries which surround Israel have a combined area three hundred times as large and a population thirty times as numerous. From November 1948 to June 1953, the governments of Egypt, Yemen, Saudi-Arabia, Lebanon, Syria, Iraq, and Jordan have been given 88 million dollars for economic development by way of U. S. grants, loans and Point Four assistance. Another 153 million dollars was contributed to Arab refugee relief (not to the individual states where the refugees are subsisting, but to a United Nations agency). But this latter sum has been spent on keeping Arabs alive who had been displaced from their homes in Israel—not on developing the Arab countries. Remittances to the Arab states from private U. S. sources have of course been negligible. The staggering financial U. S. support to Israel was noted in a magazine article "Washington Comes to Israel's Economic Rescue"[4] by Hal Lehrman, a staunch defender of U. S. Israeli policies. Mr. Lehrman showed that Israel heads the list of all countries aided by the United States on "a per capita basis, with the possible exception of Greece, in terms of total cash made available for every man, woman and child." And this calculation refers only to public U. S. funds, not to the considerably greater sums that have flown into Israel through the channels of private American philanthropy, investment and loans.

The conventional rationale for U. S. favoritism towards Israel is the new State's democratic nature. Mark Ethridge, the publisher of the Louisville *Courier Journal*, made a pertinent observation on that subject, in an address before the University of Virginia's Institute of Public Affairs, in 1952. Though a staunch defender of the Truman foreign policy in other areas, Mr. Ethridge said: "The cliché that Israel is the bulwark of democracy in the Middle East is the veriest nonsense. Israel cannot be a bulwark as long as she is propped up with gifts and loans, imported oil from Venezuela and meat from Argentina, and is not at peace and trade with her Arab neighbors."[5] Indeed, if a proportionate amount of money had gone into the Arab world, the U. S. would be amazed how much difference some twenty-five billion dollars can make in the "democratic" posture of backward countries!

More than two fifths of Israel's population are people from Arab states and from North Africa, and this proportion is steadily increasing.[6] If the Israelis from Russia and Eastern Europe (who never experienced democracy) are added to these Middle Easterners, the social basis for an indigenously democratic structure shrinks perceptibly.

The real failure of the Truman Administration was its

lack of a global plan into which all regional policies ought to have fitted. If the containment of Communism was the primary goal, all foreign policies ought to have been subordinated to this end. Once Communist expansion had been recognized as the central danger, it should have been obvious that the balance of world power rested with the Arab-Asian nations whose vast populace and natural resources separate the free and the enslaved spheres. Among these nations, the U. S. Palestine policy has made many enemies, and no friend. It was never adequately appreciated in this country that the United Nations Palestine decision had the affirmative support—and much of it lukewarm—of nations with the population of only 560 million (including the Soviet Union's 193 million). The representatives of 480 million people opposed it, while the abstaining eleven delegations represented no less than 620 million people. In other words, the U. S. pursued a course which only 33.5% of the total world population approved, while 28.9% opposed it and 37.5% had abstained from expressing their preference. The U. S. position deteriorates even more if one considers the more than 400 million people of North Africa, Burma, Manchuria, Indonesia and Japan, who were not members of the U. N. in 1947. The plain truth is that the United States has put all its eggs in one of the Middle East's smallest baskets.

The complaints of Morocco and Tunisia against France, brought before the United Nations by the Arab-Asian-African bloc, further complicated the West's relationship with these countries. On December 13, 1951, the United States voted in the U. N. General Assembly for the postponement of the Moroccan issue; in April 1952 it refused to take up the question of Tunisia in the Security Council and, a few weeks later, it refrained from joining a request for a Special Session of the General Assembly to consider these issues. The Moroccan and Tunisian questions were finally placed on the agenda of the 7th General Assembly, but in the subsequent debate and vote, the United States found it proper to espouse the French position.

At that General Assembly session a group of eight smaller powers offered a resolution inviting Israel and the Arab States to settle their differences. The Arab states opposed this proposal on the ground that past directives of the United Nations, concerning the internationalization of Jerusalem and the rights of the Arab refugees, had first to be accepted by Israel before any further negotiations could be justified. Still, the Special Political Committee adopted the resolution by 32 to 13 votes, the Soviet bloc abstaining. In the General Assembly, where a two-thirds majority was required, the resolution was defeated. Seven Latin-American countries[7] had joined the Arab side, quite likely influenced by a *New York Times* interview with David Ben-Gurion in which the Israeli Prime Minister declared that the status of Jerusalem was a settled fact and no issue for further talks. This was in clear defiance of the United Nations which had on three occasions voted for the internationalization of Jerusalem and authorized the Palestine Conciliation Commission and the Trusteeship Council to draw up the necessary statute.[8] In 1950, the General Assembly rejected a Swedish Draft resolution which would have provided an international regime over the Holy Places only, rather than over the entire city. The obvious intent of the U. N. has been effectively sabotaged to this day. With Jordan holding the old city, the new city of Jerusalem has become, for all practical purposes, the capital of Israel; however, the U. S. and some other countries, including those of South America, have refused to move their diplomatic staffs from Tel Aviv, hoping that the thrice resolved internationalization will eventually be realized.

In the final balloting on the resolution calling for direct talks between Israel and the Arab states, the Arabs also received the five votes of the Soviet bloc which, as in the voting on the North African questions, supported the Arab-African-Asian bloc against Britain, France and the United States. Each of the Arab Foreign Offices filed a protest with their respective British Ambassador against Britain's pro-Israel vote. The attitude of the Naguib Government toward the British stiffened, and U. S. prestige in the Arab countries dwindled further. Arab faith in the principles of democratic government as practiced by the West was once more weakened, and the Russians were made to appear champions of freedom.

Throughout its existence, from 1917 to 1953, the Soviet Government has been anything but pro-Zionist though shrewd tactical calculations made it vote in favor of Palestine partition. But even when supporting partition in 1947, Soviet Ambassador Gromyko reminded the Arab representatives in the General Assembly that the USSR and the Soviet people "still entertain a feeling of sympathy for the national aspirations of the Arab East. . . . The USSR is convinced that the Arab States will still on more than one occasion be looking toward Moscow and expecting the USSR to help them in the struggle for their lawful interest, in their efforts to cast off the last vestige of foreign dependence."

Within Israel, it is the Jewish Communists who express the deepest concern for the Arab refugees and object to the imposition of second-class citizenship on the Arab minority centered in and around Nazareth.

The Soviet Union's diplomatic break with Israel and the Cominform's fervid anti-Zionist propaganda could not help but please the Arabs, however suspicious their more enlightened leaders may have been of Soviet motives.

While Soviet Russia made her Eastern Zone of Germany court the Arabs, Western Germany, under U. S. influence, courted the State of Israel. After lengthy negotiations, the Bonn Government agreed in September, 1952, to pay 715 million dollars towards the cost of absorbing uprooted victims of Nazism in Israel, and to give an additional 107 million dollars to 22 Jewish organizations in the United States, as a payment for heirless and unclaimed Jewish assets in Germany. The payments are to be made in goods, over a twelve-year period, to bolster the Israeli economy. And to meet these obligations, West Germany would seek a loan—presumably in the United States.

But the claim of Jewish organizations in the United States to the property of deceased and heirless Jewish individuals in Europe—a claim resting upon the premise of the existence of a Jewish racial and national community—perpetrates the very racialism which destroyed these individuals. Restitution to surviving victims of Nazi bestiality, and to the families of those who were murdered, is a German moral obligation to individuals—not to the State of Israel or to American organizations.

The Arab states, still technically at war with Israel, claimed that such German payments to Israel would be a breach of German neutrality. Nor were the Arab leaders unmindful that the Communist East-German Government had rejected a 500 million dollar reparations claim of the Israeli Government.

Another calculated effect of the Soviet Government's quarrel with the Israeli Government was Arab panic over Israel's demand, supported by thirty-one Zionist organizations in the United States, that two and a half million Jews from behind the Iron Curtain be moved to Israel. To the Arabs, this implied Israeli expansion into the neighboring Arab countries: the "Greater Israel" idea, long held by Begin, Jabotinsky and other Zionist "revisionists," would receive an enormous impetus by such a fantastic wave of immigration.

The sweeping American analogies drawn between recent Soviet policies and the anti-Semitism of Hitler served still another Soviet objective: the more that Soviet policy was interpreted as anti-Semitism, the more deeply grew American sympathies for Israel and, conversely, the more the United States stiffened against any rapprochement with the Arab countries. And nothing could please the Soviet Government more.

CHAPTER IX

The Mugwumps and
the Cult of Doom

ALL Palestine problems revolve around the question: What is a Jew? Israel now contains a people with a common language (modern Hebrew), with a land and a government of its own, and with a common history. Israel, in short, is truly a nation.

There are people of the Judaic faith who live in Israel and are Israelis. Many more people who practice the same faith live outside that small Middle Eastern State, and clearly do not belong to that nation. There is nothing extraordinary in this. The entire Western world is populated by peoples who share religion, but not nationality, with other peoples.

Yet the attitude of the new State of Israel towards the Jews in the rest of the world, and of those Jews toward that state, involves a concept of *Jewish* nationalism, not *Israeli* nationalism.

Nationalism is a sentiment of a group of people who desire to become, or to develop even more distinctly into, a separate nation. The core of Jewish nationalism is the belief that there is a world-wide Jewish people which constitutes a distinct Jewish nation. Although the Jewish nation had ceased to exist in 70 A. D., a sentiment has persisted down through the ages that it still was alive, though in exile and without a country. And with the birth of Israel, the collective nation is said to have been "reconstituted" in that State, the reputed national home of every Jew. Jewish nationalism is that composite concept of race, nation, people, culture and community, often described with such adjectives as separate, distinct, different and chosen.

Diaspora (meaning dispersion) is the term used by Jewish nationalists to describe the status of those Jews who live outside of Israel. The term of course implies that this status is unnatural; and Zionism indeed refers to these Jews as living in the *Galut* (in exile). Diaspora nationalism insists that these exiles, wherever they may be, nevertheless constitute a nation and that they are to be "ingathered" into Israel by the process of *Kibbutz Galloyot*.

The propagation of Jewish nationalism is not confined to the Zionist movement. Historical, anthropological, sociological, psychological, theological and philanthropic factors constantly generate this nationalism. Zionism is merely its political arm. It seeks to transform Judaism, the religion, into a world-wide Jewish nation with its political center in Israel: while many Jews will not be living there immediately, the established State is, nevertheless, to be regarded as the central reality around which their existence is to revolve. The long-term goal of Zionism is the liquidation of the diaspora and the eventual return of all Jews to Zion.

Like the biblical Joseph, Jewish nationalism wears a coat of many colors. It cannot be analyzed solely in terms of conscious allegiance to Israel. There are subtler forms of allegiance, a vaguer and less tangible acceptance of unity and oneness: the waving of the Israeli flag; the singing of the "Hatikvah"; claims that Jews are "One people" and Israel "The Jewish State"; the assertion that there is a political unity amongst Americans of Jewish faith; the use of that alleged unity to pressure the American government; the many separatist *political* activities of Jews as Jews. Less subtle are the Zionist campaigns to introduce modern (not biblical) Hebrew and Israeli customs onto the American Jewish scene.

Israeli nationalism is a communal sentiment of people who live within the borders of Israel. Jewish nationalism knows no borders. Israeli nationalism is natural and understandable. Jewish nationalism is abnormal and incomprehensible.

Jewish nationalists are fervent propagandists of their secular faith. This was true even when the British still governed Palestine. I first realized this in 1944, when a young man from Henrietta Szold's office conducted me through the modern city of Tel Aviv. I was then an American soldier in the Middle East, stationed in Cairo, and had flown on leave to the U. S. rest camp of Tel Levinsky, just outside the city. I found in Palestine tremendous human achievement, turning a desert into a flourishing community, and I expressed my admiration to the guide. Whereupon he never stopped for a minute his efforts toward converting me. His love of his hardworked Palestinian soil was a wholesome manifestation of Israeli nationalism. But his attempt to make me, an American soldier on leave, feel his, a Palestinian's pride, his sense of belonging, and his responsibility for the State-to-be, was Jewish Nationalism.

While in Jerusalem, I visited Mr. and Mrs. Jacob Steinhardt, refugees from Germany who would not think of living in the United States because of "the American pogroms" about which they had been told. Mr. Steinhardt is a distinguished artist, one of Israel's finest, and the couple lived in an attractive studio house near Ben Yehudah Street. But when I saw them, they (particularly Mrs. Steinhardt) did not like Palestine. They felt little kinship with the people around them and almost yearned for Germany. Then came the proclamation of Israeli statehood and the war with the Arabs. And a few years later, it was quite a different Mrs. Steinhardt whom I met in New York at an exhibition of her husband's woodcuts and paintings. Her previous apathy towards Palestine had been supplanted by love of the nation for whose birth she had helped to fight. The overflowing idealism that now filled her soul was in no way a religious feeling. It was political love of country. She had found her new Germany in Israel. The only thing that I thought objectionable was her intense impatience with any criticism of Israel, or its leaders, and her resentment that anyone who called himself a Jew should not feel precisely as she did. More than a modicum of Jewish nationalism had crept into her Israeli nationalism. Mrs. Steinhardt was honestly convinced that Jewry in the United States was far from being safe from another Hitler—"if it happened to us in Germany, certainly it could happen to you in America."

While Americans were led to believe that an Israeli State had been set up as a refuge, and were accordingly contributing hundreds of millions of dollars, thousands of Steinhardts in Israel were led to believe that the financial support from the United States rested, not upon philanthropy, but upon an acceptance of their nationalist dogma. To those people in the new Middle Eastern State, the "Jewish People," United Jewish Appeal, and Zionism were all one and the same. It all merely represented, to them, varying facets of the distinct and separate world-wide entity, of which Israel was the embodiment.

Now it is Sunday evening, May 1945, in San Francisco. Diplomatic leaders of the victorious allied countries have gathered to set up the United Nations Organization. Many of these delegates, some of whom were thirty months later to decide the Palestine question at Lake Success, are part of a distinguished audience that overflows an auditorium. And this is what they hear: "We want to go home . . . home . . . home. We must go home!"

This was not the pathetic cry of a homeless war victim, not the wail of a lost child. This came from the lips of one of America's most gifted orators, the world-renowned Rabbi Stephen Wise, "speaking in the name of ten million Jews." His claim: that the widely scattered followers of a universal religious belief, members of many nationalities, were all descendants of the ancient Hebrews, and hence members of a world-wide Jewish nation with its center in Palestine.

No one in the United States had a more profound influence on American Jewry than Dr. Wise. As a Rabbi of the Reform Movement, he was able to reach and persuade many who would have rejected the straight Zionist approach. It was he who announced from the pulpit: "I am not an American citizen of Jewish faith. I am a Jew. I am an American. I have been an American 63/64ths of my life, but I have been a Jew for 4000 years."[1]

But the American Jews whom Rabbi Wise converted to Jewish nationalism seemed to like, personally, their "diaspora." Only a corporal's guard had availed themselves of the opportunity "to go home to Palestine." And those who did, went to colonize the Holy Land—not to found a State. When Sir Moses Montefiore visited Palestine in 1837, there lived some 9,000 Jews in Jerusalem, Safad, Tiberias and Hebron. This wealthy Englishman, who died at the age of 101, spent the last half of his long life in helping those who wished to "return for the observance of the holy religion."[2] The settlements he started, and the ones Baron Edmond de Rothschild supported after him, benefited the new colonists and threatened no Arab settler.

It was not until the decade before World War I that *nationalist* settlements were started in Palestine. The initial goal of the Zionist organization was the modest one of obtaining a "legally secured home for the Jewish people." At first, Jewish nationalists were interested in the existence, *not* the location, of such a "home." Herzl almost broke up the Zionist organization in 1903 by his willingness to accept a British offer to establish that "national home" in Uganda (or Kenya, as it is known today) in British East Africa. Just so, the British offer of an autonomous territory made by Joseph Chamberlain and Lord Lansdowne to Herzl constituted the diplomatic recognition Zionism had been seeking: it was the first time that a big power had officially negotiated with the representatives of "the Jewish people," and it came at a time when the civilized world, anguished by the Kishinev Pogrom of 1903, felt a sincere moral obligation to rescue persecuted Jews.

A young Russian from the townlet of Motol, in the province of Minsk, led the opposition at the Seventh Zionist World Congress, in 1905, that finally killed the British proposal. His name was Chaim Weizmann. Weizmann's own father had voted in favor of the Uganda proposal at the Congress of 1903, but the other delegates voted almost solidly against it, the younger Weizmann among them. When the Ugandists scored a temporary victory with the appointment of an investigating committee, the Russian intransingents walked out. Herzl, whose ingenuity and leadership had given Zionism its first impetus, died shortly thereafter, a profoundly disappointed man.

There have been other Jewish nationalists who did not insist on Zion as the only acceptable site for the Jewish State. Probably the best known of these was Israel Zangwill who broke with the Zionist World Organization when it rejected, in 1904, all colonizing activities outside of Palestine, the Uganda offer in particular. Zangwill and his followers formed the Jewish Territorial Organization "for those Jews who cannot and will not remain in the land in which they live at present." This organization was disbanded after the British had granted the Balfour Declaration.

But for Weizmann, and the Eastern European Zionists, it was Palestine or nothing. Their concept of nation was one of fated racialism: to them, what made a person a Jew was not his practice of the Judaistic faith (many of them being, in point of fact, unabashed atheists); suffice he was *born* "a Jew"—and once a Jew, always a Jew. Underlying that concept was a deep despair, a cult of exclusivity combined with a sense of doom. Its central tenets were the axiomatic conviction that anti-Semitism can not be erased from this earth, and the equally axiomatic assumption that Jews cannot live a normal life outside Israel.

This philosophy of despair has become, and has remained, the philosophy of Zionism. The State of Israel has been created by a movement which believes that Jews can live in dignity only when settled in a land of their own, a land totally Jewish in language, custom, culture, and government. Religion has not been perchance omitted from this listing: Zionism is more than ever profoundly indifferent to the Judaist faith. But in order to sell itself in a Western world, which had long ago liberated the Jews from the confinements of the ghetto, that political cult of doom assumed the vernacular of compassionate humanitarianism. Power politics were made up to look like philanthropy.

In America, it was particularly difficult to plant Zionism as a reaction to inexorable anti-Semitism. What real persecution have Jews experienced in this country, save in the recesses of their imagination? But some American Jews are able to imagine so vividly that the lash of European anti-Semitism burrowed much more deeply into their skins than it affected the inmates of Dachau. Thousands of Dachau graduates came to this country and revel in its air of freedom. Thousands of Displaced Persons refused to think that their Zion could be anywhere but here. But American Jews, who had known nothing but the comforts of this land, became Zionists. That a philosophy which insists upon reviving the self-segregating notions of Europe's ancient ghettos, should have taken any hold in the United States, where religious Judaism for generations had the opportunity of flowering with magnificence and dignity, is no doubt one of the strangest paradoxes of the age. Nevertheless, it is a fact of American life; and a fact of perilous explosiveness.

If Weizmann was the political genius of Zionism, and Herzl its philosopher, Ahad Ha-am (born Asher Ginsberg) was its spiritual father. His concern was Jewish cultural development. Without an inner rehabilitation, he argued, there was no sense in any political solution of the problems of European Jewry. He trusted that spontaneous influences would emanate from a spiritual

Jewish society, "so that the word of the Lord could go forth once more from Zion." In a letter to Weizmann, in 1918, Ha-am spoke of a "University which from the very beginning will endeavor to become the true embodiment of the Hebrew spirit of old." And seven years later, indeed, the Hebrew University of Jerusalem came into being.

The early leaders of American Zionism were humanitarians, scholars and intellectuals who, like Ahad Ha-am, were interested, not in politics and statehood, but in education and culture. Much of the early American money contributed to Palestine went to the University. Dr. Judah L. Magnes, Professor Albert Einstein, and Supreme Court Justice Louis D. Brandeis, whose attachment to Palestine centered on the University, were vigorously opposed to the conception of Jewry as a political entity.

A great legend has been built around Supreme Court Justice Brandeis by Jewish nationalism. However broadly he may have interpreted legal language on the Supreme Court bench, the Justice believed in a literal interpretation of the Balfour Declaration. As firmly as he supported the Jewish colonization of Palestine, he opposed Jewish Statehood. Once the British Government had granted the Declaration, and the development of a cultural center had commenced in the early twenties, Brandeis believed there was no longer need for Zionist political work.[3] This won him Weizmann's deep-seated enmity.

When Weizmann sought U. S. financial support for the Zionist budget, he was distressed by the low figure of $500,000—the maximum Brandeis would grant from the United States.[4] Weizmann managed to raise two million dollars the very first year; and the breach between the two men widened.

Brandeis rejected the concept of an organic unity of World Jewry and opposed a World Zionist Organization: he advocated separate and clearly defined responsibilities of autonomous country organizations rather than the centralism of one international organization. Weizmann's Palestine Foundation Fund in the United States was set up, in 1921, over the bitter protest of Brandeis whose Zionism was humanitarian, not a "folk renaissance."[5]

Weizmann himself approvingly notes that the Brandeis-Weizmann schism was popularly marked "Washington vs. Pinsk"—a rather apt formula to describe the fact that here, indeed, American free society had collided with the Russian ghetto. This is how a pro-Zionist 1949 study of the conflict[6] summarized the Brandeis position: "The Brandeis conception stripped Zionism of the literary nationalism upon which so many of its adherents thrived. He wanted to rebuild Palestine for those Jews who needed a homeland plain and simple. It was 'a Zion without Zionism,' his critics said. . . . In his concentration on Palestine, he refused strong support for Hebrew education in the countries of the diaspora and was cold towards Jewish relief organizations." Justice Brandeis looked askance at the "looseness of many budgetary practices" and the intermingling of funds collected for charitable, cultural, economic and political purposes.

And yet, in spite of this unmistakable record, the name of Justice Brandeis has been recklessly exploited by Zionism here and abroad—in this manner, for instance: "Again we must emphasize that *Camp Brandeis* (near Hancock, N. Y.) is a miniature Palestine and that the pattern of life in it is that of Eretz Israel—Reveille is sounded at 6 in the morning and at 6:10 the Stars and Stripes and the Blue-White flags are hoisted to the tunes of 'Star Spangled Banner' and the 'Hatikvah.' " Regrettably, none of the Justice's family and friends protested against the abuse of his name for an enterprise that teaches American youngsters allegiance to a foreign flag.

On the death of Chaim Weizmann (November 9, 1952), Professor Albert Einstein was informally offered the Presidency of Israel. Prime Minister Ben-Gurion instructed Israeli Ambassador, Abba S. Eban, to ascertain whether Einstein would accept if elected. Dr. Ezriel Carlebach, the editor of *Maariv*, largest newspaper in Israel, nominated Einstein with the assertion, "he belongs to us, not to Princeton University."

But even the least careful study of Dr. Einstein's attitude towards Israel should have shown how little he did belong to "us." Dr. Einstein was always intensely interested in the Hebrew University. When Dr. Weizmann went on his first visit to the United States, in April 1921, Professor Einstein was invited to come along, with "special reference to the Hebrew University."[8] This was the time of Weizmann's fight with Brandeis over the scope of Zionism, and Einstein privately sympathized with the Brandeis position which "reflected a denial of Jewish nationalism" (Weizmann's words). Yet Einstein's sole interest was the University, and he refrained from participation in the political battle royal. In 1950, when the American Joint Board of Directors merged with the Weizmann Institute of Science, he became its President. His statements in support of the Hebrew University were continually blown up by Zionist publicity into endorsements of Zionism. They never were any such thing.

Testifying before the Anglo-American Committee of Inquiry in January, 1946 (in answer to the specific question whether refugee settlement in Palestine demanded

a Jewish State), Dr. Einstein stated: "The State idea
is not according to my heart. I cannot understand why
it is needed. It is connected with narrow-mindedness and
economic obstacles. I believe it is bad, I have always been
against it." He derided the Jewish Commonwealth concept as "an imitation of Europe, the end of which was
brought about by nationalism."

In 1948, Einstein publicly and wholeheartedly supported the views of the Dr. Magnes who favored the
establishment of an Arab-Jewish bi-national State in
Palestine and attacked Zionist terrorism and violence.
In a letter to the *New York Times*, Dr. Einstein thus
endorsed the position of Dr. Magnes and his followers:
"Besides the fact that they speak for a much wider circle
of inarticulate people, they speak in the name of principles which have been the most significant contribution
of the Jewish people to humanity."[9]

On April 1, 1952, Dr. Einstein spoke (in a message
to the Children To Palestine, Inc.) of the necessity to
curb "a kind of nationalism" which has arisen in Israel
"if only to permit a friendly and fruitful co-existence
with the Arabs." Olivia Terrell, Executive Secretary of
the organization, later admittedly censored this portion
of Einstein's message in the press release. Her explanation: "Our only concern is with the welfare of children
. . . not with any political aspects. A Children-To-Pal-
estine dinner is no place for a statement like that."[10]

This act of Zionist censorship took me to Princeton
to seek Professor Einstein's views on the incident. Dr.
Einstein told me that, strangely enough, he had never
been a Zionist and had never favored the creation of the
State of Israel. Also, he told me of a significant conversation with Weizmann. Einstein had asked him: "What
about the Arabs if Palestine were given to the Jews?"

And Weizmann said: "What Arabs? They are hardly of any consequence."

Professor Einstein's *Out of My Later Years* (N. Y.: Philosophical Library, 1950), contains this unequivocal statement of his position: "I should much rather see a reasonable agreement with the Arabs on the basis of living together than the creation of a Jewish state. Apart from practical considerations, my awareness of the essential nature of Judaism resists the idea of a Jewish state with borders, an army, and a measure of temporal power no matter how modest. I am afraid of the inner damage Judaism will sustain."

In his authoritative book,[11] Professor Philipp Frank speaks of Einstein's deep opposition to nationalism which found succinct expression in his opposition to "substituting a Jewish nationalism for a German nationalism." According to Dr. Frank, Einstein had the goodhearted weakness to lend his name to the *whole* of the Zionist platform though he believed in only *one* of its planks. He hesitated to rebuke Zionists here or in Israel for frequent manipulations of his views. In his modest manner, he declined the Israel Presidency on the limited ground that he was not qualified in the area of human relationships. And the Zionists continue to use Einstein's name to enhance their prestige and their political purse.

There is a considerable symbolic meaning in the accidental fact that Weizmann, the creator of modern Zionism, was a great chemist. For his political Zionism was concocted of the strangest and often hardly compatible elements: the clannishness of the nationalist Jew; the propitiatory uneasiness of the "reluctant Jew" (Waldo Frank, in his *The Jew In Our Day*,[12] calls him "inertial Jew"); the conscience of a disturbed Christian world; the philanthropy of the rich; the need of the poor to cluster together; the generosity of America; the orthodoxy of the religious Judaist; the political passion of the atheist; the modern dread of loneliness; the pride of the socially frustrated and therefore politically ambitious intelligentsia; the romanticism of the "cultural Jew"; the hardboiled greed of the metropolitan professional politician. All these, and more, components Weizmann mixed thoroughly, and then he added the masterful final touch—the coloring of humanitarianism which protected his extraordinary concoction against any analytical criticism.

Alone, the Zionists would never have settled Palestine. Palestine was settled by the coalition efforts of Anglo-Saxon Christians (such as Balfour, Lloyd George, Winston Churchill), who were powerfully moved by the Anglo-Saxon's devotion to the Old Testament, and outstanding non-Zionist Jewish families of the Western world, whose Judaic traditions made philanthropy the crowning justification of their wealth. But the Montefiores, the Rothschilds, the Schiffs, the Warburgs, the Rosenwalds, the Marshalls, the Lehmans and the Morgenthaus have, until a few years ago, always detested political Zionism.

In a speech at the Menorah Society Dinner in December, 1917, Chief Judge Irving Lehman, brother of U. S. Senator Herbert H. Lehman, welcomed the position of the British Government on Palestine, but added that "ardent Zionists though some of you may be, I feel that you agree with me that politically we can be part of one nation only, and that nation is America."[13] And: "Not as a group apart must the Jews survive here, but they must maintain here, as elsewhere, their ancient ideals and traditions and contribute to the culture of the American people, of which they form an integral part, the

strength of their ideals and the strength of their traditions." Judge Lehman recognized that the problem of
Judaism—unsolved to this day—was how to keep the
faith alive now that "it has become a part and not, as
formerly, the whole of our lives." He went on: "I cannot for an instant recognize that the Jews as such constitute a nation in any sense in which that word is recognized in political science, or that a national basis is a
possible concept for modern Judaism. We Jews in America, bound to the Jews of other lands by our common
faith, constituting our common inheritance, cannot as
American citizens feel any bond to them as members
of a nation, for nationally we are Americans and Americans only, and in political and civic matters we cannot
recognize any other ties. We must therefore look for
the maintenance of Judaism to those spiritual concepts
which constitute Judaism."

Henry Morgenthau, Sr. (the father of the man who
now heads the Israeli Bond drive), stated in his autobiography: "Zionism is the most stupendous fallacy in
Jewish history. It is wrong in principle and impossible
of realization; it is unsound in its economics, fantastical
in its politics and sterile in its spiritual ideals. Where it
is not pathetically visionary, it is cruel, playing with the
hopes of a people blindly seeking their way out of age-
long miseries."

Jacob Schiff, Julius Rosenwald, Felix Warburg and
Henry Morgenthau, Sr., would not have permitted all
the Hitlers in the world to change their basic philosophy.
These men were not just non-Zionists; they were passionate antinationalists. How chagrined they would be
to see those who inherited their fortunes and their good
names, so cruelly deceived and exploited by nationalists
in humanitarian clothing! Weizmann, by the way, ex-

plains, rather cynically, how it happened that so many antinationalist U. S. Jews erected on the American scene the very props of a separatist movement of which they wanted no part: "Those wealthy Jews who could not wholly divorce themselves from a feeling of responsibility toward their people, but at the same time could not identify themselves with the hopes of the masses, were prepared with a sort of left-handed generosity, on condition that their right hand did not know what their left hand was doing. To them the university-to-be in Jerusalem was philanthropy, which did not compromise them; to us it was National Renaissance. They would give—with disclaimers. We would accept—with reservations."[14]

These reservations were carefully concealed from the donors. Weizmann realized the enormity of his task, and his need to win the financial support of antinationalist U. S. Jews. To Louis Marshall, he had this to say (when Marshall suggested that it would cost half a billion dollars to build up Palestine): "We'll need much more. The money is there, in the pockets of the American Jews. It's your business and my business to get at some of it."[15]

And get at it the Zionists did. In 1929, the Jewish Agency (the official liaison between Palestine Jews and Jewry outside) was enlarged to include Americans whose deep concern for coreligionists abroad had heretofore been expressed solely through the philanthropy of the Joint Distribution Committee. Many heretofore antinationalist U. S. Jews were now neutralized to be merely non-Zionists. More stubborn anti-Zionists soon tired of being outvoted in the Jewish Agency and surrendered their seats, which were immediately filled by nationalists.

In 1939, the non-Zionist Joint Distribution Commit-

176

tee (J.D.C.) and the Zionist United Palestine Appeal virtually merged in a single fund-raising drive, the United Jewish Appeal (U.J.A.). The J.D.C. then received approximately 60 per cent of funds raised. Yet the 1952 agreement between the two groups gave the J.D.C. about 20 per cent of the first 55 million dollars raised, and less than 10% of all receipts above that figure. The overwhelming remainder now goes to the United Israel Appeal (successor to the United Palestine Appeal). The nationalists had captured the fund-raising machinery.

The American Jewish Committee, whose purpose is "to prevent the infraction of the civil and religious rights of Jews in any part of the world," was formed with the same non-nationalist intent originally behind the J.D.C., and by some of the same men. The A.J.C. courageously resisted the continued pressure to bring about a Zionist-controlled holding company of all Jewish organizations, "speaking for American Jewry." At the UN Conference at San Francisco, A.J.C. Chairman, Judge Joseph Proskauer, frowned on the Zionists lobbying for statehood. While the A.J.C. theoretically still opposes the Zionist brand of Jewish nationalism, practically, however, the A.J.C. has become the most effective force in promoting nationalist political goals, both before and since the creation of Israel.

For many years, Rabbi Stephen S. Wise had been on the closest terms with President Roosevelt—until the President became tired of his dramatic antics and incessant rantings over "inadequate political support being given to the Zionist cause." Wise became too virile a desk-pounder even for the sympathetic Roosevelt. When F.D.R. refused to see Wise, non-Zionists filled the gap. Eugene Meyer, former Chairman of the Board of the Reconstruction Finance Corporation and owner of the

Washington Post, frequently acted as an intermediary between A.J.C. and the White House. Under Truman, a much more direct liaison was maintained between the White House Executive Office and the Committee. In his report[16] to the annual meeting, the A.J.C. President boasted "of the ready access to the White House and of serving as a catalyst between our Government and the Jewish Agency." The Zionists would have been powerless without A.J.C. help in the crucial days of November, 1947, when extra votes were needed to insure a two-thirds majority in the United Nations.

The American Jewish Committee has vigorously opposed anti-Zionist criticism. Its pamphlets, justifying the Israeli position both on the Arab refugee problem and on the internationalization of Israel (in direct opposition to the United Nations), have been widely distributed. In its own words, the A.J.C. "continues to stimulate pro-Israel feeling among the American people, particularly over radio and television."[17] Speaking to a group of Yiddish writers and journalists, A.J.C.'s Mr. Jacob Blaustein told his listeners that "American Jews must labor with all their might to guarantee the existence of the Israeli State. . . . Israel's failure would be a terrible blow for American Jews. . . . "[18] This A.J.C. leader also referred to the assistance given to Israeli diplomats in Washington by his organization, and assailed the Rosenwald group for raising an "artificial issue of 'divided loyalty'." The American Jewish Committee helps forcefully in the U.J.A. drive and was the vital force behind the Israeli Bond sale in the U. S.

A few times, the A.J.C. clashed with the official leaders of political Zionism—usually when openly Zionist organizations tried to gain undue organizational advantages in relationship to Israel. In its official statements, the A.J.C. still proclaims an antinationalist philosophy. But political attachment to Israel is the only feasible test for judging what constitutes Jewish nationalism. And, short of political allegiance to Israel, the A.J.C. encourages political nationalist activities. The "I-am-not-a-Zionist-but" approach of the A.J.C. has helped the Israeli Government more than any openly Zionist activity in America. For the overwhelming majority of American Jews, who are neither Zionists nor anti-Zionists, have been impressed and swayed by the A.J.C.

The Weizmann-Silver-Wise school of Zionism has been able to make gigantic strides in the United States only because of these mugwumps in U. S. Jewry. For in Zionism as elsewhere, it is not the over-zealous bearer of a membership card who accomplishes most for the party. It is the fellow traveler. Because it recoiled from translating its doubts about Zionism into positive opposition, American non-Zionism has become the fellow traveler of Jewish nationalism.

CHAPTER X

Israelism — A New Religion?

THE average Jew has only the scantiest personal knowledge of his religion, Judaism. A heritage has been handed down, for generations, from parent to child and learned by rote: "You are different— you are a Jew—you must help other Jews." This, rather than positive metaphysical insight, is all the average Jewish child ever learns about its being Jewish.

The predisposition to accept nationalism as religion is deeply ingrained in such a child. The mind will retain, even after maturity, irreconcilable contradictions so long as they have been implanted before the logical faculties became dominant.

Zionism has striven to supplement the early conditioning that Jewish children receive at home. This is the Zionist educational program as explained by Louis A. Falk, Vice-President of the Zionist Organization of America: "We must expand our educational activities. We must strengthen the youth movement and spread Hebrew education throughout the land; support institutions in which the teaching is carried out in our spirit; improve the existing Zionist Summer Camps and build new ones under Z.O.A.'s auspices; organize a net of evening courses throughout the country, headed by professional (Zionistically speaking) pedagogues; strengthen the Hebrew press and institute chairs for Hebrew in the American Colleges and Universities. . . . "[1]

The "right" kind of a Sunday school text book for those who attend religious instruction could of course play an important role, but the nationalist objective can be better accomplished in summer camps, when the children are more relaxed and more receptive. Camp directors throughout the country are sent a selective range of program material from the Camp Service Bureau of the Zionist Youth Commission. Most of these pamphlets bear the imprint of the Jewish National Fund, an indirect beneficiary of the U.J.A. The purpose of the various programs is to develop in the child during the summer months an emotional and personal identification with Israel's national development. The material involves the children in Israeli map-making, painting murals of Israel's scenery, and building models of Israeli's colonies. By brush, paint and paper, hammer, chisel and scissors, youthful American summer campers are to be familiarized with Israel's geography, her agricultural and industrial community, her political and military institutions.

Children of age level five to eight are given twelve Palestine landscapes to be finished with water colors or colored crayons. Among other games offered for the camps are jig-saw puzzles of Israel and playing cards portraying great Zionist leaders and historic places in Israel. For youngsters bent on stage-acting, full-length plays are mailed out, dealing with events and personalities of Jewish history and surcharged with Jewish nationalism. A special dramatic program for Herzl Day in commemoration of the father of Zionism is stressed. The camp libraries are offered, free of charge, books and magazines about the pioneer youth movement in Israel and travelogues of modern life in the Gallilee. Palestinian songs, folk-dance series, films and film slides are distributed, mostly rental free. Among the film titles: *Homecoming 1949; Land of Hope; Israel in Action;* and *If I Forget Thee.* Finally, the camps are offered trained counselors "especially skilled in introducing Jewish content into camp activities."

The American Zionist Youth Commission[2] overseeing this program is a joint agency of the Zionist Organization of America and of Hadassah. In behalf of the latter, thousands of women throughout the country think they are doing unpolitical philanthropic works in the interests of oppressed coreligionists abroad, and few of these women realize how much of the money they collect goes into the nationalist indoctrination of their own children. The Zionist circular letter that offers Zionist indoctrination material to American camps quite appropriately ends on quoting the maxim: "As the twig is bent, the tree will grow." Further twig bending includes the persistent attempts to introduce modern Hebrew into the public high schools and, through the "Halutziut" movement, to urge young American Jews above the age level of 18 to go to Israel, at least for a training period.

After the United Jewish Appeal (U.J.A.) fell under the virtual control of Zionist-minded leadership, it became increasingly difficult to determine how many millions of U. S. charity dollars go each year to Jewish nationalism for propaganda purposes. Nor is it possible to estimate the subtle nationalist conditioning performed with a million-dollar advertising that purports to seek philanthropy. All that advertising copy is aimed to make the reader feel he is part and parcel of Israel, for instance by asking him to "help the greatest homecoming in history . . . to strengthen Israel's economy and democratic way of life." But charity dollars are also being used for political indoctrination in a much more direct manner. The United Israel Appeal is the source of revenue for the Jewish National Fund and the Palestine Foundation Fund,[3] nationalist Israeli institutions whose open purpose has always been to help build a Jewish State. The United Israel Appeal turns its share of U.J.A. money over to the Palestine Foundation Fund which finances the World Zionist Organization, including its executive arm, the Jewish Agency. It was the Jewish Agency which argued the case for a Jewish State before the United Nations in 1947. It is now registered with the U. S. Justice Department as a foreign agent. As the New York Yiddish Daily, the *Morning Journal*,[4] pointed out, U.J.A. money is finding its way directly into the Treasury of the State of Israel through the purchase of government-owned land by the Jewish National Fund.

Another aspect of this intermingling of philanthropic and political funds was discussed by the *Menorah Journal*,[5] a scholarly monthly magazine of Jewish opinion. For years, the United Jewish Appeal of Greater New York (a corporation separate from the national U.J.A.) distributed part of the money it raised to agencies in this country. Its newspaper appeals were couched entirely in terms of aid to Jewish refugees abroad; and the charitable contributors, many of them Christian, never knew that 7 per cent of the funds collected went to Jewish defense agencies such as the Anti-Defamation League operating in the United States. (While this practice ceased in New York City, it continues in Washington, D. C., and elsewhere.)

Religious symbols have been deliberately used to

heighten the impression that the small sovereign Middle East State of Israel is actually identical with world Jewry. The Zionist Organization of America proclaimed the Jewish New Year of 1952 as Jerusalem Year and regional Zionist branches were directed to induce U. S. municipalities to name a street or avenue after Jerusalem. At Passover 1952, full-page advertisements of the United Jewish Appeal carried the emblazoned caption: "Wherefore is this day different from all other days?", a political play on the venerable question prescribed for the religious Passover service.

Any country in the world that faces an economic crisis tries to obtain a foreign loan from another government or through the Export-Import Bank. In some instances, securities are sold directly to citizens of other countries as an investment opportunity; bankers and specialists in international finance, rather than leaders of a particular segment of foreign communities, are normally concerned with the floating of such bond issues. Yet none of these normal practices in the marketing of securities has been pursued in the instance of Israel: Israel Bonds have been sold exclusively through the nationalist appeal to an alleged "special responsibility of the Jewish people" in the U.S.A.

To dispel all possible misunderstandings, Israeli Finance Minister, Eliezer Kaplan, told the Knesset that Israel's position was different from countries who had not succeeded in selling their bond issues in the United States, because there were five million Jews in America "whose fate is linked with ours." The bond issue prospectus, filed with the Security Exchange Commission in Washington, recited the nationalist version of Jewish history: that the State of Israel "brought to realization hopes and prayers that had their origin many centuries ago; the exodus from Palestine scattered the Jews in all directions, but for many centuries they sought to live as close to their homeland as possible." In a letter dated January 11, 1951, former Secretary of the Treasury Henry Morgenthau, Jr. opened the Israel Bond drive with the assertion that it was a matter of the utmost "patriotism as Americans and as Jews to see to it that this Israel Government Bond issue is a success." But, one may politely ask, since when is the private financing of a foreign government a patriotic American duty?

Zionist propaganda has constantly equated adherence to Judaism with financial support of Israel. A series of advertisements called on Jewry to "Give a bond for Chanukah," implying that the spirit of this holiday imposed upon Jews everywhere the support of Israel. On the eve of another Jewish holiday, Purim, Chairman Morgenthau said in the Bonds of the Israel Government (B.I.G.) *Newsletter*:[6] "On Sunday, March ninth, an unusual event will take place in hundreds of Committees throughout America. On that day just prior to Purim, thousands of men and women will visit the homes of neighbors to solicit their purchase of Israel Bonds. The cable (attached) from the President of Israel makes clear the importance which Israel attaches to this enterprise which is so vital for the economic growth of the country." For Rosh Hashonoh and Yom Kippur, the most sacred holidays of Judaism, synagogues throughout the nation were called upon in 1952 "to mobilize their strength for the State of Israel and to sponsor the sale of Israel Bonds *during synagogue services*." The chief rabbi of Israel, Dr. Halevi Herzog, had urged this action in a letter read at a rally at the Israeli Exhibition, attended by U. S. rabbis and synagogue leaders. The head of the Mizrachi Organization (the American Zionist religious

party) declared that letter to be of "historical significance," while another leading Orthodox rabbi declared
it was the "religious duty of all Jews to buy the bonds
on the awe-inspiring and holy days."[7] Orthodox rabbinical authorities sanctioned this extraordinary exploitation of holiest holidays as being "within the framework
of traditional observances." But the prophet Isaiah would
have observed: "Behold, in the Day of Your Fast, Ye
pursue your Business."[8]

The pressures, propagandistic, economic, and otherwise, to purchase Israel Bonds have been enormous. Synagogues, B'nai B'rith Lodges, Hadassah groups and country clubs have been mobilized as bond salesmen. For
most U. S. Jews it has been made practically impossible,
short of social suicide, to resist the compulsions to buy.
More than 32,000 crowded Brooklyn's Ebbets Field on
the night of April 30, 1952, for an extraordinary celebration. Mr. Morgenthau presided, Mrs. Roosevelt, Mayor
Impellitteri, Israeli Ministers Dov Joseph and Golda Myerson and Rabbi Goldstein, were among the speakers.
Billy Rose staged the event and the star-studded program included Milton Berle, John Garfield, Hazel Scott,
Sid Caesar and others. This was Israel's fourth anniversary. Even in Texas, where folks allegedly think of themselves as Texans first, the "largest attendance in the history of the Jewish community of San Antonio" was
noted at a similar "Independence Day" celebration at
the Municipal Auditorium.[9]

Governor Theodore F. McKeldin of Maryland, who
placed President Eisenhower's name in nomination at
the Chicago Republican Convention, was enrolled in the
Bond Drive. The Governor wrote that the purchase
of bonds involved no act of allegiance to Israel. But his
curiously defensive analogy between "American Jews"

who purchase Israel Bonds and other Americans who purchase "British, Argentine, or other foreign bonds" just as curiously overlooked the pressuring propaganda and religious appeals behind the Israel Bond drive. Purchasers of other foreign bonds have not been pushed into their investment via any duality of status—the principal appeal in the selling of Israel Bonds.

Paying Israel's way either by contribution or bond purchase does not end the alleged obligation of Americans "as Jews." As Zionism sees it, it is also their duty to engage in U. S. politics as a Jewish bloc "to create a climate of public opinion favorable to Israel's legitimate political and economic needs"[10]—the pledge with which the new President of the Zionist Organization of America responded to a cabled message from Israeli Prime Minister Ben-Gurion. American Jewry was warned "that only an alert and militant Zionist Organization can swing American public opinion to come to Israel's aid and exert pressure on our Administration of the kind which proved successful in 1947 and 1948 and without which the State would not have come into being. . . . Every Jew the world over will see his status enhanced or reduced by what Israel accomplishes."[11]

Where such political action is not taken by Jews voluntarily, Zionists have moved "to democratize[12] the Jewish communities," another way of saying *to capture* local community councils and local funds. A priority for Israeli needs over the requirements of American institutions was the confessed goal.[13]

The assumption of responsibility for the State of Israel has not been confined to Zionist groups. The American Jewish Congress, the American Jewish Committee, and other organized bodies of U. S. Jewry have added their strength to Israel's political cause. A virtual air lift has been operating to bring Cabinet members and other important Governmental officials from the new Middle East State to this country. At times it might have been easier to obtain an Israeli cabinet quorum in New York, or in Washington, than in Tel Aviv.

Another unique facet in the "tale of two countries" is important. Every political party in Israel has its own political counterpart in this country; and the Zionist political parties in the United States perform as the U. S. branches of those Israeli factions. The principal ones are the General Zionists (better known as the Zionist Organization of America), the Mizrachi, the Labor Zionists, the Revisionists and the Progressive or Labor Zionists Leftists. The Israeli opposite numbers are the General Zionists (sometimes split into wings A and B), the Mizrachi, the Mapai, the Herut and the Mapam. In the meetings of the World Zionist Congress, each Israeli party and its American facsimile work closely together for their particular economic, political and social creeds.

The intensity of Zionist pressure is most noticeable in New York City where billboards on streets and subways fiercely put the stamp of nationality on Judaism. At one end of the Eighth Avenue subway entrance at Columbus Circle, one could find a large poster: "Give to the U.J.A.: Give to the U.J.A.: Give to the U.J.A."; an equally imposing poster on the other side plugged: "Buy Israel Bonds—Pay More Than 3½%." Down a block or two, a tremendous fifty-foot U.J.A. banner spans Broadway imploring those both to the north and to the south "to give." And across town, plush Fifth Avenue stores disrupt the otherwise commercial decor of their display windows with a small, elegant "Give to the U.J.A." flag. The metropolitan press is filled each day with such stories as "1800 at Eddie Cantor's Birthday Party Buy $2,616,000 in Israel Bonds to Get In." Or it may be a full-page advertisement calling for the "maintenance of the Z.O.A. colonies in Israel." On one day, the *New York Times* carried stories of the Zionist Council's new five-year plan; the needs of the Joint Distribution Committee to help Jews in Europe; the visit of the Tel Aviv Police Chief to the United States in connection with the Bond drive; statements of the Israel Foreign Minister regarding the country's objectives in the controversy with the Arab States; and a half-page advertisement: "Get Bonds at the Israeli Exposition."

In the *New York Times Index* for 1947, 1948, and 1949[14] Palestine (without "Jewish" listings) was accorded more pages than Great Britain and France combined. Indonesia, with a population of 78 million people, achieved its independence on November 2, 1949, after prolonged fighting with the Dutch, and protracted United Nations negotiations in which the United States was heavily involved; but that crucial country's listings in the *New York Times Index* totalled 3 pages against the 10 pages given to Palestine and Israel the same year. In 1950 and 1951, the *Times* space given Israel still exceeded Great Britain's news allotments.

The press and radio rarely distinguish between the words "Jew" and "Israeli," "Judaism" and "Zionism"— in other words, between religion and nation. They talk of the *Jewish* State, the *Jewish* Flag, the *Jewish* Premier, etc. This deplorable semantics of the U. S. press is just what the Zionist doctor ordered: in such way, U. S. Jewry is inexorably linked to Israel at any moment of Israeli crisis. And, of course, each year, as the one before, the Zionist cry is: "This is the year of crisis." That cry has become as much a part of the American scene as the ritual throwing out of the ball at the start of the season or the opening of the Metropolitan Opera. The head of the American section of the Jewish Agency was honest enough to say, at least to other Zionists: "All the campaigning which is today based on the thesis that 'this is the last difficult year' is a dangerous method of propaganda. The truth is that Israel will need help for years and years."[15]

William Zuckerman, editor of the *Jewish Newsletter*, dubbed the climate of the American Jewish community as "Campaign Judaism," which, he said "has almost consciously emptied itself of all higher aspirations and spiritual needs and has willingly limited itself to the role of a financial milk cow for others. . . . How can a community such as this, whose highest ideal is mechanical fundraising, be the source of nobility and greatness? Can the interminable big-and-even-bigger Bond and UJA drives, the Hadassah teas, the gaudy banquets, the garish publicity and appalling bad taste, be the soil from which greatness will spring? Can salesmanship, even when clothed with the mantle of philanthropy, be anything but shallow and sterile?"[16]

The significance of all these manifestations is that, for the past ten years, Yahweh, the God of Judaism, has been supplanted in the Jewish American life by nationalist-minded politicians. The Decalog's Second Commandment once committed the Jews: "Thou shalt have no other Gods before me. Thou shalt not make unto thee any graven image." In contemporary Judaism, the worship of the State of Israel is crowding out the worship of God.

CHAPTER XI

Operation "Ingathering"

I N SOLEMN policy declarations, David Ben-Gurion publicly announced what Jewish nationalists have privately been saying since the days of Herzl: that *all* the world's Jews must "go home." These were not extemporaneous remarks of an irresponsible person; these were statements of the Prime Minister of the sovereign State of Israel who, as the top leader in the World Zionist movement, speaks with ultimate authority on Zionist dogma.

On August 31, 1949, David Ben-Gurion had this to say to a group of Americans visiting Israel: "Although we realized our dream of establishing a Jewish State, we are still at the beginning. Today there are only 900,000 Jews in Israel, while the greater part of the Jewish people are still abroad. *It consists of bringing all Jews to Israel. We appeal to the parents to help us bring their children here. Even if they decline to help, we will bring the youth to Israel;* but I hope that this will not be necessary."

How many of these American children did he want? Mr. Ben-Gurion explained this upon his arrival in the U.S., in May 1951. He envisaged an influx of an additional four million Jews into Israel in the next ten years, and he left little doubt from where the bulk of these new settlers were expected to come. The large immigration waves from Iraq, Yemen and Bulgaria had subsided, and Israel made clear that she no longer wanted the weak and infirm, but the healthy youth from the United States. Ben-Gurion asserted that the "establishment of a new state was never the fulfillment of Zionism and that the movement was more necessary now than ever."[1] He pointed out that, whereas the sovereignty of the State was limited to citizens within its borders, the Zionist movement embraced all Jews throughout the world.

In December 1951, the Israeli Premier discussed in the Knesset immigration problems of Israel. He charged American Zionist leadership with having gone bankrupt after the founding of the State, because they had failed to migrate in large numbers. Ben-Gurion cried: "There were not five leaders who got up to go to Israel after the State was established. I don't maintain they would have been followed by masses, but they would have proved that Zionism was not void of meaning, at least in the eyes of its leaders."[2]

In a rebuttal to this charge, Benjamin Browdy, then President of the Zionist Organization of America, pointed to the ten trade schools and the business college that had been established for Israel in this country, to the recruiting of skilled Americans for teaching in Israel, to the shipment of U. S. food, clothing and materials. He could also note his movement's attempts to instill what Browdy called "an exodus psychology" within U. S. Jewry as proof that they were not merely "charity Zionists." Dr. Israel Goldstein, in the guise of voicing Israeli complaints against American Jews asked: "What are American Jews waiting for? Are they waiting for a Hitler to force them out? Do they imagine that they will be spared the tragedies which have forced Jews of other lands to emigrate?"[3]

In his parliamentary address Mr. Ben-Gurion had taken the immigration problem off the humanitarian level. It was now squarely posed as an Israeli national manpower problem—no longer as a philanthropic responsibility. The Premier said that Israel needed nurses, teachers and other technicians, and went on: "I am sure they will come. There are economic factors to induce them. A Jewish engineer in America will not easily obtain employment in a non-Jewish firm and there are not enough Jewish firms to absorb all intellectuals." Here at last was the crescendo to the doom music of Herzl, Weizmann, Wise, Silver, and all Zionist theoreticians.

Any American Jew ought to have resented the innuendo of a foreign politician that his, the American Jew's, attachment to the United States could be altered by job trouble or the manpower needs of a foreign nation. No bigot could have made a meaner charge. And how did the American Jewish Committee protect U. S. Jewry against the outrageous assertion of the leader of a foreign state that the relationship of American Jews to the United States was anything but unqualified and permanent? After Ben-Gurion's first "ingathering" declaration, Jacob Blaustein, the A.J.C. President, went to Israel for a retraction—only to reassure, on his return, that everything was all right. And so it was—for Jewish nationalism. The movement continued to march along the chosen "ingathering" path.

From the outset, immigration to Palestine has been artificially stimulated. For even Europe's Displaced Persons had to be powerfully "convinced" that Israel was the only place where they could build their lives anew. There were, in 1948, between 100,000 and 114,000 displaced Jews in the American Zone of Germany; from among that group, more than 55,000 applications for emigration to the United States had been filed by the fall of 1947, and a majority of these people specified a preference of going anywhere but Palestine.[4] This was in the face of most intense propaganda work of the Jewish Agency amongst the inmates of the D.P. camps. In a report to the Zionist-controlled American Jewish Conference (which included every organization save the American Jewish Committee), Chaplain Klausner discussed quite frankly how to deal with these stubborn Displaced Persons. Worked out after consultations with the former Advisers on Jewish Affairs to the U. S. High Commissioner, Judges Simon Rifkind and Louis Levinthal and Rabbi Philip Bernstein, the Klausner report submitted this pertinent observation: "I am convinced that the people must be forced to go to Palestine. They are not prepared to understand their own position nor the promises of the future. To them, an American dollar looms as the greatest of objectives. By 'force' I suggest a program. It is not a new program. It was used before, and most recently. It was used in the evacuation of the Jews from Poland and in the story of the 'Exodus.' "

"The first step in such a program," the Klausner report went on, "is the adoption of the principle that it is the conviction of the world Jewish community that these people must go to Palestine. The second step is the transmittal of that policy to the Displaced Persons. The third step is for the world Jewish community to offer the people the opportunity to go to Palestine. By opportunity, it is to be understood that any means put at the disposal of the people is to be considered an adequate opportunity. Those who are not interested are no longer to be wards of the Jewish community to be maintained in camps, fed and clothed without their having to make any contribution to their own subsistence. To effect this program, it becomes necessary for the Jewish community at large to reverse its policy and instead of creating comforts for the Displaced Persons to make them as uncomfortable as possible. The American Joint Distribution Committee supplies should be withdrawn. I have taken the time to indicate the type of help that the Joint has been giving. My purpose was to be able to indicate that the supplementary aid of the Joint may be termed 'luxury items' in that this aid serves as a means to put the individual in business. A further procedure would call for an organization such as the Haganah to harass the Jew. Utilities would be tampered with and all protection now given by the Adviser on Jewish Affairs, D.P. Chaplains, and Agency personnel be withdrawn. Of course, it is to be understood that there are certain problems that persist even in the most normal of societies which must be cared for by one or more agencies."

"It must be borne in mind," continued Rabbi Klausner, "that we are dealing with a sick people. They are not to be asked, but to be told, what to do. They will be thankful in years to come. Too many times have I been cursed in the evening, while moving masses of people, only to be thanked the following morning for having transferred them from an abominable site to a more comfortable location. The cooperation of all agencies is imperative. The principle must be whole-heartedly accepted by all Agencies involved. The AJDC must set aside the funds now allocated to Germany to be used for the execution of this program. If this program is not accepted, let me assure this Conference that an incident will occur which will compel the American Jewish community to reconsider its policy and make the changes herein suggested. At that time, there will have been much more suffering, a greater wave of anti-Semitism and a tougher struggle to accomplish what might perhaps be accomplished today."

The then Adviser on Jewish Affairs to the High Commissioner in Germany, William Haber, called attention, in a letter to the Conference, to Klausner's "all consuming passion for Zionism" which explained his resentment against the Displaced Persons for not seeing that Israel was their only hope. Haber agreed without reservation that these people ought to be evacuated, but took issue with the suggestion that the D.P.'s be made uncomfortable and be harassed. Mr. Haber referred to the "somewhat compulsory form" of conscription for the Palestine Army that already was being applied in the camps, and to the "social pressures" used to persuade young and able-bodied D.P.'s "to volunteer" for the Haganah.

Reports that acts of terror and discrimination were committed in D.P. camps against Jews who disagreed with Zionism had been received from time to time in the United States. An important U. S. labor leader reported in the summer of 1948[5] that Jewish relief organizations responsible for administering the camps were engaged in a general campaign "to force D.P.'s to accept Zionism, to join the Palestine Jewish Army, and to give up legitimate political differences." The means employed towards these ends included confiscation of food rations, dismissal from work, smashing of machines sent by Americans to train D.P.'s in useful skills, taking away legal protection and visa rights from dissenters, expulsion from the camps of political opponents and, in one instance, even the public flogging of a recalcitrant recruit for the Israel Army. Trucks of the Jewish Agency were known to drive through the Jewish camps in Germany, "picking up" boys and young men. Strange transports left Germany every week for France where, as a first step en route to Israel, the herded people were kept in camps established at Marseilles. In Germany's D.P. camps, stories were spread that pogroms were taking place in parts of the United States. Artist Steinhardt and his wife, of whom I have told in a previous chapter, would stop believing in the reality of anti-Semitic violence in the United States only after their visit to this country.

In this manner, the "ingathering of the exiles" began. At the Israeli Cabinet meeting of August 15, 1948, Premier Ben-Gurion stated: "Generations have not in vain suffered and struggled to see only 800,000 Jews in this country. It is the duty of the present generation to *redeem* the Jews in the Arab and European countries." After the 1949 Israeli elections, Ben-Gurion stated this objective in a different manner: "We must save the remnants of Israel in the Diaspora. We must also save their possessions. Without these two things, we shall not build this country."

The Arab-Israeli war afforded an opportunity for "redemption." After the European D.P. camps were emptied, more than 80 per cent of the subsequent immigrants came from the Soviet-Satellite countries and the Arab States of the Middle East and North Africa. Where these Jews did not willingly immigrate, a combination of pressure and propaganda forced them to move.

In the instance of the 110,000 Iraqi Jews, their life was made miserable by the intensified political conflict between a small hard core of Zionists in their midst and the Moslem Government. The Jews had been brought to the land of Iraq by Nebuchadnezzar after the destruction of the Kingdom of Judah. Here the Babylonian Talmud had been written and the captives had found the "peace of the city" prophesied for them. Here their leaders served as counsellors and advisers to Sultans and Pashas, and had gained civic and financial prestige. Here the Jewish community enjoyed economic and religious freedom for centuries. In the twenties there had been a Jewish Finance Minister in the cabinet. There were some sixty synagogues. In fact, representatives of Middle Eastern Jewry, including Iraqi's, had appeared before the Anglo-American Committee in 1946 to express the fear that their friendly relations with Mohammedan Arabs were endangered by political Zionism. And at that time, there were more persons of Jewish faith in the Arab countries, including North Africa, than in the Promised Land.

There were forces within the Jewish Iraqi community which were stirred by Zionist agents who sought to make Iraqi Jewry conscious of their ties with Palestine. The Jewish Community Council in Baghdad had attacked Zionism on several occasions. Iraqi's Chief Rabbi, Khedouri Sassoon, who had guided his flock for forty-eight years, issued a statement which said: "Iraqi Jews will be forever against Zionism. Jews and Arabs have enjoyed the same rights and privileges for 1000 years and do not regard themselves as a distinctive separate part of this nation." Despite these warnings, Zionist agents effectively produced trouble in Iraqi. Rabbi Sassoon himself was badly beaten by coreligionists.

With the outbreak of the war between Israel and the Arab States, Israel became the proclaimed enemy of Iraq, and many innocent Jews were mistaken for Zionists. It is hard to assess all the facts except that passions flared on both sides, leading to incidents. Acts of extremists led to a gradual deterioration of relations between the Iraqi Jews and Moslem. The breach widened when the Iraq Parliament passed the Option Law permitting those who wished to leave to do so, but not making the exodus mandatory.

As Foreign Minister Tewfik Sweidi, who as prime minister had promulgated the law, explained to me in Baghdad in June, 1953: "We could not help but feel that some Jews had become foreigners and were potential fifth columnists. We protected them but gave them the choice of going to Israel or remaining as loyal citizens of Iraq. At the end of the first eleven months only 30,000 had registered for emigration. One of the buses carrying Jews to the airport was bombed—Zionists were accused of this act—and within two months more than 80,000 had expressed the desire to depart."

One of the approximately 4,500 who still remain in Iraq told me: "Many parents who left did so only because their more Zionist-minded children insisted that they quit the country for Israel." At the end of the exodus, a cache of bombs and guns was found concealed in a synagogue.

To Americans, Operation Ali Baba (as the exodus from Iraq was named) was a challenge to give money for the rescue of oppressed peoples. But for more than 100,-000 Iraqi Jews, this was a forced rescue from the land in which their fathers had prospered for many centuries. As Dorothy Thompson has pointed out, these "rescued" Jews from Iraqi were imitating their ancestors, the Biblical exiles in Babylon—only in reverse: these new Israeli settlers now sat by the river of Jordan and wept for their homes in Babylon.

The Yemenite Jews came from a medieval Middle Eastern civilization which they shared with their Moslem neighbors. It has been reported that only five people in all of Yemen owned automobiles, and one of them was a Jew. This medieval state on the Red Sea was built on a quasi-caste system in which the Jews, centuries ago, had taken over the arts and crafts (to a certain extent also small shopkeeping) and were engaged in agriculture. It has been said that these Yemenite Jews held a key position because in Yemen "the artisan is king."[6] At any rate, their existence as artisans led to extreme solidarity and strictest religious discipline. They lived the old Talmudic law to the letter and bore the closest resemblance to the original Jews of Palestine by whom they had been converted to Judaism. Like other Yemenites, the Yemenite Jews lived, by Western standards, under sub-normal conditions; but the Yemenite Jews were no worse off than their neighbor.

These Yemenite Jews were transported to Israel, in an operation colorfully labelled "The Magic Carpet," in two stages (December 1948 to March 1949, and July 1949 to September 1950), at a cost of approximately 5½ million dollars. The Near East Air Lines handled this air lift with five Skymasters and one Tudor. These medieval people, most of whom had never seen a plane before, wished to hurry to Israel largely for religious reasons: once the State was created, it was quite natural for these primitively pious Jews to see the Messianic promise in their speedy return to the land of the Bible. But once in Israel, the Yemenite was immediately labelled with the usual clichés of prejudice such as "childish," "imbecilic," "shiftless," "dirty" and "unwilling to work."

Oriental Jews now constitute approximately 45% of Israel's total population. More than 665,000 newcomers had swarmed into Israel until the Jewish Agency aban-

doned, in November 1951,[7] unrestricted immigration
for selective immigration with an admitted preference
for the young, the able-bodied, and those with special
professional skills.

Despite this temporary curtailment of immigration,
the "ingathering" goal of Jewish nationalism has not
altered a whit. Speaking before the Annual Convention
of the Labor Zionists of America in July, 1952, Israeli
Foreign Minister Sharett said that Israel must have a
population of not less than four million.[8] But, he added,
for the truly desirable influx, Israel was now looking
to the countries of North and South America. The Foreign Minister was merely spelling out what his chief
had previously announced in broad principle to the
World Zionist Organization: "This State is the only one
which is not an end in itself, but serves as a means for
the fulfillment of Zionism, the ingathering of the exiles.
It is not a State for its citizens alone, but for the whole
Jewish people." At the same time, incongruously
enough, the United Jewish Appeal issued an emergency
call in behalf of the most recently "ingathered" 240,000
Israelis who desperately needed shelter.

South America, indeed, has not been neglected as a
supply source of future Israeli citizens. As a first step,
the Jewish community in Mexico has been reduced to
an Israel colony. There, the Zionists control most Jewish communal institutions, including the important
school system, and dominate all funds. This did not just
happen. When they were raising money for the United
Zionist Fund (the Mexican equivalent of the U.J.A.)
the Zionists published the names of those Jews who had
not yet contributed. Other advertisements warned that
no Jew who wished to visit Israel could obtain a visa
without proving that he had contributed adequately to

the United Zionist Fund. A gathering of Mexican Jews was told that the "pogrom" from which the Costa Rican Jews had been barely rescued would, sooner or later, be the lot of all Jews in Mexico; therefore, "it is only sound policy to provide themselves with a place of refuge and especially a refuge for their possessions,"[9] and an investment in Israeli Bonds would naturally be a good means of transferring their Mexican property.

It has taken the Zionists in Mexico five years to expunge all opposition to their totalitarianism. In the Spring of 1948, the United Zionist Fund in Mexico City announced that those who refused to contribute, or failed to contribute sufficiently large sums, would be judged at an "open trial." The names of the "guilty" were read at a pre-trial meeting attended by over 500 men and women. "There was great tumult in the hall and people were standing ready with pencil and paper to record the names as they were read."[10] A jury of eleven had been hand-picked two weeks before the first "trial" which began on June 16. *Die Stimme*, in its issue of June 19th, describes the "lynch spirit" stirred up by Zionist "prosecutors" of "delinquents." One of the accused was badly beaten.[11] While the "trial" proceeded, the Zionist head-man in Mexico City conducted "back-stage bargaining negotiations with those willing to pay last-minute hush money rather than face public denunciation."[12]

The following sanctions were imposed upon those declared guilty:

(1) Exclusion from all social institutions of which the delinquent is a member or would like to be a member;

(2) Demand on all his friends to break off relations with him;

(3) Refusal of all local institutions to accept any contributions to any enterprise from the guilty one;

(4) "The names of all declared guilty to be sent to
the Government in Israel in order that they be
inscribed in the list kept for that purpose";

(5) No local Jewish publication to be permitted to
publish any defense of persons judged guilty.

The Kangaroo Court of Mexico City has been extended into other Jewish communities of Latin America.
In Montevideo, recalcitrant Uruguayans who, in 1949,
refused to contribute the 2 per cent tax levied by Zionist leaders on all their wealth, were denied entrance to
the synagogue and the right to obtain the service of a
Rabbi or Cantor at marriage, death and circumcision
ceremonies.[13] Essentially the same outrage was reported
from Brazil, Argentina, and Peru.[14] In Argentina, the
largest and most powerful Jewish fraternal and burial
society announced that Jews who did not give to the
fund would not be buried in Jewish cemeteries.[15]

At the Mexican "trial," the head of the Mexican
branch of the Joint Distribution Committee took the
floor to incite the crowd and urge sanctions. The "de-
fendants" subjected to this kangaroo court formed a Defense Committee, appealed to American organizations
for assistance, and protested to the main office of the
Joint Distribution Committee.[16] In a reply to their letter,
the Secretary of the Latin American J.D.C. washed his
hands of "strictly a community matter" and asserted
"that, as you probably know, similar fund raising efforts,
and methods similar to those about which you complain,
have been employed by communities in this country."[17]
Moses A. Leavitt, executive vice-chairman of the Joint
Distribution Committee added in a reply of his own:

"We have nothing to apologize for and obviously we cannot jeopardize the lives of people overseas by refusing to accept funds which any Jewish community feels it wishes to offer to us. . . . "[18]

Operation "Ingathering" has been codified by the lawmakers of Israel. This is Article 3 of the proposed Constitution not yet adopted, as there has been no decision yet whether Israel is to have a written Constitution like the United States or an unwritten one like Britain: "The state of Israel is designed to be the National home of the Jewish people and shall admit every Jew who desires to settle within its territory subject to such regulatory provisions as may from time to time be enacted by the Chamber of Deputies." The Knesset on July 5th, 1950, implemented this constitutional provision with the Law of Return which endows every Jew with the right to come to Israel for permanent settlement.

The new Nationality Bill of Israel went into effect on July 14th, 1952, (coincidentally, as Norman Thomas pointed out, "Bastille Day in France, the beginning of Jewish emancipation in the Western democratic states a century and a half ago").[19] Under this law, all Jews of Israel automatically become citizens of the State, but none of the 170,000 Arabs in that country can so become an Israeli citizen without proving first that he was a Palestinian citizen up to May 14, 1948, and that he had lived there continuously since the establishment of the State in Israel, or entered Israel legally after the establishment. To become a naturalized Israeli citizen, the Arab must fulfill six requirements—from which a Jew in Israel, or anywhere else in the world, is exempt—such as giving proof that he has resided in Israel for three of the five years preceding the application, possesses knowledge of the Hebrew language, and has renounced prior nationality. Of course, only a small proportion of Israel's 170,000 Arabs can offer the proofs necessary for automatic citizenship.[20]

While the Arab born in Palestine is thus deprived of equality of citizenship, the American Jew (or the Jew from any other country) residing in Israel is automatically endowed with Israeli citizenship regardless of whether or not he renounced his original citizenship. The new law made it explicitly incumbent upon him to disclaim this Israeli "endowment." Most Americans living in Israel rushed to reject the privilege of dual citizenship, specifically declaring their unwillingness to become Israeli citizens.[21] U. S. consulates have been besieged by U. S. Jews seeking confirmation that their American citizenship was in good order. The precarious position of American Jews in Israel was further complicated by the McCarran Act which stipulates that Americans lose U. S. citizenship by service in a foreign army. Inasmuch as a number of Americans (males between the ages of 18 and 45, and American women between the ages of 18 and 35) have been subjected to Israel's universal draft and permitted to serve without swearing allegiance to Israel, their U. S. citizenship was seriously jeopardized.

The second-largest group of Israeli residents who showed a stubborn unwillingness to become Israelis are Tunisian and Moroccan Jews "rescued" into Israel by various "ingathering" techniques.

About the Israeli Nationality Act, U. S. Socialist Norman Thomas had this to say: "An Arab, without too much exaggeration, can complain that the Jews were practicing Hitlerism in reverse. He can certainly maintain that the volume of Jewish criticism of the bad Mc-

Carran Immigration Bill—now, alas, a Law—in America, comes with extraordinary bad grace from such American Zionists as might support or apologize for Ben-Gurion's law of nationalism." Verily, the Israeli Knesset ignored the Biblical direction: "And ye shall love the stranger, for ye were strangers in the land of Egypt, and as one of the citizens shall be unto you the stranger that sojourneth in your midst, ye shall love him as thyself."

Jewish nationalists have defended the Israel Nationality Law in this rather hard-boiled and somewhat Nazi-like manner: "No one will deny that essentially the (Nationality) Law of Israel contains some discrimination against the Arabs, because Jews become citizens automatically, while Arabs must bring proof. But the discrimination is a result of an event which has been delayed for over a thousand years. The Nationality Law is the first law of its kind in a land which was in our times taken over by sword and conquest. Let us not deceive ourselves; one is either against such historical 'primitivism' in our times, or one accepts it and remembers that everything that happens, no matter how unpleasant the happening, characterizes a land in the process of being created after it was conquered in order to re-establish the historical home of the Jewish people."[22]

Most Americans would vehemently resent any doubt of the indivisibility of their citizenship, but the U. S. Zionists do not find the idea of an American Jew's automatic citizenship in Israel altogether repellent. Something else disturbs them much more. Not so long ago, this mordant definition of a "Zionist" was making the rounds: "A Zionist is a Jew who will give money to a second Jew to send a third Jew to Israel." And the Amer-

ican Zionist was suddenly facing the fact that *he* might
be that third Jew. To bring about the exodus of other
Jews from their countries was fine; but most U. S. Zionists balk at the idea that the "ingathering" might include
themselves. Theirs is strictly an "after you, my dear
Alphonse" attitude. Only some three thousand American Zionists have made their permanent homes in Israel.
The rest, no matter how imbued with a love of their
"homeland" over there, seem to prefer activities in its
behalf in the comfort of the United States.

This has temporarily discouraged the Israeli leadership, but it has not daunted their plans. The forced "ingathering" of the Iraqi and other Middle Eastern Jewry
is a pattern which the Zionists would like to repeat in
the West, though they have not managed as yet to create the necessary incidents to explode Western Jewish
communities. That they will continue to try is proven
by an article in *Davar*, the official organ of the Socialist-
Labor (Mapai) Party in Tel Aviv, the newspaper of
Israel's governing party. Here is what was said in Prime
Minister Ben-Gurion's own paper: "I shall not be
ashamed to confess that, if I had power, as I have the
will, I would select a score of efficient young men—
intelligent, decent, devoted to our ideal and burning
with the desire to help redeem Jews, and I would send
them to the countries where Jews are absorbed in sinful
self-satisfaction. The task of these young men would
be to disguise themselves as non-Jews, and, acting upon
the brutal Zionism, *plague* these Jews with anti-Semitic
slogans, such as 'Bloody Jew,' 'Jews go to Palestine,' and
similar 'intimacies.' I can vouch that the results, in terms
of a considerable immigration to Israel from these countries, would be ten thousand times larger than the results

brought by thousands of emissaries who have been preaching for decades to deaf ears."[23]

As Israeli leaders have complained, too few American Zionists have practiced what they preach. Nevertheless, they still preach. They still are an integral part of a world organization pledged to a task which will not be completed until, to use the words of Rabbi Silver, "the process of ingathering of the exiles encompasses the entire Jewish people."

The future of the American Jew was carefully charted in Jerusalem during the 23rd World Zionist Congress of 1951, the first to convene since the establishment of the State of Israel. Fifty-four years had passed since the Basel Platform of 1897. A new program had to be formulated. For, if the creation of a sovereign state had been the only goal of Zionism, its work would be judged completed and the organization would have to be disbanded. But meeting in Israel, at a safe distance from the American press, the heart and core of Zionism was laid bare, undisturbed by fears that a forthright exposition of true Zionist goals might endanger American fund raising.

The nationalization of one part of the "Jewish people" had been achieved, and the remaining problem was how, not whether, to "nationalize" the Jews who still lived *outside* Israel. Because of the vital financial contributions and the political assistance they had rendered and were continuing to render Israel, American Zionists demanded a decisive role in governing Israel's affairs. Rabbi Silver and his friends argued that they were the fountainhead from which flow American dollars, and they demanded an equal voice in "management." Mrs. Golda Myerson, on the other hand, pressed Ben-Gurion's official contention that "the only persons who had the right to influence Israel policy were those who lived in this country." The Israeli Zionists insisted that the tag "exiles" be applied to all Jews outside Israel, while the U. S. Zionists refused to accept personal residence in Israel as the sole criterion for control. The following resolution, adopted by a vote of 286 to 0, finally pleased everyone: "The task of Zionism is the strengthening of the State of Israel, the ingathering of the exiles in Eretz Israel and the fostering of the unity of the Jewish people."

The original wording "the redemption of the Jewish people *through* the ingathering of the exiles," was deleted. The call for "ingathering" had been toned down to make it *one* task of Zionism, rather than the *sole* instrument of Jewish redemption. In such manner, those who did not wish to be "ingathered" themselves, at the moment, were enabled to continue their proselytizing of American Jewry.

Another resolution unanimously called upon the youth of the Jewish communities, particularly those in the United States, to emigrate to Israel. The American Zionists, sensitive to U. S. public opinion, indicated that they would concentrate on youth education, which would ultimately result in emigration to Israel, rather than an *open* recruiting of immigrants in the United States. Mrs. Samuel Halprin, head of the Hadassah, opposed direct recruiting of youth for pioneer work in Israel *now*. "In ten or fifteen years it may be right and proper. But now? Is this the correct timing?"[24]

But the head of the American section of the Jewish Agency, Dr. Nahum Goldmann, was able to say triumphantly after the Jerusalem meeting: "We accomplished a great job. American Jews have always been asked for money and came through beautifully. Now we shall ask them for children, and I am confident they will come through after much education and effort."[25]

The 23rd World Congress strengthened the links between Zionists inside and outside Israel. The World Zionist Organization won a grant of both a special legal status within Israel with a voice in important areas of the State's internal development, and recognition outside of Israel as the agency through which the State could make its demands on "the Jewish people." However, Prime Minister Ben-Gurion stipulated certain conditions for granting that special status, the most important of them being the "collective obligation of all national Zionist Organizations to aid the Jewish state *under all circumstances and conditions even if such an attitude clashes with their respective national authorities*."[26] At the World Congress, this was referred to as "unconditional cooperation with the State and the Government of Israel." Israeli opponents warned that the granting of a special status to the Zionist World movement will estrange many Jews outside of Israel "who will with some justification fear the charge of double loyalty."[27]

The momentous meaning of the Prime Minister's stipulation was emphasized by the President of the Zionist Organization of America as a pledge "to mobilize World Jewry in behalf of the Jewish State, and to keep it mobilized as a striking force at all times." The grant of special status, according to Ben-Gurion, "in effect enabled the Zionist organization to act in place of the state (of Israel) in matters of emigration and settlement." It also gave organized Zionism, at least in the sphere of "ingathering," actual control over non-Zionist Jewish organizations which were interested in re-settlement work.

For this reason, the non-Zionist American Jewish Committee balked, at its meeting of 1951, against the

World Congress arrangements, and the Knesset was sufficiently impressed to postpone implementing legislation until November 1952. Moreover, the Zionist Organization of America is the alter ego of the General Zionists, an Israeli party which has vied for political supremacy with Ben-Gurion's Socialist Mapai Party. It was not until Ben-Gurion had moved to appease the financially potent American Zionists and had brought the General Zionists into the Israeli Government that the World Congress agreements were given any effect. But once the new coalition government was formed, in deference to U. S. Zionism, the path was cleared for a speedy enactment of the political pact between World Zionism and Israeli Government.

The Middle East State of Israeli and the Zionist movement of the world are now contractually united in the pursuit of their common "ultimate goal and principal purpose—the ingathering of the exiles" (meaning, among others, more than five million American citizens of the Jewish faith). This is the official wording of Is-raeli-Zionist policy. And as if to dispel all possible doubts of those Jews who still cling to the illusion that their contributions to Zionist causes are merely philanthropic donations, the Chairman of the Jewish Agency, Mr. Berl Locker, made in 1950 this formal statement before the Action Committee of the World Zionist Organization: "Israel's flag is *our* flag and it is often necessary to suffer for a flag. We must see to it that the Zionist flag which has begun to fly above the State of Israel is hoisted aloft *over the entire Jewish people* until we achieve the completion of the ingathering of the exiles."[28]

This is clear and unequivocal language. The Zionists at least cannot be accused of dodging the issue: they demand, openly and consistently, the allegiance of

American Jews to the flag of Israel. Zionism may be a heretical creed, but the Zionists have at least the courage of their convictions. The truly objectionable, the pathetically irresponsible people are those American Jews who reject Israel's claim to their allegiance, and yet, support the Zionist crusade—simply because they refuse to face the facts and to live by the principles they profess.

CHAPTER XII

The Racial Myth

I T IS strange that the fallacious obsession of a van-
quished enemy should dominate the surviving
group's philosophy. It was Hitler who, in imposing
Nazism on country upon country, said: "You are not
a German—you are a Jew. You are not a Czech—you
are a Jew. You are not a Pole—you are a Jew. You are
not a Frenchman—you are a Jew." And Nazi law defined how many generations back a modicum of special
blood would establish future membership in the race.
But Nazism was at least consistent. To Hitler, it was
not only "once a Jew, always a Jew," but also "once
a German, always a German." It was the contention of
the Third Reich that, throughout the world, a person
of German ancestry had a perpetual obligation to the
German state and could not shed his German allegiance.
And this was so because, for Nazism, every German belonged to his distinct and chosen Aryan race.

There is no reputable anthropologist who will not
agree that Jewish racialism is as much poppycock as
Aryan racialism. As far back as December 1938, the
American Anthropological Association, at its annual
conference in New York, condemned Aryanism as a

fallacy and stated that both, "Aryan" and "Semitic," were *linguistic* terms without any *racial* significance. Race involves the inheritance of specific physical features by large groups of mankind, such as hair texture, head form, color of eyes and skin, stature, the shape of the nose, etc. Hitler, Weizmann, cartoonists and other creators of "Jewish" prototypes notwithstanding, there is no Jewish or Semitic race.

Anthropological science divides mankind into three recognized races: Negro, Mongolian or Oriental,[1] and Caucasian or White (although some authorities refer to a fourth race—the Australoids).[2] Each race is divided into branches and subdivisions possessing special characteristics, invariably present, from generation to generation. Members of the Jewish faith are found in all three races and in their subdivisions.

The terms Aryan and Semite have no anthropological connotation. "Aryan" refers to a group of Indo-European languages, including Russian, English, German, French, Persian, and the language spoken by the Hindus of Northern India. The principle Semitic languages, closely related to the Hamitic languages of ancient Egypt (the Coptic and Berber tongues), are Hebrew, Syrian, Abyssinian and Arabic. The ancient Assyrians, Phoenicians and Babylonians also spoke Semitic languages. The Semitic-speaking peoples are members of the Caucasian race.

The word "Semite" originally designated a descendent of Shem, one of the sons of Noah, and has been applied to certain ancient (no longer existing) people as well as to Arabs and Jews. Incorrect semantic usage has given a *racial* meaning to a linguistic term, and a further malapropism has included in that meaning all followers of the Judaistic faith, most of whom do not understand

ancient or modern Hebrew. And, surely, a knowledge
of Yiddish could not make a person a Semite: that dialect (rather than a language) is a combination of the dialect spoken in lower Germany with Hebrew and Slavic.[3]

As races have intermarried throughout history, mankind has become more and more an admixture of strains.
Even "the proud Anglo-Saxon race" is a misnomer: very
few English can claim the pure blood of the Angle and
the Saxon invaders; most others will have to be satisfied
with Celtic and Iberian forebears.[4] The Jews have min-
gled most: Until the middle of the fifth century B. C.,
intermarriage was a normal phenomenon in Israelite
life, and the ensuing Judaist proselytizing over the globe
brought peoples of all races into the Jewish faith.

Today, to trace anyone's descent to ancient Palestine
would be a genealogical impossibility; and to presume,
axiomatically, such a descent for Jews, alone among all
human groups, is an assumption of purely fictional significance. Most everybody in the Western world could
stake out some claim of Palestinian descent if genealogical records could be established for two-thousand
years. And there are, indeed, people who, though not
by the widest stretch of imagination Jewish, proudly
make that very claim: some of the oldest of the South's
aristocratic families play a game of comparing whose
lineage goes farther back into Israel. No one knows what
happened to the Ten Lost Tribes of Israel, but to speculate on who might be who is a favored Anglo-Saxon pas-
time, and Queen Victoria belonged to an Israelite Society that traced the ancestry of its membership back to
those lost tribes.

Twelve tribes started in Canaan about thirty-five centuries ago; and not only that ten of them disappeared—
more than half of the members of the remaining two

tribes never returned from their "exile" in Babylon. How then, can anybody claim to descend directly from that relatively small community which inhabited the Holy Land at the time of Abraham's Covenant with God?

The Jewish racial myth flows from the fact that the words *Hebrew, Israelite, Jew, Judaism,* and the *Jewish people* have been used synonymously to suggest a historic continuity. But this is a misuse. These words refer to different groups of people with varying ways of life in different periods in history. *Hebrew* is a term correctly applied to the period from the beginning of Biblical history to the settling in Canaan. *Israelite* refers correctly to the members of the twelve tribes of Israel. The name *Yehudi* or *Jew* is used in the Old Testament to designate members of the tribe of Judah, descendants of the fourth son of Jacob,[5] as well as to denote citizens of the Kingdom of Judah,[6] particularly at the time of Jeremiah[7] and under the Persian occupation.[8] Centuries later, the same word came to be applied to anyone, no matter of what origin, whose religion was Judaism.

The descriptive name *Judaism* was never heard by the Hebrews or Israelites; it appears only with Christianity. Flavius Josephus was one of the first to use the name in his recital of the war with the Romans[9] to connote a totality of beliefs, moral commandments, religious practices and ceremonial institutions of Galilee which he believed superior to rival Hellenism. When the word *Judaism* was born, there was no longer a Hebrew-Israelite state. The people who embraced the creed of Judaism were already mixed of many races and strains; and this diversification was rapidly growing.

From the very outset, *Israel* signified something other than a racial kinship. There is plenty of evidence upon which scholars support the lineal diversity of even the earliest Hebrews. Their name comes from the word *Ibhri*, meaning one who comes from beyond, or from the other side. Abraham earned the name for himself when he crossed the Euphrates River on his way from Ur of the Chaldees to Palestine, then known as Canaan. *Abram* (the passer-over or immigrant) is the sense in which *Hebrew* is used in the Book of Genesis.[10] The reference to his tribe as to Hebrews is therefore appelative (carrying a connotation of foreignness) and in no manner ethnic or racial. Biblical students are agreed that the Exodus story of Moses leading a united people out of Egypt into the Promised Land is the simplification of a long and complicated history of tribal invasions of Canaan (Palestine). One Hebrew tribe may have drifted down into Egypt and become enslaved, while others were attacking the outlying Canaanite cities. Most scholars assume three such migratory waves. There is much dispute over their historical dates, but certainly a period of three to six centuries separated Abraham from Moses.

Few historical figures have been so deeply shrouded in mystery as was Moses. Of unknown origin, he married Zipporah, the daughter of a Midianite[11] priest, Jethro. It was at the home of his father-in-law that he discovered Yahweh and learned the ritual of worshiping the God of the first monotheistic faith. Was Moses of Egyptian blood, as some historians, such as James Henry Breasted, maintain?[12] His name could have been derived from the Egyptian *Mose*, meaning child, which appears in the name of such rulers of the Nile as Ah-Mose and Ra-Mose (Greek translation and contraction turning it into "Ramses"). Who were the people Moses brought to the threshold of Canaan? Partial light is shed on their origin by the Biblical story of Joseph. There was at the time (1600-1500 B. C.) a famine in the fertile crescent

(Palestine, Syria, Lebanon), and certain nomadic peoples, undoubtedly of Babylonian and Aramean ancestry, moved into Egypt. Subsequently enslaved, or otherwise dissatisfied with their lot, they left the land of the Nile together with other Semitic-speaking people such as the Moabites, Edomites and Ammonites. Moses, who had been exiled earlier, for some reason returned to his birthplace after Yahweh had revealed Himself to him through the burning bush at Mount Horeb in Sinai.

Canaan was only gradually absorbed, and the blood of the invaders was blended with the Canaanite blood, itself a composite of many strains. The tribe of Judah grew out of an Israelite-Canaanite marriage. Joseph married Osnath, and the tribes of Ephrain and Manasseh were largely Egyptian. A whole clan of Simeon was called Saul after the son of a Canaanite woman. The Old Testament, in the books of Joshua, Judges, Samuel, and the Kings, tells how the newcomers to Canaan mixed with the Philistines and the Hittites. Half of those today calling themselves "Jews" may be descendents of these Hittites, another of the conquered nations or tribes of Canaan. And the most direct descendents of the ancient Hittites are today the Christian Armenians.

Carefully drawn pictures on ancient Egyptian monuments portray a substantial fraction of Hebrews as having had blue eyes and blonde hair—physical characteristics of the tall fair-haired Amorites, one of the seven peoples who inhabited Canaan before and after the first Hebrew invasion. The dynasty of David descended from Ruth, a daughter of the Moabites.[13] Still later, there were many non-Israelite converts amongst those returning from the exile in Babylon. Moreover, innumerable Judeans had intermarried, both in Babylonia and at home, with their conquerors and other "foreign" peoples. This brought down upon them the wrath of Ezra who lists the non-Israelite strains[14] whose daughters and offspring must be banished by their Israelite husbands and fathers. This offspring included Canaanites, Hittites, Perizzites, Jebusites, Ammonites, Moabites, Egyptians, and Amorites.[15]

Despite the narrow nationalism of some post-exilic leaders, Judaism became a tremendous proselytizing force[16] in the pagan world. Those who carried the religion of Yahweh to other parts of the globe were hardly more than a drop in the ocean of foreign peoples who had never possessed any racial, lingual or cultural affinity with Israel, and, nevertheless, became members of the Judaic monotheistic faith. These converts included such diverse peoples as Yemenites and Greeks, the Queen of Sheba, the people of Adiabene (a Hellenistic state on the Tigris). Conversions to Yahweh in Rome had carried Judaism through Italy into France, the Rhone Valley and the Rhine Basin. Mass conversions of Germanic tribes spread Judaism into Central and Eastern Europe, particularly Poland and Western Russia. Friedrich Hertz, in his *Race and Civilization*, notes that, "not withstanding all obstacles even in the Middle Ages and modern times,"[17] there have been occasional conversions in Slavic countries which account for unmistakable Slavic facial characteristics of Polish and Russian Jews. Conversions to Judaism are reported in Hungary as late as 1229.[18]

Perhaps the most significant mass conversion to the Judaic faith occurred in Europe, in the 8th century A. D., and that story of the Khazars (Turko-Finnish people) is quite pertinent to the establishment of the modern State of Israel. This partly nomadic people, probably related to the Volga Bulgars,[19] first appeared in Trans-Caucasia in the second century. They settled in what is now Southern Russia, between the Volga and the Don, and then spread to the shores of the Black, Caspian and Azov seas. The Kingdom of Khazaria, ruled by a *khagan*, or *khakan*, fell to Attila the Hun in 448, and to the Muslims in 737. In between, the Khazars ruled over part of the Bulgarians, conquered the Crimea, and stretched their kingdom over the Caucasus farther to the northwest to include Kiev, and eastwards to Derbend. Annual tributes were levied on the Russian Slavonians of Kiev. The city of Kiev was probably built by the Khazars. There were Jews in the city and the surrounding area before the Russian Empire was founded by the Varangians whom the Scandinavian warriors sometimes called the Russ or Ross (circa 855-863).

The influence of the Khazars extended into what is now Hungary and Roumania. Today, the villages of Kozarvar and Kozard in Transylvania bear testimony to the penetration of the Khazars who, with the Magyars, then proceeded into present-day Hungary. The size and power of the Kingdom of Khazaria is indicated by the fact that it sent an army of 40,000 soldiers (in 626-627) to help Heraclius of the Byzantines to conquer the Persians.[20] The *Jewish Encyclopedia* proudly refers to Khazaria as having had a "well constituted and tolerant government, a flourishing trade and a well disciplined army."

Jews who had been banished from Constantinople by the Byzantine ruler, Leo III,[21] found a home amongst these heretofore pagan Khazars and, in competition with Mohammedan and Christian missionaries, won them over to the Judaic faith. Bulan, the ruler of Khazaria, became converted to Judaism around 740 A. D. His nobles and, somewhat later, his people followed suit. Some details of these events are contained in letters exchanged between Khagan Joseph of Khazaria and R. Hasdai Ibn Shaprut of Cordova, doctor and quasi foreign minister to Sultan Abd al-Rahman, the Caliph of Spain. This correspondence (around 936-950) was first published in 1577 to prove that the Jews still had a country of their own— namely, the Kingdom of Khazaria. Judah Halevi knew of the letters even in 1140. Their authenticity has since been established beyond doubt.

According to these Hasdai-Joseph letters, Khagan Bulan decided one day: "Paganism is useless. It is shameful for us to be pagans. Let us adopt one of the heavenly religions, Christianity, Judaism or Islam." And Bulan summoned three priests representing the three religions and had them dispute their creeds before him. But, no priest could convince the others, or the sovereign, that his religion was the best. So the ruler spoke to each of them separately. He asked the Christian priest: "If you were not a Christian or had to give up Christianity, which would you prefer—Islam or Judaism?" The priest said: "If I were to give up Christianity, I would become a Jew." Bulan then asked the follower of Islam the same question, and the Moslem also chose Judaism. This is how Bulan came to choose Judaism for himself and the people of Khazaria in the seventh century A. D., and thereafter the Khazars (sometimes spelled Chazars and Khozars) lived according to Judaic laws.

Under the rule of Obadiah, Judaism gained further strength in Khazaria. Synagogues and schools were built to give instruction in the Bible and the Talmud. As Professor Graetz notes in his *History of the Jews,* "A successor of Bulan who bore the Hebrew name of Obadiah was the first to make serious efforts to further the Jewish religion. He invited Jewish sages to settle in his dominions, rewarded them royally . . . and introduced a divine service modeled on the ancient communities. After Obadiah came a long series of Jewish Chagans (Khagans), for according to a fundamental law of the state only Jewish rulers were permitted to ascend the throne."[22]

Khazar traders brought not only silks and carpets of Persia and the Near East but also their Judaic faith to the banks of the Vistula and the Volga.[23] But the Kingdom of Khazaria was invaded by the Russians, and Itil, its great capital, fell to Sweatoslav of Kiev in 969. The Byzantines had become afraid and envious of the Khazars and, in a joint expedition with the Russians, conquered the Crimean portion of Khazaria in 1016. (Crimea was known as "Chazaria" until the 13th century). The Khazarian Jews were scattered throughout what is now Russia and Eastern Europe. Some were taken North where they joined the established Jewish community of Kiev. Others returned to the Caucasus. Many Khazars remarried in the Crimea and in Hungary. The Cagh Chafut, or "mountain Jews," in the Caucasus and the Hebraile Jews of Georgia are their descendants. These "Ashkenazim Jews" (as Jews of Eastern Europe are called), whose numbers were swelled by Jews who fled from Germany at the time of the Crusades and during the Black Death, have little or no trace of Semitic blood.

That the Khazars are the lineal ancestors of Eastern European Jewry is a historical fact. Jewish historians[24] and religious text books acknowledge the fact, though the propagandists of Jewish nationalism belittle it as pro-Arab propaganda.[25] Somewhat ironically, Volume IV of the *Jewish Encyclopedia*—because this publication spells Khazars with a "C" instead of a "K"—is titled "Chazars to Dreyfus": and it was the Dreyfus trial, as interpreted by Theodor Herzl, that made the modern Jewish Khazars of Russia forget their descent from converts to Judaism and accept anti-Semitism as proof of their Palestinian origin.

For all that anthropologists know, Hitler's ancestry might go back to one of the ten Lost Tribes of Israel; while Weizmann may be a descendant of the Khazars, the converts to Judaism who were in no anthropological respect related to Palestine. The home to which Weizmann, Silver and so many other Ashkenazim Zionists have yearned to return has most likely never been theirs. "Here's a paradox, a paradox, a most ingenious paradox": in anthropological fact, many Christians may have much more Hebrew-Israelite blood in their veins than most of their Jewish neighbors.

Race can play funny tricks on people who make that concept the basis for their likes and dislikes. Race-obsessed people can find themselves hating people who, in fact, may be their own racial kith and kin. The most persuasive argument the Jewish nationalist could advance for Zionism is based on the hypothesis of a "Hebrew-Semitic race." But most members of such a "race" would be found amongst the Arabic peoples of the Middle East, the overwhelming majority of whom do not profess the Jewish faith. The Arabs, bitter enemies of the Israelis who have returned to their reputed "racial home," most closely resemble those Jews who are indigenous to Palestine and the Middle East; for they are of purer Hebrew-Israelite blood than most of those who have been "ingathered."

It is Saudi Arabia's King Ibn Saud who is the modern Semitic prototype of the patriarch Abraham. The allegation that Arabs are anti-Semitic is somewhat ludicrous.

The Moslems of the Arab world call the Middle East Jews "the sons and daughters of my uncle." Conversely, anthropologists have not the slightest doubt that most German Jews in the Holy Land resemble other Germans much more closely than their Palestinian coreligionists of Khazar or Yemenite origin.

W. Z. Ripley, in his *Races of Europe*, points out that the "original Semitic stock must have been in origin strongly dolichocephalic," that is to say, African, from which it follows that about nine-tenths of the contemporary Jews are as widely different in headform from that "parent stock" as they possibly could be. Anthropologist Friedrich Hertz speaks of a Jewish "racial compound," and Eugene Pittard, Professor of Anthropology at the University of Geneva, notes in his *Race and History* that the Jews "constitute a very powerful religious and social community[26] whose elements are extremely heterogeneous."[27] Dr. Pittard categorically states: "There is no more a Christian race than a Musulman race, and neither is there such a thing as a Jewish race."[28] The same conclusion is reached in a 1952 study of the United Nations Educational, Scientific and Cultural Organization.[29] Columbia University anthropologists say in "The Races of Mankind":[30] "Jews are people who acknowledge the Jewish religion. They are of all races, even Negro and Mongolian. European Jews are of many different biological types. . . . The so-called Jewish type is a generalized type common in the Near East in countries bordering on the Mediterranean."

It is, in fact, the unanimous conclusion of all anthropologists, from Weissenberg, Hertz and Fishberg (themselves Jews), to Boas, Ripley, Mead, Pittard and others, that wherever Jews are found, they closely resemble the people amongst whom they live. Even those of common family names, supposedly traceable to the ancient Hebrew tribes, such as Levites (Levy) and Kohanim

(Kohn, Cohen, Cohn), have little physical resemblance to one another. There is not one racial characteristic common to all who profess to be Jews.

Weissenberg suggests two most common types of Jews—the Semitic or dark type, of Mediterranean origin, with a fine nose; and the Armenoid type, with a coarser nose and an appearance of blondness—the Tartar-Khazar type, mostly found in Eastern Europe. The Armenians and the people of Anatolia are rather proud possessors of what is called a "Jewish nose." Julian Huxley[31] notes that the Armenoid, with his heavy nose and pronounced nostrils, resembles the ancient Hittites.

The results of Jewish migration and hybridization with other peoples are spectacularly evident in Israel where Jews have brought, from every segment of the globe, the widest range of racial traits. On my first visit to Jerusalem in 1944, I was struck by the overwhelming visual proof that ridicules Jewish racialism. At a glance, I could distinguish the Ashkenazim of Poland from the Sephardic Jews of the Iberian Peninsula or North Africa, the Yemenite Jews, the German Jews—all different, not only in anthropological features, but also in dress, language, manners and mental attitudes. The common denominator of persecution did not change the fundamental fact that, in essence, they were Poles, Portuguese, Germans, etc. The Sephardic Jews from Southern Europe bear the physical traits of such Mediterranean people as the Arabs, Italians and Greeks. The Western European Jew resembles his coreligionist in Eastern Europe as little as the Spaniard resembles the Slav. Forty-five per cent of the Polish Jews have light eyes, and 29 per cent of the Lithuanian Jews blond hair.[32] The physical differences between the European, Indian, Yemenite and Ethiopian Jews are greater than those between Teutons, Slavs and Latins. There are tall blond Jews with blue eyes from Central Europe and the Baltic and Scandinavian countries; woolly-headed Algerian Jews; brown Falasha Jews with the curly hair of Abyssinia; the yellow Jews of China; and the black Tamels of India, who have dwelt in the heart of Asia for seventeen centuries.

Jean-Paul Sartre, the French existentialist, wrote of a German friend of his, a Jew who was blond, lean, and phlegmatic, and amused himself, at the beginning of the Nazi regime, by going out with SS men one of whom bragged: "I can tell a Jew a hundred yards away."[33] But another German friend of Sartre's, a Corsican Catholic, was short and fat, had dark curly hair, and a Bourbon nose. So, naturally, German children called him "Jude" and threw stones at him. And indeed, there are as many Jews who do not resemble the "Jewish Prototype" as there are Christians who do. Certain physical characteristics, which can be found in Christians as well, will identify the Jew only because of a cultural association with acquired mannerisms, names, bearing, and manner of speech. These "Jewish traits" are accentuated by Jewish herding-together: they result from social isolation and protracted inbreeding which has tended to perpetuate patterns as in "ruling dynasties, castes and in areas of local isolation."[34] These traits are anything but racial; and they disappear where integration is practiced.[35]

Within the Jewish fold in the United States, there are constant and ample manifestations that Judaism is merely a religious kinship. Just as it is said of the Cabots and the Lowells in the land of the cod, the German-American Jew speaks only to the Sephardic-American Jew, who speaks only to God; and they both look with disdain upon the Ashkenazim Jew from Poland or Russia. But the cultural chasm and basic differences amongst

Jews of varied ethnic origin has shown nowhere worse than in Israel. When Israelis speak of the "disturbing colored problem," they are referring to the Oriental Jews from the Middle East and North Africa. The Israeli of German or French origin often insists that he has a little more in common with the Zulus of deep Africa than with the Yemenite Jews. And the irony deepens when the descendants of converted Khazars become reluctant to accept as equals[36] "ingathered" brethren who can stake out a relatively plausible claim to ancient Palestinian descent.

The Jewish immigrants from Yemen resisted the attempts of the Israeli Government to enroll their children in the non-religious school system. In Yemen, girls marry at the age of 12 and even younger, and men are allowed several wives. When the Israeli Parliament outlawed polygamy in 1950 and set 17 as the minimum age for marriage, the Yemenite resentment was just as deep as that of some Oriental immigrants to Israel who were now forcibly restrained from sacrificing live animals in their religious rites.[37] The Iraqis, most of whom entered Israel in 1950 and 1951, now constitute more than one tenth of the Israeli population (being outnumbered only by the Poles and Roumanians). They have bitterly complained of discrimination. In July 1951, Iraqi Jews staged in Tel Aviv a mass demonstration against "race discrimination in the Jewish state, the first of its kind."[38] Whenever assaults occur on the dark streets, certain Tel Aviv papers customarily report "The assault is thought to have been committed by a North African"—a reference to the 50,000 new Jewish immigrants from Morocco, Tunisia and Algiers. In November 1951, a group of 130 Indian Jews expressed the desire to be repatriated to India. In Israel, they claimed, they were being forced to do the lowest kind of labor, were called "black" by the rest of the populace.[39] They even insisted they were permitted only black bread. Speaking for this group of Indians, Isaac Joseph, an insurance salesman, said: "In India there is no discrimination. In Israel we are Easterners and apparently inferior."

Despite such fierce internal variances and stresses, a fictional Jewish oneness is presented to the outside world. This unity is cemented by anti-Semitism. For the average Jew it is, from childhood, a world of "we" and "they." He is brought up, at home and in religious school, to believe in *being* something ("be proud you are a Jew") rather than to *believe* in something ("be proud of Judaism"). Little wonder he is such easy prey for the Zionists whom Professor Arnold J. Toynbee has succinctly called "a fragment of a fossil."

CHAPTER XIII

Shadow and Substance

I T IS not Palestine alone that has been partitioned. A vast number of American Jews were split in two by the same political act. And no one has stated the ugly problem—the problem of a citizen's insufferable dual loyalty—more succinctly than Israel's Jewish Agency in this official statement: "Once there is a (Jewish) State, clashes inevitably arise with the needs and demands of other countries to which Jews owe loyalties. The problem of *double loyalty* cannot lightly be dismissed merely by saying that it does not exist. . . . It will become more difficult to fight in behalf of Israel's political demands when these demands do not conform with the policy of the State of which the Jews are citizens." To which Prime Minister Ben-Gurion, addressing the Zionist Action Committee in Jerusalem, added: "Zionists in other countries ought to have the courage to stand up for the State (of Israel) even if their Governments are against it."

An American citizen's right to sympathize with Israel, and give aid to the needy in that country, can be challenged by no reasonable person. But this is not the conduct to which Zionism has been committing American Jewry. Zionism, with fantastic success, has been pledging American Jewry to the unreserved political support of a sovereign foreign State.

This, and this alone, is the issue: Will American Jews allow Zionism to separate them from America as a special collective whose fate is outside and beyond the American fate? This, I repeat is the sole issue; and it cannot much longer be hidden behind the banal contention that, after all, America's Irish are fully free to display their special passions for Ireland—and why, then, should not America's Jews, too, be free to feel the same way about Israel? The sentimental affection that Americans of Irish (or Italian, or French) birth have for their country of origin offers no analogy to the feeling toward Israel exhibited by many American Jews. The Irish are a nation, and Judaism is a religion. The Irish who are in the United States left Ireland only in recent generations, while the Jews left Roman Palestine two millenniums ago, centuries before the first Angles and Saxons set foot on England, and they have come to America not from Israel, but from every country in Europe.

An even more telling point of difference is, simply and clearly, that no Irish Government has ever dared demand from America's Irish one tenth of the allegiance the Israeli Government demands from America's Jews as a matter of course; or claim one tenth of the sovereignty over "Diaspora Irish" the Israeli Government has stipulated of "Diaspora Jews" in Israel's constitutional law. Would an Irish Chief of State have dared declare the "ingathering" of America's Irish, as an Israeli Chief of State has declared the "ingathering" of the world's Jewry to be the supreme political goal of Israel? It is beneath anybody's self-respect to go on pretending that

Zionism was merely an attempt to enrich American folklore by promoting a Jewish counterpart to the St. Patrick's Day Parade. Zionism is a hard-headed political creed which proposes to subject America's Jews to the sovereignty of Israel.

Unlike the thousands of American Jews who blind themselves to that disturbing fact with a fuzzy indifference, and with protestations of their solely philanthropic ties with Israel, most American Zionists know what they want and what they are doing. Speaking to American Zionists on "The State and the Future of Zionism" in 1950, Ben-Gurion thus defined their duties: "The basis of Zionism is neither friendship nor sympathy but the love of Israel, of the State of Israel. . . . It must be an unconditional love. There must be complete solidarity with the State and the people of Israel."[1]

And this is not just the conduct expected of those who, by a conscious act of dedication, have pledged their allegiance to the State of Israel. In Ben-Gurion's eyes, all Jews, all over the world, are implicitly Zionists; the job of the ubiquitous Zionist machine is merely to make this fact explicit. And the success of that tireless effort can be measured in the educational field as, for instance, reported by Charles G. Spiegler, a New York high school and college teacher, in the *Chicago Jewish Forum, United Jewish Appeal,* Vol. IV, No. 1, January 18, 1949. Mr. Spiegler tells of a questionnaire "submitted to two-hundred average American high school students between the ages of 15 and 16" in which he asked these questions: "Do you eventually want to visit Israel? Why?" All students, of course, wanted to visit Israel. But why? Among the answers Mr. Spiegler proudly quotes: "I want to see what my homeland is like"; and: "It is our country." The same article describes an emotional intensity, translated into action, which is as deep or deeper than any feeling expressed toward the United States: "There are thousands, even as young as eight or nine, who stand on street corners, march through trains, enter swank business offices, where they deliver sincere one-minute talks on why every Jew must help."

In a bulletin of the Washington Heights, N. Y., Sunday School of the Y.M.H.A. and Y.W.H.A. (*Sunday School Life*, Chanukah Issue), one reads this extraordinary pledge of young Americans: "Here Is Our Pledge, Israel: I pledge my loyalty to God, to the Torah and to the Jewish people and *to the Jewish state. . . .* "

When a questionnaire was issued to the pupils of the public school system in Galveston, Texas, 102 students answered the question "What is your nationality?" with: "Jewish."

The final word on this subject has been said by Woodrow Wilson almost forty years ago: "You cannot become true Americans if you think of yourselves in groups. America does not consist of groups. A man who thinks of himself as belonging to a particular national group has not yet become an American. And the man who goes among you to trade upon your nationality is not worthy to live under the Stars and Stripes."[2] But that man still "goes among us"—and he is even a teacher in America's public school system! And he, the Zionist, is not unduly impressed by Woodrow Wilson's injunction that the trader "upon your nationality is not worthy to live under the Stars and Stripes"; he proudly hoists, on American soil, the Flag of Israel. (An editorial in the magazine of the Intercollegiate-Zionist Federation of America proclaimed officially: "Of course the Israeli flag is a flag of a foreign state. So is Hebrew the language of that state, Chanukah one of its holidays. . . . *But all these are ours as well.* The future of the Jews is bound up with that of Israel.")

His own compliance with Jewish unity involves the non-Zionist in these declarations and activities of the Zionists. The failure to appreciate that Israel is as much a foreign state as France or Germany has led Jews into pitfalls which others not afflicted with the aged duality would easily have seen. Dual loyalties do not necessarily involve the conscious process of reasoning: "*This* is in the interests of the United States; *that* is in the interests of Israel, and I choose *that*." This is the obvious, rare case. Much more common is the unconscious choosing of *that* without any consideration of *this*.

In 1948, when the recovery of Europe through the Marshall Plan was the fundamental keystone of American bipartisan foreign policy, the core of an envisioned reconstructed Europe was to be Britain. Strong Communist Parties in Italy and France were doing everything in their power to interfere with the operations of the Plan, while the Russians themselves were creating obstacles by means of the airblock of Germany.

At this time there was an attempt to mobilize American public opinion behind a boycott of British goods. Signs were plastered in stores throughout New York City, and the Sons of Liberty Boycott Committee was formed. From the pulpit and in resolutions, support was given to this anti-British activity. This was, in practical effect, as much an attempt to sabotage foreign policy, as were any of the Communist efforts in Europe. While Uncle Sam was pouring out hundreds of millions from the national coffers to place her closest ally in a better dollar position, there were many Jews who cancelled plans to include England on their trips abroad because they refused to leave dollars there.

The problem of how to use Germany in the common defense against Communism is a complicated enigma. It was not easy to arrive at the decision that Germany should be rearmed and integrated into the Western European community. The spectre of a remilitarized Germany was frightening in itself without adding to it Jewish sensitivity and the prejudices of the state of Israel toward the successors to the Hitler Government. Zionism injected the issue of the special Jewish peril into the question, even coupling the indemnification rights of Israel against Germany. When the Knesset in Israel recessed as a protest against the signing of the peace treaty between West Germany and the Western Allies, no Jewish group stepped forward to disassociate itself from what was publicly stated to be "the Jewish position."

On still another occasion the split personality revealed itself. In the fall of 1949, the question of the internationalization of Jerusalem rested on the agenda of the United Nations' General Assembly. Israel's Foreign Minister Sharett, on his arrival in the United States from Tel Aviv, called for the support of "World Jewry" for Israel's position. American Jews were called upon by their leaders to take a "High Holiday Oath" not to forsake thee, Jerusalem. The major rabbinical bodies were announced as solidly united against internationalization. A campaign carried this view to the Congress, the State Department, and the American Delegation to the United Nations.

During the debate and ensuing vote the United States sided with Israel. Having been outvoted in the General Assembly, the United States abided by the majority decision and warned Israel against making any rash moves. In direct defiance of the U. N. resolution—a reaffirmation of the 1947 decree—Premier Ben-Gurion declared in Tel Aviv that his government offices were being transferred to the Holy City. As one voice, Jewish organizations sided with the foreign government in a much publicized statement: "The Jews fully support the Jews of Israel in whatever steps they may take to defend the integrity and centrality of Jerusalem as their 'National Capital.' "

Amazingly enough, Zionism has been successful in persuading non-Jewish America, or at least most of America's politicians and press, that the Jews have a special dispensation from the otherwise universal American tenet, "America does not consist of groups." Small wonder that American Jewry seems axiomatically convinced of its special destiny above and beyond the destiny of America. It is, of course, an immensely perilous assumption; but it is deeply rooted in the history of Judaism—an experience in which the religious substance and the nationalist shadow blend most confusingly.

*　　*　　*

Religion, to the theologian, is a set of metaphysical doctrines concerning the nature of the universe and the meaning of human life. In a less technical sense, religion involves man's attitude towards a controlling supernatural power that demands reverence and organized worship. Judiasm is of course a religious faith, but very few of those who think of themselves as Judaists possess true title to that designation. Statistics on U. S. synagogue membership vary, but no reliable source places the total membership above one and a half million.[3] Adding an approximate 250,000 who worship at least on the two High Holy Days, New Year (Rosh Hashonoh) and

Day of Atonement (Yom Kippur), there is a total of 1,850,000 practicing Judaists in America. In other words, of the more than five million Americans who list themselves as Jews, three-and-a-quarter million, or 65 per cent, do not participate in the synagogue.

Attendance at worship, of course, is quite a different thing from synagogue membership. Only one half of the Conservative synagogues (modified Orthodox) are holding daily service, and this mostly for mourners.[4] Fifty-seven per cent of the synagogues reported less than fifty regular worshippers, seventy per cent less than one hundred. While young people were notably absent from religious service, the synagogues served as centers of their social life. Clearly, what links together American Jewry is something other than religion. To put it bluntly, an individual is counted as a member of the Judaic faith because he feels at home with people who also consider themselves to be Jews.

In his *Basic Judaism*,[5] Milton Steinberg speaks of "the seven strands of Judaism," of which only two are truly concerned with God, the universe and man, with a moral code for individuals and society. The other five are solely concerned with rites, custom and ceremony, law and literature, and with social institutions through which these find expression—for the most part hang-overs from ancient times when the word "Jew" referred to both a religion and a nation. There are few Jewish Holidays which are holy days in the spiritual sense, and not mere anniversaries of some event in Jewish *national* history (such as the destruction of the Temple or Esther's successful campaign against Haman). In that sense, recent attempts to link Jewish Holidays with economic and political needs of Israel are by no means against the traditional grain.

Judaism has no dogma and no precisely stated credo which an adherent must profess. The belief that he is of a different, chosen and distinct people—in other words, that he is a Jew—has, for the individual, gradually assumed the place of defined theological convictions. Aside from being the first monotheistic creed, the true attractiveness of Judaism always rested in its simplicity. The prophets' idea of justice and the moral law gave Judaism its chance to grow from a national deism into a universal creed. But in historic reality, Judaism has shrunk to a nationalist rite.

The personification of Jesus gave Christianity a spiritual warmth which formalistic and legalistic Judaism has always lacked: A "God with a face" is a Divine Being of immediate and intimate meaning to humans. Moses was only another man with few characteristics of sanctity, and the Jewish prophets were never accorded the status the apostles hold in Christianity. To counterbalance such advantages of Christianity, Judaism could have stressed its direct approach to God, without the oppressive need of an intermediary. However, gradually the "Jewish people" itself became the intermediary between Yahweh and those who would worship him: the "chosen people" concept smothered universality.

In response to the growing appeal of Christianity, the older faith became increasingly exclusive and secular. Proselytizing ceased and emphasis shifted to Judaism's imaginary blood ties with an extinguished Hebrew-Israelite nation. Practices prevailed over beliefs. The mores of a vanished people were handed down from generation to generation. The Jewish historian, Heinrich Graetz, thus described the Talmud: "The sublime and the common, the great and the small, the grave and the ridiculous, the altar and the ashes, the Jew and the heathen, be discovered side by side."[6] (Kosher dietary laws are to these days based upon sanitary necessities of two millenniums ago.)[7] Though these codifications bore only the barest touch of spirituality, they were accepted in lieu of a religion and observed in proud respect for historic practice—an expression of "oneness" of the so-called Jewish people rather than a set of theological convictions.

Patriarchs and rabbis, jealously ruling their walled-in sovereignties of the ghetto, developed a nostalgia for that portion of the Jewish past which knew of noble warriors, kings and nationhood. The sacred mission of carrying a universalist message to all people was buried under ceremonial concepts of peoplehood, concepts which persecution and prejudice made even more stubborn. The Kingdom of God, the transfigured society, came to mean a clannish promise for the privileged few. Particularism triumphed, and Judaism made a "racial hoard of God."

Thus, the Zionist movement found it quite easy to transform the spiritual concept of a return to Zion into a literal rebirth of a political past. But its very success is now confronting Judaism with this ultimate alternative: Can Judaism survive as a religious force, divorced from Israel, proving that the nation-concept was merely a historic means of keeping a spiritual faith alive? Or will Judaism, having served its purpose as the handmaiden of nationalism, now have to fade away?

Yet the heart of the universal Judaistic faith in a universal God is still beating. In the words of Micah[8] and Leviticus:[9] "It hath been told thee, O Man, what is good and what the Lord doth require of thee—only to do justly and to love mercy and to walk humbly with thy God. . . . Love thy neighbor as thyself." And in the words of Isaiah: "For my house shall be called a House of prayer for all people."[10] These remain the unfulfilled goals of Judaism—and of mankind. The need for the spiritual revival of Judaism was never greater. By returning to active proselytizing and competing with other religions for the inner convictions of man, the American rabbinate could offer concrete evidence that a vibrant Judaistic faith yet exists.

In this one sense, the establishment of the State of Israel may yet prove to have been a providential blessing: now that those Jews who crave their separate nationhood can go to Israel, the last reason has been removed for the pernicious Jewish duality outside the Holy Land. Now each American Jew has been given a free choice to be either an American of Jewish faith or a nationalist Israeli in his own Middle East State. He can not be both. For him who cherishes the clannishness of particularism above everything else, there is only one honorable course—to emigrate to Israel. And the American Jew, who desires to harmonize his special religious beliefs with the universal pattern of American existence, will now have to cut all political ties with Zionism and the State of Israel. For American Judaism can survive only when it is so completely divorced from Israel as American Protestanism is divorced from England.

CHAPTER XIV

Agenda for Jews

THERE are millions of Arabs around Israel, and the young State must learn what so many Jews have never learned—to live not only within but *with* their environment. Today, the Arabs of the Middle East think themselves committed to an unending struggle against Zionism.

"When we die, we shall pass the torch to our children" is the new Muslim motto. And yet, there still is reasonable hope for a peaceful coexistence of Arabs and Israelis —provided Israel desires such coexistence and International Zionism does not endanger it. The reconciliation agenda for Jews (and it would be an Arab's job to sketch those for Arabs) are inextricably set by the errors of the past and the needs of the future.

Above all, Israel must achieve complete national normalcy by ceasing to be the Jewish and becoming the Israeli state. The State of Israel, to be normal, must solemnly withdraw all claims to the fealty of anybody but its own citizens. For unless a State's sovereignty ends at its borders, it is an abnormal fraud and a dangerous freak. Unless the State of Israel severs its umbilical ties with private political and propaganda organizations *outside* its borders, it deserves neither the recognition of the civilized world nor the co-operation of its Arab neighbors.

Specifically, Israel must, for a start, at least execute the various decrees of the United Nations which created that State. These orders stipulated an economic union of Palestine, an international rule over the city of Jerusalem which is the holy home of three world religions, and a just settlement of the Arab refugee problem. They also provided certain boundaries for the new nation.

No nation has ever been under a greater moral obligation to alleviate the plight of refugees than the State of Israel. Not only did Israel's political acts create that plight for the Arabs of Palestine, but the international rationale for the very existence of Israel was the world's desire to save refugees. Who, then, if not Israel must fully honor the right of displaced persons to return home in peace? And, just as clearly, full compensation must be granted to those Arab refugees whose return is not feasible. A United Nations Commission should supervise the assessment of their sequestered Palestine property and enable these refugees to find permanent reintegration in Arab lands. If need be, Israel should finance that restitution out of the reparation funds she is receiving from Germany.

The economic union of a politically partitioned Palestine was proposed by the United Nations just as much in the interest of Israel as in the interest of Arab Palestine. For, without such a union, the new State can never overcome its "reliance on gift capital and political motivations behind many of the development schemes with little regard to economic consideration."[1] To assume a trusted place in a peaceful Middle East, Israel must settle down to peaceful and mutually beneficial trade with her Arab neighbors. That trade, and not perpetual aid from

American Jewry, is Israel's road to economic viability.

Once the Arab refugee problem has been solved, Jerusalem internationalized, Palestine's economic union established, and Israel's sovereignty clearly confined to her territory, all other differences between Israelis and Arabs could be easily resolved in neighborly coexistence. Confronted with Israel's good will, the Arab world would learn to accept what it now considers an insufferable reversion of two Arab millenniums. And no longer incited by the "Arab Peril," busy Israelis might soon silence the fanatics in their midst who preach imperialistic Israeli expansion into Arab lands. (As a matter of fact, most *sabras*, or native-born Israelis, are even today totally indifferent to both Jewish nationalism and, *alas*, Jewish religion.) The Shalom Aleichem, the "peace be with you" of Hebrew, would then merge with the Salaam Alaikum of the Arabic.

As to American Jewry, they must realize, fast and unequivocally, that the survival of Israel is solely Israel's responsibility. American Jews who want to share in that responsibility will have to do so in Israel; that is, become Israeli Jews. They cannot live with one foot in the United States and one foot in Israel. It can not be repeated often enough that there is, for an American Zionist, no honorable way other than to have the courage of his conviction and invest himself as well as his capital in Israel.

American Jews who want to remain just that—Americans of the Jewish faith—will then at last be able to normalize their lives. An end will be put to all those "drives" which disguise a fanatical nationalism, tied to a foreign State, as philanthropy. For American Jews, to live normally will mean to free themselves of the spell of "unity"—the fallacious contention that Jews are less divided on secular issues than Baptists or Presbyterians, and that their security depends on the maintenance of this fiction. It will mean, above all, that American Jews can live at inner ease with their countrymen: When the last reservation is erased in their minds, when Jewish Americans are satisfied in their hearts that this, the United States, is their home for ever, they will have achieved the inner strength to laugh at the fossils of bigotry.

The desire of some Jews to maintain Israel as their insurance policy, "because it can also happen here," can only lead to increased misunderstanding. The establishment in a sensitive part of the world of what is claimed to be the political center of the "Jewish people" has already added, not lightened, existing tensions and prejudices. And as Caroll Binder, the editor of the *Minneapolis Star*, pointed out at the time of partition: "If the struggle for a Jewish State would eventually have to cost the democratic countries the oils of the Middle East, the Jews of the United States would most properly have to pay dearly for it."

Jewry will also have to insist on somewhat tidier semantics in America—on a clear distinction between Israelis, Zionists and Jews. The U. S. press notwithstanding, the Government of Israel is *not* Jewish; nor is the State of Israel. A synagogue is Jewish. So is the Decalogue. *Jews* are individuals who profess Judaism. Officers and citizens of the sovereign State of Israel are *Israelis;* and some of them are Jews. Also, some individual American Jews are Zionists, which means that they are on their way to exchange American for Israeli nationality. Except for those individuals, who propose to do what all Americans once have done—namely, to assume a new citizenship—American Jews are Americans who worship God in Judaistic ways. And the U. S. press had better clean up the sloppy language of the headlines.

There is no effective provision in international law by which the Israeli Government can be forced to repeal legislation that impairs the indivisibility of the citizenship of Jewish citizens of other nations. The American of Jewish faith has little means of protecting himself against claims of attachment made by a foreign government and its various agencies, short of divorcing himself completely from everything Jewish. But what an individual American citizen cannot redress through legal process, the U. S. Government surely could achieve politically. For instance the U. S. Government might seek the repeal of Israeli laws that establish abnormal ties, such as the automatic right of Jews alone to Israeli citizenship and the imposition of dual citizenship on Jewish Americans in Israel. If as in the past our government hesitates to reject, in a solemn and strong declaration of U. S. policy, all Israeli claim to any kind of special relationship with Jewish Americans, America will remain paralyzed in the Middle East.

Yet a real and lasting change of America's attitude towards the Middle East can be brought about only by a change of the climate that conditions American Jewry. This country's political obsession with "the Jewish vote" will haunt the nation's foreign policy in the Middle East, perhaps catastrophically, until American Jewry itself exposes the fraud. To that end, American Jews must make unmistakably clear that the Zionist speaks for no one but himself. With this action American foreign policy for the Middle East could be liberated to develop in the national interest.

From Haym Solomon of the American Revolution through Judah P. Benjamin, Secretary of State for the Confederacy, down to the present, there have been many who have made vital contributions to the American melting pot: Flexner; Brandeis, Cardozo and Frankfurter; Gershwin and Berlin; Pulitzer and Ochs; Louis Untermeyer, Fannie Hurst and Edna Ferber; Heifetz, Elman, Zimbalist, Milstein; Horowitz, Rubinstein and Serkin; George S. Kaufman, Moss Hart and Elmer Rice; the Guggenheims, Schiffs, Strausses, Lewisohns, Warburgs, and Rosenwalds. Some of these were born here and others were not, but the attainments of all these men and women were as individual Americans and not as part of a separate people.

The American Jew wants integration, not segregation. He measures the friendship of his Christian fellow citizens, not by what they are willing to do for the foreign State of Israel, but by their devotion to the Christian Commandment of love for their neighbor. The American Jew, irrevocably committed to the political ideals of America and the Commandments of his God, wants no special rights. He wants equal rights. His personal God is the God of Moses, his national home America.

Notes and Index

Notes

CHAPTER I

1. The number of those who returned is not known. There was no single mass return but a dribbling back, a little at a time.

2. See *Jewish Encyclopedia*, VI, 602.

3. Amos 9:7.

4. In the coronation ceremony of Elizabeth II, the Archbishop of Canterbury anointed his sovereign saying: "And as Solomon was anointed by Zadok, the priest. . . ."

5. See Dr. Julius Morgenstern, *As a Mighty Stream* (Philadelphia: Jewish Publication Society of America, 1949).

6. Nevill Barbour, *Nisi Dominus, A Survey of the Palestine Controversy* (London: Harrap, 1946), cited on p. 20.

7. Max L. Margolis and Alexander Marx, *A History of the Jewish People* (Philadelphia: Jewish Publication Society of America, 1927), p. 525.

8. *Ibid.*, p. 233.

9. *Ibid.*, p. 289.

10. *Universal Jewish Encyclopedia*, X, 531; also Vol. IX.

11. "Jews" called the Spanish peninsula a "Sepharad."

12. Salo W. Baron, *A Social and Religious History of the Jews* (3 vols., 1937).

13. Elmer Berger, *A Partisan History of Judaism* (New York: Devin-Adair, 1951).

14. Baron, *op. cit.*

15. Chovevei Zion, or Lovers of Zion, formed in 1881.

16. Allen Tarshish, *Not by Power* (N.Y.: Bookman Associates, 1952), p. 239.

17. *Yearbook*, Central Conference of American Rabbis, I, 80–125.

18. Naomi Wiener Cohen, *The Reaction of Reform Judaism in America to Political Zionism* (1897-1922) (Publications of the American Jewish Historical Society, June, 1951), p. 365.

19. *Ibid.*, p. 371.

20. *Ibid.*, p. 368.

21. Solomon Grayzel, *A History of the Jews* (Philadelphia: Jewish Publication Society, 1947).

22. Dr. David Philipson and Dr. Isaac Landman, before a hearing of the Committee on Foreign Affairs of the House of Representatives, relative to The Fish Resolution. (See *The Reaction of Reform Judaism*, pp. 389–90.)

23. *American Jewish Year Book*, 1943.

24. Resolution of the General Syrian Congress, Damascus, July 2, 1919.

CHAPTER II

1. See Barbour, *Nisi Dominus: A Survey of the Palestine Controversy* (London: Harrap, 1946).

2. *Palestine Royal Commission Report*, Cmd. Paper 5479, *Great Britain Parliamentary Papers* (London, 1937), p. 23.

3. David Lloyd George, *The Truth About the Peace Treaties* (London: Gollancz, 1938), II, 1121.

4. *Ibid.*, II, 1117.

5. *The American Zionist*, February 5, 1953.

6. *Palestine Royal Commission Report*, p. 23.

7. J. W. V. Temperley, *History of the Peace Conference*, IV, 170.

8. See William I. Cargo, *The Origins of the Balfour Declaration*, Vol. XXVIII, "Papers of the Michigan Academy of Science, Arts and Letters" (1942), pp. 597–612.

9. Chaim Weizmann, *Trial and Error* (New York: Harper and Brothers, 1949), p. 192.

10. Parliamentary Debates, House of Commons, Vol. 326, col. 2330.

11. Weizmann, *op. cit.*, p. 203.

12. In David Lloyd George's *The Truth About the Peace Treaties* (pp. 1133–34), Montagu is quoted by his Chief as saying that he had "striven all his life to escape from the Ghetto."

13. Weizmann, *op. cit.*, p. 163.

14. Albert M. Hyamson, *Palestine: a Policy* (London: Methuen, 1942), p. 110.

15. See J. C. Hurewitz, *The Struggle for Palestine* (New York: W. W. Norton, 1950), pp. 18–20.

16. Nahum Sokolow, *History of Zionism* (London: Longman's 1919), I, pp. xxiv and xxv.

17. Lloyd George, *op. cit.*, II, 1132.

18. Albert M. Hyamson, *op. cit.*

19. Lloyd George, *op. cit.*, II, 1137.

20. *Great Britain Parliamentary Papers*, 1922, Cmd. Paper 1700, pp. 12–21.

21. Hyamson, *op. cit.*, n., p. 112. For similar assurances, see also Earl Balfour's defense of the Mandate in the House of Lords, June 1922, reported on page 95 of Hyamson.

22. Charles H. Levermore, *Third Year Book of the League of Nations* (1922), p. 137.

23. The Preamble of the Mandate contained Weizmann's "reconstitute the national home," but Article II used the exact phraseology of the Balfour Declaration.

24. *Great Britain Parliamentary Papers*, 1939, Comm. Paper 5964.

25. Lloyd George, *op. cit.*, pp. 1141–42.

26. For more on the Hogarth Message, see George Antonius, *The Arab Awakening* (Philadelphia: Lippincott, 1939), pp. 267–8; also Barbour, *op cit.*, n. p. 69.

27. Antonius, *The Arab Awakening*, p. 268.

28. *Letters of T. E. Lawrence*, edited by David Garnett (London: Jonathan Cape, 1939), p. 269.

29. Hyamson, *op. cit.*, p. 103.

30. The Commission consisted of Dr. Henry Churchill King, President of Oberlin College, and Mr. Charles R. Crane, Chicago industrialist and member of the American Commission to Russia in 1917. The report was suppressed until December 1922 when the *N. Y. Times* and *Editor & Publisher* made it available.

31. Official survey of the Anglo-American Committee of Inquiry.

32. *Times* (London), Nov. 15, 1945.

33. Anglo-American Committee of Inquiry, *Report to the United States Government and His Majesty's Government of the United Kingdom* (Pub. by Department of State, 1946), Preface.

34. Three of the signers of these unanimous recommendations later became the most ardent Christian supporters of Jewish Nationalism: Bartley Crum, R. H. S. Crossman and James G. McDonald reversed their position complete, even before Israel became a political reality.

35. Anglo-American Committee of Inquiry, Recommendation, No. 3, p. 4.

36. Weizmann, *op. cit.*, p. 201.

37. *New Palestine*, October 27, 1944.

38. Hurewitz, *op. cit.*, p. 249.

39. For a full discussion of the refugee problem, see Morris L. Ernst, *So Far So Good* (New York: Harper, 1948), pp. 170–77.

40. *Ibid.*, p. 176.

41. Fiscal Year 1942, only 10% of quotas used; 1943, 5%; 1944, 6%; 1945, 7%.

42. *Yiddish Bulletin*, Free Jewish Club, May 19, 1950.

43. *New York Times*, October 27, 1946.

44. The Supreme Council of the allied powers agreed to assign the Mandate for Palestine to Great Britain, April 25, 1920. The draft Mandate was confirmed by the Council of the League of Nations, September 29, 1923.

45. Weizmann, *op cit.*, p. 290.

46. The founder of this group, Abraham Stern, was a Pole who had settled in Palestine in 1925. He is reputed to have written Hebrew poetry between acts of greatest violence and was killed in 1942 by Palestine Police.

47. Weizmann, *op. cit.*, pp. 437 and 438.

48. Anglo-American Committee of Inquiry Recommendations, No. 10 at p. 12.

49. United Nations, *Official Records of the 2nd Session of the General Assembly* (Lake Success, 1947), II, 139.

CHAPTER III

1. On the author's 1953 visit to the Middle East, he encountered an eye witness to this violence who is an Arab refugee in Lebanon.

2. "Ad Hoc Committee of the Palestinian Question," Summary Record of Meetings, 25 September-25 November, 1947,

United Nations Official Records of the Second Session of the General Assembly (New York, Lake Success), p. 40.

3. *Plenary Meetings of the General Assembly*, II, 1312.

4. *Ibid.*, p. 1317.

5. *Ibid.*, p. 1319

6. *Ibid.*, p. 1357.

7. *Ibid.*, p. 1365.

8. *Ibid.*, p. 1364.

9. *Ibid.*, p. 1327.

10. Emanuel Newmann, in *American Zionist*, Feb. 5, 1953.

11. *Plenary Meetings of the General Assembly*, II, 1314–15.

12. *Dallas Morning News* of Dec. 1, 1947: "There is mordant humor in the fact that philanthropic world thought has been manoeuvered into a cul-de-sac. . . . Palestine is as much of a catastrophe as a problem."

13. *Forrestal Diaries* (Viking Press), pp. 346–47.

14. *Plenary Meetings of the General Assembly*, II, 1426.

15. The only condition of the Dutch and Surinam Governments was that the area of 500,000 acres was to be settled by the refugees *as Surinam citizens*, in equality with others in the Netherland territory, and not as any kind of "Jewish citizens."

16. Weizmann, *Trial and Error*, p. 459.

17. The General Assembly stipulated a date "not later than August 1" for the termination of the Mandate, but the Mandatory Power, anxious to relieve itself of the burdensome responsibility, withdrew even earlier.

CHAPTER IV

1. See Mallory Browne's dispatch in the *New York Times*, February 21, 1948.

2. See *New York Times*, February 20 and February 21, 1948.

3. Editorial of March 22, 1948.

4. February 26, 1948.

5. *Ibid.*, April 18, 1948.

6. Weizmann, *Trial and Error*, p. 477.

7. See *New York Times*, March 22, 1948: "Revolt on Truman Emerges"; also *New York Times*, March 25, 1948.

8. See *Official Records of the Second Special Session of the*

General Assembly, Vol. I, Plenary Meetings of the General Asembly, April 16-May 14, 1948, Summary Record of Meetings (New York, Lake Success).

CHAPTER V

1. Resolution of the 76th Congress, adopted on June 30, 1922. A Convention of December 3, 1924, between Great Britain and the United States, safeguarded American interests in the Holy Land.

2. House Resolutions, 418 and 419, 78th Congress, Second Session (1944).

3. *Hearings Before Committee on Foreign Affairs, House of Representatives, on the Wright-Compton Palestine Resolutions, Washington, D. C. (February 8, 9, 15, 16, 1944)* (U. S. Government Printing Office, 1944), p. 144.

4. *Papers Relating to the Foreign Relations of the United States, The Paris Peace Conference* (1919), XI, 150-55.

5. *Paris Peace Conference.*

6. *Papers Relating to the Foreign Relations of the United States, The Paris Peace Conference* (1919), XI, 150-55.

7. *Ibid.*

8. Letter, Hon. Henry L. Stimson, Secretary of War to Hon. Sol. Bloom, Chairman Foreign Affairs Committee, House of Representatives, Washington, D. C., March 17, 1944.

9. James F. Byrnes, *Speaking Frankly* (New York: Harper, 1947).

10. Elliott Roosevelt, *As I Saw It*, p. 245.

11. *The American Zionist*, Feb. 5, 1953.

12. *Ibid.*

13. Alfred Steinberg, "Mr. Truman's Mystery Man," *Saturday Evening Post* (December 24, 1949).

14. *Forrestal Diaries* (New York: Viking Press, 1950).

15. *Ibid.*, p. 309.

16. *Ibid.*, pp. 344-45.

17. *Ibid.*

18. *Ibid.*

19. *Ibid.*, p. 346.

20. *Ibid.*, pp. 376-77.

21. *Ibid.*, p. 363.

22. *Ibid.*, p. 364.

23. *Ibid.*

24. *My Mission to Israel*, Simon and Schuster, N. Y., 1951.

25. *Forrestal Diaries*, pp. 440–41.

26. James G. McDonald, *My Mission to Israel*, p. 17.

27. *Ibid.*, p. 25.

28. *Ibid.*, p. 32.

29. *Ibid.*, p. 52. (A complimentary copy of this book was sent to every Rabbi in the United States.)

30. In "*Lying In State*" (N. Y.: Doubleday, 1952), former U. S. Ambassador to Egypt, Stanton Griffis, contends (p. 213) that the Israeli Government knew the murderers of Count Bernadotte who were given passports by the Czechoslovak Government within 24 hours after Bernadotte died.

31. His supporters spelled the name "Beigin," whereas the official spelling was "Begin."

32. *Washington Evening Star*, December 1, 1948.

33. *Ibid.*

34. *Chicago Daily News*, December 8, 1948.

35. Menachem Begin, *The Revolt: Story of the Irgun* (New York: Henry Schuman, 1951).

36. *Ibid.*, p. 164, note 1.

37. *New York Times*, September 28, 1947.

CHAPTER VI

1. *New York Times*, October 26, 1952.

CHAPTER VII

1. *New York Times*, October 24, 1952.

2. Commenting on an editorial entitled "The Charge of Bigotry," which appeared in the *Herald-Tribune* during the Dulles-Lehman Senatorial campaign, the author wrote to his old friend Whitelaw Reid, the publisher of the paper. A significant portion of that letter read: "The support given to Jewish nationalism has undoubtedly been one of the factors in nurturing the very religious and racial issues which you rightly decry. . . . By emphasis, yes even shading and coloring, your writers have presented an over-glorification of what

actually exists in Israel, and thus you have inflamed the emotions of your readers. Day by day your paper has encouraged Jews to think as Jews and to be more conscious of their Jewishness in the secular sense. . . . "

3. *Public Opinion Quarterly*, Spring, 1948.

4. Arnold K. Isreeli, *Pro-Arab Propaganda in America* (Feb., 1952).

5. *New York Times*, September 12, 1949.

6. September 30, 1949.

7. A. Forster and B. Epstein, *Trouble Makers* (New York: Doubleday, 1952).

8. *The Facts* (Civil Rights Division of Anti-Defamation League, 1948), Vol. III, Part V.

9. *Ibid.*

10. This use of a stock apologetic phrase universally attributed to anti-Semites reads like an innuendo.

11. *The Facts*, Vol. III, Part V.

12. *Time*, October, 1951.

13. *Hearings before the Committee on Foreign Affairs, House of Representatives, Washington, D. C.*, February 8, 9, 15 and 16, 1944 (Washington: U. S. Govt. Printing Office), p. 210.

14. Rabbi Benjamin Mintz, President of the World Mizrachi, warned Reform Judaism that any attempt to introduce their creed in Israel would be met by a "war" (*Jewish Newsletter*, August 4, 1952).

15. *New York Times*, September 29, 1952.

16. *The Reader's Digest, The American Mercury, The American Legion Magazine, Human Events.* On other subjects, articles of mine have appeared in the *Foreign Policy Association Headline Series*, the *Washington Post* and the *Washington Star.*

CHAPTER VIII

1. *Nazi-Soviet Relations 1939-1941; Documents from the Archives of the German Foreign Office*, ("Department of State Publications," 3003), pp. 217–59.

2. These colleges are preparatory schools.

3. This included a 135 million dollar loan from the Export-Import Bank, technical assistance aid, and grants under the Mutual Security Program.

4. *Commentary*, October, 1952.

5. *New York Times*, July 2, 1952.

6. The oriental influx into Israel was 6% of immigrants in 1948, 46% in 1949, 50% in 1950 and 70% in 1951. Including the Arabs, there are now more Orientals than Occidentals in Israel.

7. Colombia, Costa Rica, Dominican Republic, Guatemala, Haiti, Honduras, Venezuela.

8. In November 1947, the General Assembly recommended the establishment of Jerusalem as a separate entity administered by the U. N. with the Trusteeship Council as the administering authority. At its second session in April, 1948, the Trusteeship Council completed a draft of the Statute, but postponed formal approval and transmitted the text to the Second Special General Assembly for advice. At that time, violence broke out in Jerusalem, and the General Assembly requested the Trusteeship Council to take action for the protection of the City, but failed to give further instructions concerning the Statute. The Trusteeship Council reported to the General Assembly that the parties had agreed to a cease-fire within the walled City, and recommended appointment of a special Municipal Commissioner. The General Assembly approved this recommendation, but shortly thereafter armed conflict broke out and the Commissioner was never able to function effectively. On December 11, 1948, the General Assembly established the Palestine Conciliation Commission and requested it to draw up a plan for the internationalization of Jerusalem. This plan was prepared during 1949 by the Palestine Conciliation Commission and presented to the 4th General Assembly. However, on December 9th, 1949, the General Assembly reiterated its decision of November, 1947, concerning Jerusalem and requested the Trusteeship Council to proceed with the preparation of a Statute. No action was taken on the Palestine Conciliation Commission plan. At its 6th session in April, 1950, the Trusteeship Council completed

its draft Statute but did not take steps to implement it, due to disagreement between the parties concerned.

CHAPTER IX

1. *Newsweek*, May, 1949.
2. Barbour, *Nisi Dominus*, p. 33, cites this phrase from Sir Moses Montefiore's diary.
3. Weizmann, *Trial and Error*, p. 219.
4. *Ibid.*, p. 262.
5. *Ibid.*, p. 268.
6. *The Realities of American-Palestine Relations* (Public Affairs Press, 1949).
7. Dr. Beracah Reis-Reichel, "Life in the Brandeis Camp," *The Morning Journal* (New York: April 7, 1946).
8. Weizmann, *op cit.*, p. 266. Einstein's secretary who accompanied him to the United States was Simon Ginsberg, son of Ha-am, the cultural Zionist.
9. *New York Times*, April 18, 1948. Rabbi Leo Baeck co-signed the letter.
10. New York *Daily News*, April 1, 1952.
11. Dr. Philipp Frank, *Einstein* (New York: Knopf, 1947).
12. (Boston: Little Brown, 1944.)
13. Originally published in *Menorah Journal*, Feb. 1918, and reprinted in *Menorah Journal*, autumn 1950, pp. 116–18.
14. Weizmann, *op cit.*, p. 77.
15. *Ibid.*, p. 309.
16. *Annual Reports of American Jewish Committee*, 1950 and 1951.
17. *Look* magazine, June, 1952.
18. *Forward* (New York), March 13, 1950.

CHAPTER X

1. *Dos Yiddish Folk* (official organ, Z. O. A., N. Y.), October, 1951.
2. A holding organization of Young Judes, Junior Hadassah, and the Inter-Collegiate Zionist Federation of America.

3. Keren Kayemeth, the Jewish National Fund, purchases land for agricultural settlers, while the Keren Hayesod, the Palestine Foundation Fund, finances immigration.

4. *Morning Journal* (New York Yiddish daily), December 2, 1949.

5. See "Our Philosopher-Protectors," *Menorah Journal*, Autumn, 1947; also "An Inquiry into the Joint Defense Appeal etc.," in same issue, and "Mid-Century Inventory," Autumn 1950.

6. Vol. II, No. 5 (1952).

7. *The Day* (New York), September 4, 1952.

8. Isaiah 58:3.

9. B. I. G. (Bonds of Israel Government) *News*, New York, Vol. II, No. 8, (1952).

10. Address of Rabbi Irving Miller, at the 55th Annual Convention of the Z. O. A., at Manhattan Center, 1952.

11. *Bulletin*, Manhattan Chapter, Zionist Organization of America (1951).

12. An executive of the Jewish Agency interpreted this frankly as an effort "to Zionise world Jewry . . . to establish Zionist hegemony over the developing Jewish communities throughout the world."

13. Dr. Nahum Goldmann claims Zionist credit for checking a "tendency" to worry about domestic needs and to resist the priority for Israeli needs. See *Mid-Century Inventory*, p. 131, reporting on the meeting of Zionist leaders in New York, May 24, 1950.

14.

1947 New York Times Index:		*1948 New York Times Index:*	
Palestine	27 pages	Palestine	24 pages
Great Britain	11 pages	Israel	2 pages
France	13 pages	Great Britain	5 pages
Greece (Truman Doctrine proclaimed)	11 pages	France	6 pages
		Greece	4 pages
"Jewish" & "Jews" (listings)	6 pages	"Jewish" & "Jews" listings	3 pages

1949 New York Times Index:

Palestine	7 pages	France	3 pages
Israel	3 pages	Greece	2 pages
Great Britain	5 pages	"Jewish" & "Jews"	
		listings	3 pages

15. *The New Partnership. Zionism and the State*, a report on the Sessions of the Actions Committee in Jerusalem, May, 1950, published by the Jewish Agency in Palestine (11 E. 66th Street, New York City).

16. *Jewish Newsletter* (New York), Vol. VIII, No. 18 (Sept. 1, 1952).

CHAPTER XI

1. *New York Times*, May 30, 1951.
2. *Ibid.*, December 13, 1951.
3. *The Day* (New York), March 15, 1950.
4. Chaplain Klausner says in his report on "Jewish Displaced Persons in the American Occupied Zone of Germany" to the American Jewish Conference, May 2, 1948: "The Jews as a group are not overwhelmingly desirous of going to Palestine . . . we may predict that perhaps 30% of the people will go to Palestine." In his letter of May 26, 1948, William Haber, Adviser on Jewish Affairs to the High Commissioner in Germany, disputes Klausner's estimate and claims accuracy for the Jewish Agency figure of 70%, but admits that a great number of the people who registered for migration to Palestine also registered for migration to other countries.
5. *The New Leader*, letter of Louis Nelson, then Manager, Knit Goods Workers Union, later Vice-President of the International Ladies Garments Workers Union (New York, August 21, 1948).
6. See S. D. Goiten, "The Transplantation of the Yemenites: The Old Life They Led," *Commentary*, July, 1951.
7. During the following year, the number of persons who migrated to Israel was not much greater than the number of those who emigrated from Israel.
8. *Forward*, July 5, 1952.
9. See *Foreois* (Mexico City), September 1, 1952, and *Jewish Newsletter* (New York), October 27, 1952.

10. *Die Stimme* (Mexico City), June 9, 1948.

11. See Correspondence of Mexican Defense Committee, sent to all Jewish organizations, particularly the letter of June 23, 1948, from Mexico City.

12. *Die Stimme*, June 9, 1948.

13. *Jewish Post*, April 22, 1949.

14. See *Imprensa Israelita* (Rio de Janeiro), July 23, 1948; *Nossa Voz* (San Paulo), July 28, 1948.

15. Jewish Telegraphic Agency, Buenos Aires, August 2, 1948.

16. See letter of Defense Committee, August 11, 1948.

17. See letter, Philip Skorneck, Secretary, Latin American Committee of the American Jewish Joint Distribution Committee, New York, July 12, 1948.

18. See letter, Moses A. Leavitt, Executive Vice-Chairman, American Jewish Joint Distribution Committee, July 19, 1948.

19. *Council News*, American Council for Judaism, September, 1952.

20. The discrimination of the Citizenship Law was attacked by the *Haaretz* (Tel Aviv), April 3, 1952; *Forward* (New York), April 26, 1952; and *The Day* (New York), May 3, 1952.

21. See *Forward*, New York, July 16, 1952.

22. *Jewish Morning Journal* (New York), September 15, 1952.

23. Quoted in *Kemper*, Yiddish paper (New York), July 11, 1952.

24. Reported in Zionist *Newsletter*, Nov. 27, 1951.

25. *Press Bulletin*, 23rd World Zionist Congress (Jerusalem), Aug., 1951.

26. Jewish Telegraphic Agency, Aug. 8, 1951.

27. See "Official Minutes," 23rd World Zionist Congress, 1951.

28. "Mid-Century Inventory," *Menorah Journal*, Autumn, 1950, p. 131.

CHAPTER XII

1. The indigenous American population, the Indians, belonged to the Mongolian race.

2. Australians who were on the island before Europeans ar-

rived. See Diana Tead and Jane Eakin Kleinman, *What Is Race* (Paris: UNESCO House, 1952).

3. Jews of the Middle Ages used Hebrew characters in writing the spoken language of their environment. Ladino is the corresponding language mixture of Spanish and Hebrew.

4. See "Statement on the Nature of Race and Race Differences by Physical Anthropologists and Geneticists," *What Is Race:* "We agreed that all races were mixed and that intra-racial variability in most biological characters was as great if not greater than inter-racial variability."

5. I Chron. 4:18. The feminine form "Jehudijah" is used here.

6. II Kings 16:6 and 25:25.

7. Jer. 32:12; 38:19; 40:11; 43:9.

8. Neh. 1:2; 3:33; 4:6; Esther 2:5; 3:4; 5:13.

9. Flavius Josephus, *History of the Jewish War*, written in both Hebrew and Greek, in seven volumes.

10. Gen. 14:13.

11. Sometimes called Kenite.

12. James H. Breasted, *The Dawn of Conscience* (New York: Scribner, 1933), p. 350.

13. *Ruth* 13:22.

14. *Ezra* 9 and 10.

15. *Ezra* 9:1.

16. See *Encyclopedia Britannica*, XIII, 165 (1952); also *Universal Jewish Encyclopedia*, pp. 1-3 (1943).

17. Frederich Hertz, *Race and Civilization* (London: Trench and Trubner, 1928).

18. William Z. Ripley, *Races of Europe* (New York: Appleton, 1898), p. 392.

19. *Universal Jewish Encyclopedia*, VI, 375-78.

20. *Jewish Encyclopedia*, IV, 1-7 (1903).

21. Constantine VI, the Son of Leo III, married the Khazar Princess, Irene.

22. Heinrich Graetz, *History of the Jews* (Philadelphia Jewish Publication Society, 1895), III, 140-41. Also in the popular edition published in 1919 where it was stated that the Khazars were of pagan and not Israeli descent (III, 109).

23. Henry Hoble Hall, *Why Palestine* (New York, 1946), p. 14. (Pamphlet.)

24. In addition to Schecter and Graetz, see *History of Jews in Russia and Poland*, S. M. Dubnow (Jewish Publication Society of America, Philadelphia, 1916), pp. 19-29; Margolis & Marx, pp. 525-26; *Encyclopedia Britannica* (1952), XIII, 362–63; Ripley, p. 391.

25. See, for example, the *Trouble Makers*, an Anti-Defamation League report by Arnold Forster and Benjamin R. Epstein (New York: Doubleday, 1952), p. 96.

26. Eugene Pittard, *Les Races et L'Histoire* (Paris: La Renaissance Du Livre, 1924), p. 413.

27. *Ibid.*, p. 430.

28. *Ibid.*, p. 430. See also Appendix III of *What is Race*, a pamphlet published by UNESCO (Paris, 1952).

29. *What is Race.*

30. Ruth Benedict and Gene Weltfish, *The Races of Mankind*, Public Affairs Committee, New York, 1943 (New York: Viking, 1945), p. 177.

31. Julian Huxley and A. C. Haddon, *We Europeans* (London: Jonathan Cape, 1953).

32. *What is Race*, p. 74.

33. Jean-Paul Sartre, *Jew and Anti-Semite* (New York: Schocken Books, 1948), pp. 61–62.

34. Hertz, *op. cit.*, p. 135.

35. *Ibid.;* also, Benedict and Weltfish, *op. cit.*, p. 177.

36. See Dr. Joseph B. Schechtman, "Is There Discrimination in Israel," *Alliance Review*, March 1952, and January 1953, published by the American Friends of the Alliance Israelite Universelle, New York.

37. Leonard J. Schweitzer, "Israel, a Kingdom Divided," *The Sign*, January, 1953.

38. Schechtman, *op. cit.*

39. See *New York Times*, November 22, 1951; January 12, 1953; March 27, 1952; and March 31, 1952.

CHAPTER XIII

1. Action Committee, World Zionist Organization, Jerusalem, April 25, 1950.

2. Address in Philadelphia, May 10, 1915, from *The Public Papers of Woodrow Wilson*, Vol. 2, Part 1.

3. See *American Jewish Yearbook* 1951 and 1952, prepared by the American Jewish Committee and published by the Jewish Publication Society of America, Philadelphia. Dr. Mordecai M. Kaplan, the head of the Reconstruction Movement, places the number at only 600,000. According to the 1951 *Yearbook*, affiliated with national organizations were 500 orthodox synagogues (with a membership of 100,000 families); 400 modified Orthodox or Conservative synagogues (with 150,000 families); and 400 Reformed with houses of worship (with 100,000 families). In addition, there were 2,000 independent congregations of various sizes, mostly Orthodox.

4. See *American Jewish Yearbook*, 1952, p. 156. Thirty-one per cent of the congregation members claimed "quite regular attendance," seven per cent "never," forty-one per cent "occasionally" and twenty-one per cent "often, but not regular."

5. (New York: Harcourt Brace, 1947).

6. Heinrich H. Graetz, *History of the Jews*, II, 632.

7. In *A Partisan History of Judaism* (New York: Devin-Adair, 1951), Dr. Elmer Berger points out that Exodus 34:26 is the only authority for these laws and that interpretations of later rabbis greatly broadened the biblical interdictions regarding food, in order to make Judaist practices still more different.

8. Mic. 6:8.

9. Lev. 19:18.

10. Isa. 56:6.

CHAPTER XIV

1. *Report of the United Nations Special Committee on Palestine*, Chapter I, p. 32.

Index

DATE DUE